Advances in Contemporary Educational Thought Series
Jonas F. Soltis, Editor

The Cultural Dimensions of Educational Computing:
Understanding the Non-Neutrality of Technology

C. A. Bowers

Power and Criticism:
Poststructural Investigations in Education

Cleo H. Cherryholmes

The Civic Imperative:
Examining the Need for Civic Education

Richard Pratte

Responsive Teaching:
An Ecological Approach to Classroom Patterns
of Language, Culture, and Thought

C. A. Bowers and David J. Flinders

RESPONSIVE TEACHING

An Ecological Approach to Classroom Patterns of Language, Culture, and Thought

C. A. BOWERS AND DAVID J. FLINDERS

Teachers College, Columbia University
New York and London

Published by Teachers College Press, 1234 Amsterdam Avenue
New York, NY 10027

Library of Congress Cataloging-in-Publication Data
Bowers, C. A.
   Responsive teaching : an ecological approach to classroom patterns of language,
culture, and thought / C. A. Bowers and David J. Flinders.
      p. cm.—(Advances in contemporary educational thought ; v.)
   Includes bibliographical references.
   ISBN 0-8077-2998-1 (alk. paper).—ISBN 0-8077-2997-3 (pbk. : alk. paper)
   1. Classroom management.   2. Interaction analysis in education.
3. Psycholinguistics.   4. Human ecology.   I. Flinders, David J., 1955–
   . II. Title.   III. Series.
LB3013.B645   1990   89-36673
371.1'024—dc20   CIP

ISBN 0-8077-2998-1
ISBN 0-8077-2997-3 (pbk.)

Printed on acid-free paper

Manufactured in the United States of America

97 96 95 94 93 92 91 90   8 7 6 5 4 3 2 1

Contents

Foreword

The classroom. It is the center of instructional activity in our society. It is where teaching happens. In this century of educational science, the classroom has been carefully observed and thoroughly studied by educational researchers bent on laying bare its secrets to discover how teaching and learning are accomplished. The dominant approach to this research has been positivist, and one of its central practical purposes has been to provide a knowledge base for teachers to use in the management and control of their classrooms. In recent years a new form of research, most often called qualitative research, has challenged the dominantly quantitative approach. Qualitative researchers stress the need for educators to understand the human motives, feelings, meanings, norms, customs, and implicit rules that govern the variety of interactions in classrooms. They eschew an objective search for generalizations and seek instead the subjective meanings that explain the actions of people in real-life situations. They do not seek technical applications, and their studies usually focus on a single case. Sometimes they also speak to the political and ethical forces at work in classrooms.

The tension between these two approaches has most often been portrayed as an incompatible, incommensurable, contradictory set of bipolar philosophical assumptions. A few have argued for a possible methodological accommodation between them and for a multiple representational view of different dimensions of social reality. These philosophical arguments and practical attempts at accommodation lack something the sociologist Robert Merton, in a different context, once called a "middle range." I believe Bowers and Flinders offer just such a "middle range" in this book, and it is this that makes their contribution an advance in contemporary educational thought.

Although they deal not so much with new ideas about the relationships between culture, language, and thought, they provide a rich, new way of putting them together in the "middle range," bring-

ing the theoretical to bear directly on the illumination of our understanding of the culture and politics of everyday classrooms. They use
individual case studies and numerous concrete examples that provide
teachers with sophisticated ways to think about teaching their subject
matter. They argue that teachers can use this conceptual framework
to interpret what goes on in their classrooms in pedagogically, culturally, and politically sensitive ways.

There is neither grand theory nor precise methodological description in this study. There is, however, a cogently argued-for theoretical framework and a sophisticated use of concepts and insights
from seminal thinkers that should provide a heuristic for methodological extrapolations by researchers in their study of classrooms.
There is also a needed but not fanatical political-critical agenda dealing with such serious contemporary problems as gender and ethnicity in education. Above all, there is a full and rich rendering of a
"middle range" conceptual framework for teachers to use in thinking
about acting responsively and responsibly in the classroom. Based on
an ecological point of view derived mainly from Bateson, it calls for a
shift from our currently dominant cultural metaphors, which foster a
destructive individualism, to ecological metaphors that not only include us in nature, but also connect epistemology with ethics and human beings to each other in love and commitment. It urges teachers
to help students develop a mind set of connectedness.

Bowers and Flinders have written a book about teaching that
both researchers and teachers have much to learn from. Their initial
argument is straightforward: The dominant scientific (they call it
Cartesian and technicist) approach to research on the classroom has
produced useful techniques for teachers, but also has blinded them to
other modes of interpretation of the ecology of the classroom. These
alternative modes, when supported by an appropriate conceptual
framework, can provide teachers with a more sensitive and reflective
means of teaching in a pluralistic cultural setting full of politically and
ethically relevant choices. Bowers and Flinders develop the needed
ancillary conceptual framework, using as major beams and trusses
such theorists as Bateson, Birdwhistell, Geertz, and Foucault and
such concepts as language, culture, ecology, metaphor, nonverbal
communication, primary socialization, framing, solidarity, power,
and politics.

Their emphasis is always on the teacher who has the professional
responsibility of educating the uninitiated. They also stress the importance of developing a knowledge base for teachers that goes beyond the technical and includes the social, cultural and political. They

end with the claim that all of our current debates over the purposes of education are headed in the wrong direction because they share a belief in progress and rationality based on individualism when we should be thinking about the best form of education for living together.

It is a book worth reading, heeding, and learning from.

Jonas F. Soltis, Editor
Advances in Contemporary
Educational Thought Series

Preface

The two key words in the title of this book are *responsive* and *ecology*, which seem naturally to go together when talking about environmental issues. We think they also go together when thinking about educationally meaningful classrooms. The words, however, were not chosen casually. Thinking of the classroom as an ecology, that is, in terms of interactive relationships and patterns, is the best way of understanding the interconnection of behavior and learning. Put another way, the mental and behavioral processes should not, in our judgment, be viewed as distinct. The ecology of mental and behavioral processes is further complicated by the fact that students and teachers give individualized expression to cultural patterns: Behavior is largely a matter of communicating in culturally prescribed ways, while thought processes and the use of language are also deeply influenced by culture. To make matters even more complex for the teacher, the behavior and thought processes of students increasingly reflect the cultural diversity of the larger society.

This is where the word *responsive* becomes especially pertinent. The professional judgments of the teacher should be based on an understanding of how the student's behavior and thought processes involve, to a larger extent than is generally recognized, the reenactment of cultural patterns. Being responsive, as we use the term here, thus means to be aware of and capable of responding in educationally constructive ways to the ways in which cultural patterns influence the behavioral and mental ecology of the classroom.

As we have such a long tradition in education of thinking of the classroom not as an ecology of cultural patterns communicated through thought and behavior, but as made up of individuals whose thought and behavior can be objectively observed and judged, it is important to acknowledge the intellectual traditions we consider as foundational to an approach to teaching that responds to culture. The sociology of knowledge (particularly as set forth by Peter Berger,

Thomas Luckmann, and Alfred Schultz) is basic to understanding the role of language in transmitting the cultural patterns to the next generation and to the reasons so much of this learning occurs at a taken-for-granted (unconscious) level. Cultural anthropologists, such as Clifford Geertz, Ward Goodenough, and Mary Douglas, have provided us a vocabulary for thinking about just how much of human experience is encompassed by the word *culture* and the double-binds that we can get into when thinking about the culture of others as well as ourselves. Cultural linguists (Ron and Suzanne Scollon and Deborah Tannen, among others) as well as people working in the area of the metaphorical nature of language (Donald Schon, Michael Reddy, and Mark Johnson in particular) have helped us understand some of the encoding characteristics of language that are essential to the teacher's knowledge base. However, Gregory Bateson is the theorist who has enabled us to reframe the contributions of these different strands of thinking into a conceptual framework that allows both student behavior and thought processes to be understood in a new way. Recognizing that the mental process is not limited to what occurs in the head of the individual, and that behavior is really a form of communication about relationships, helps to provide a sense of conceptual coherence to what we are trying to understand.

Our own extensive classroom observations, in California and Oregon, as well as the classroom ethnographics of a longer list of people than we cite here, provided examples of how so much of what occurs in the classroom involves the reenactment of cultural patterns that are often mistakenly attributed to the conscious intent of students and teachers. Sometimes the misreading of these patterns contributes to instances that come near to being complete breakdowns in communication—as Susan Philips (1983) demonstrated. The classroom teachers who generously opened their classrooms to us deserve special thanks. We were not always able in the time allowed by school schedules to explain the connection between the theoretical framework we were building and the way that the classroom observations would lead to refinements in the theory and to preliminary recommendations of responsive teaching practices.

Courtney Cazden's recommendation that classroom ethnographies be used as part of the teacher's professional knowledge base, as well as our reading of the works by researchers associated with the KEEP program in Hawaii about the use of culturally sensitive research in adjusting teaching style to the primary culture of students, further convinced us we were on the right track. But it was the work with students, especially graduate students, that provided much of the impetus we needed to keep going. In addition to sitting through a course based on an ecology of the classroom perspective, they participated in a special seminar that had led to video documentation and other materials essential to helping student teachers connect theory to the professional judgments they will make in the classroom. James Dorward, Petra Munro, Joan Weston, Anthony Catalano, Tracy Faulconer, Maggie McBride, Karen Froude-Jones, Loretta Pence, Susan Victor, Leslie Conery, and Gretchen Freed-Rowland kept the discussions lively and helped us recognize the need to provide students with visual documentation of classroom patterns. We also want to thank our colleagues Diane Dunlap and Rob Proudfoot for bringing articles to our attention at especially critical times. Several key people helped us recognize the problems associated with introducing student teachers to a responsive approach to the classroom by incorporating some of our ideas into their courses: Nancy Meltzoff, Douglas Cooper, and Douglas Lamoreaux. Don DeWitt helped co-teach the first course on ecology of the classroom; as the theoretical connections were only partially understood, he deserves a special thanks for helping us during the most preliminary phase of our work.

The supportive relationships that characterized our own ecology over the months it took to write this book involved other key participants. Our spouses, Mary Bowers and Lynn Flinders, provided encouragement and insightful comments as the work progressed. The editors at Teachers College Press helped eliminate the sources of frustration and delay that often accompany the transition from a raw, partially formulated idea to a completed book manuscript. Lastly, we want to thank Sevilla Ludwig for her skillful typing of the manuscript. Her cheerfulness and commitment to "getting it right" made for a wonderful working relationship.

Responsive Teaching

*An Ecological Approach to Classroom Patterns
of Language, Culture, and Thought*

CHAPTER 1

A Context for Professional Knowledge

Let us begin with the classroom. Once the students are at their desks, Susan Krebs[1] quickly takes roll, walks to the center of the room, glances from side to side, and clasps her hands close in front of her, a ballpoint pen intertwined between her fingers. She pauses, "OK, let's get started. . . ." Her arms are held close to her sides, her back straight, and her weight shifted onto the heels of her shoes. She stands perfectly still, a posture that signals the beginning of class. "OK, OK, let's get together now. I'm going to give you your vocabulary assignment today, but first I want to talk about our reading and the clue sheet I gave you last week." She holds up a sheet of paper divided into two sections (the top half labeled QUESTIONS, the bottom half labeled CLUES), then continues:

> "We've talked about how this novel is like a mystery, and I asked you to write down all the questions you had as you read, and all the clues. Well, I'm beginning to see there's a very fuzzy line between questions and clues. Every time we find a clue, it just raises more questions. This idea of clues and questions was just an experiment—a way to help us keep track of what's going on in the book. There's still a lot we don't know. This story is like a puzzle we're trying to fit together, isn't it? OK, let's go over chapters 5 and 6 together."

Susan directs their discussion by raising specific questions and calling the students' attention to particular passages. Eventually she provides closing comments and then distributes mimeographed copies of their vocabulary assignment, again addressing the class:

---

[1] All the teachers described in this book have been given pseudonyms in order to protect confidentiality.

1

"We only have thirty vocabulary words this week. That's quite a small number when you think about how many words there are in English . . . almost a million, I believe. Words are like people; new ones are always being born, others are growing old and dying. But, of course, it's a very slow process. The dictionaries are at the back of the room."

No, the dictionaries have recently been moved to the front of the room, and several students are quick to inform Susan of her absent-mindedness. At this point a young Hispanic girl in the back row sits upright in her chair and, in playful mimicry of Susan's tone of voice, remarks, "Why, Ms. Krebs, we really must be more precise in our use of language." The class immediately recognizes that the girl is using a skillful imitation of "teacher talk" to turn the tables on Susan, and Susan joins her students by responding with a knowing smile and appreciative laughter.

In starting with a descriptive account wherein the issues of classroom control and instruction blend into the daily routines of teaching, we want to make two points. The first relates to D. C. Lortie's observation that the teaching profession has no codified body of knowledge and skills. As he succinctly put it, "No way has been found to record and crystallize teaching for the benefit of beginners" (1975, p. 58). In the intervening years a massive amount of research on classroom management techniques and effective teaching procedures has attempted to remedy this deficiency. We believe this effort has yielded only limited benefits; because of guiding technicist and behavioral assumptions, it may actually have set back the effort to expand the foundations of the teacher's professional knowledge.

The second point is that the classroom, as demonstrated in our descriptive account, must be understood as an ecology of language processes and cultural patterns. These include the use of the spoken and written word; the use of personal and social space (proxemics) as part of the message exchange system; the body language of movement, posture, and facial expression (kinesics); the changes of voice pitch, tempo, and intensity—as well as intruding sounds and pauses. This ecology of relationships involves message exchanges of an exceedingly subtle and complex nature. At the most obvious level can be seen the processes of primary socialization, framing, negotiating, maintaining the order of turn-taking, and the use of humor to strengthen solidarity in the classroom. Less obvious are the implicit cultural patterns of thought, behavior, and inner response that influence both what is communicated in the classroom and how it is communicated. Understanding the deep cultural foundations of the language dynamics of the classroom, which we see as including the thought process, behavior patterns, and patterns of communication, is an essential aspect of the teacher's professional knowledge.

Although the classroom management–teacher effectiveness perspective has dominated teacher education over the last decade, we feel that it involves an exceedingly limited way of understanding the dynamics of classroom life. The conceptual underpinnings of this approach, which are largely technicist and behavioral in their orientation, are also inadequate for addressing the educational issues that arise from the increasingly self-conscious cultural pluralism of American society. Thus our primary task will be to lay out the theoretical foundations for understanding the culturally ladened interactive processes of the classroom and how teachers can use this understanding to enhance educational processes. We will not be rejecting the legitimate insights and discoveries of the people who have advanced the classroom management–teacher effectiveness framework of understanding; on the contrary, their insights need to be integrated into a body of professional knowledge that is grounded in a more contemporary understanding of the cultural nature of the individual, language, and the rational process.

The conceptual underpinnings of the classroom management–teacher effectiveness perspective (what we will refer to as the management paradigm) can be easily recognized in the prescriptive guidelines that appear in both teacher-training textbooks and summaries of classroom research. In terms of Susan Krebs's classroom, as well as thousands of others spread across the country from Kotzebue, Alaska, to New York City, the primary responsibility of the effective teacher is to establish clearly the rules and procedures that govern activities in the classroom. As stated by Daniel Duke and Adrienne Meckel in *Managing Student Behavior Problems*, "rules constitute one of the central features of school organizations." Thus, for them, "Goal Number 1" is to "create an awareness on the part of all who work and study in the school that it is an organization governed by rules" (1980, p. 45). The effective classroom manager who minimizes disciplinary problems, and thus increases the time spent on instructional activities, must conceptualize in advance the behaviors expected during each type of school activity. These activities include transitions between hall and classroom as well as transitions between learning activities in the classroom (from seatwork to lecture situations to participating at the blackboard or in the lab), test taking, listening to lecture presentations, involvement in group discussions, and so forth. This means, according to Randy Sprick's (1986) survival guide (his term), *Discipline in the Secondary Classroom,* that teachers should write "four or five positively stated rules that reflect [their] expectations" for "how students should conduct themselves for each type of activity" (p. 4).

The concern with establishing control over the activities occurring in the classroom (creating a "work system," to use Walter Doyle's phrase; 1986, p. 413) can lead, in the case of some interpreters of the management paradigm, to an exceedingly high degree of standardization of classroom procedures. For example, Sprick (1986) identifies six procedures to be followed in conducting the first ten minutes of class:

> Stand at the door to greet students; when you are ready to begin class, get everyone's full attention before you start; present class rules and consequences for misbehavior; take attendance; explain your procedures for assigning and collecting work; explain your grading system. (p. 8)

Presumably these recipe-like guidelines are meant for the first meeting of the class. As the class progresses teachers are expected to draw on a body of professional knowledge that includes a five-step procedure for "teaching students how to behave" (p. 9).

This control orientation is also reflected in the massive amount of research done over recent years on classroom organization and management. In summarizing this research, Walter Doyle states that "both policy-directed and descriptive studies indicate that life in classrooms begins with the creation of a work system and the setting of rules and procedures to hold the system in place, and that a considerable amount of energy is devoted to this process." The professionalism of teachers, he concludes, is only demonstrated when there is "a willingness and an ability to act when rules are broken. For this reason, reprimands and consequences play a central role in the role-setting process" (1986, p. 413).

It is not our purpose here to assess the merits of all the findings or the quality of research that underpins the classroom management paradigm; suffice it to say that this view of what should constitute the basic core of the teacher's professional knowledge includes insights that deserve to become part of commonsense classroom practice. It has also led to some highly questionable recommendations, such as the one that effective teachers should utilize a method of instruction that involves more "low-level," factually oriented questions, rather than the "high-level" questions that foster relational thinking, and avoids discussing or using pupil answers and questions (Medley, 1979). Nor do we wish to engage in a direct discussion of the philosophy of education that is taken for granted in the classroom management paradigm, even though we think it is based on fundamentally incorrect assumptions about the purpose of education in a democratic society. Rather, the main task, as we see it, is to make explicit what we regard as the distinctive characteristics of the body of professional knowledge that is derived from the classroom management paradigm and to identify how this way of thinking is rooted in an intellectual tradition that was established long before the constitutive nature of culture and language was fully understood.

ORIGINS AND ASSUMPTIONS OF THE MANAGEMENT PARADIGM

The classroom management paradigm involves a pattern of thinking that was identified in *The Homeless Mind* as a technological mode of consciousness (Berger, Berger, & Kellner, 1974). Its roots can be traced back to such influential thinkers of the seventeenth century as Francis Bacon (1561–1626), who identified knowledge with power, efficiency, and industrial utility; René Descartes (1596–1650), who helped lay the foundations for a way of thinking about a mechanical universe that could be subdivided into ever smaller components parts whose movements could be observed and measured; and Isaac Newton (1642–1727), who demonstrated the explanatory power of a mathematical and thus abstract way of understanding natural phenomena. It was also influenced by John Locke's way of thinking about language and the nature of the individual, as well as by an impressive list of philosophers, sociologists, and psychologists who over the past century and a half have modernized and strengthened the foundations of a mechanistic way of thinking—about the person, the environment, and the processes of the social world. Although we could use a variety of labels that would help situate historically the classroom management paradigm—Cartesianism and positivism being the two most inclusive—we will use the label of "technicist" to communicate the growing importance given to reducing every aspect of experience, including the dynamics of the classroom, to technique that can be rationally formulated for the purpose of improving prediction, control, and efficiency. Before explicating the essential characteristics of the technicist pattern of thinking we see in the classroom management literature and prescriptive practices, we want to make another point about its origins.

Masculine Orientation

Recent feminist literature dealing with the connection between gender and ways of thinking has helped clarify how historically men have translated the distinctiveness of their own experiences into the philosophical arguments that have served as guidelines for thinking about the nature and purpose of the rational process as well as our relations with each other and the environment. Historical studies by feminists even suggest that the transition from the organic and interdependent sense of reality of the Middle Ages to the mechanistic view of the universe that has become the foundation of our current scientifically based knowledge and technological development was precipitated by a period of great social and psychological turmoil during which feminine qualities were associated with madness, witchcraft, and the satanic (Bordo, 1987). Although there were other agendas to be achieved during that critical transitional period in Western thought, such as the secularization of moral judgment, the masculinization of thought was the major philosophical achievement of this period. This accomplishment required representing the individual in an entirely new way—as free from the forces of culture, tradition, and emotions. The view of the individual as a separate agent allowed the newly discovered capacity for detached observation and rational judgment to be exercised. To observe meant to set at a distance, which authorized the exercise of power based on personally detached (objective) judgment. Evelyn Fox Keller summarizes the new boundaries that separated the self as knower from the world as known:

> The scientific mind is set apart from what is to be known, that is, from nature, and its autonomy is guaranteed . . . by setting apart its modes of knowing from those in which that dichotomy is threatened. In this process, the characterization of both the scientific mind and its modes of access to knowledge as masculine is indeed significant. Masculine here connotes . . . autonomy, separation, and distance . . . a radical rejection of any combining of subject and object. (1985, p. 79)

The autonomy (and isolation) of the rational individual, according to feminist writers, requires a mechanistic view of the universe as a defense against feminine qualities, where a sense of meaning and personal identity are acquired through relationships characterized by nurturing, caring, listening, empathy, and responsibility (Gilligan, 1982; Chodorow, 1978). The relevance of this connection between gender and cognitive style to our discussion of the classroom management paradigm not only relates to the practice of equating the teacher's professionalism with the exercise of power and control through the use of techniques. It also relates to understanding the basic limitations of the classroom management paradigm; that is, how it downplays both the importance of the caring and nurturing relationships of the classroom and the need to utilize multiple sources of knowledge that come from being attuned, for lack of a better word, to the myriad forms and levels of message exchanges that make up the ecology of the classroom. Furthermore, we think the lack of attention given to the importance of teachers' adopting a self-reflective stance, whereby the contribution of their own attitudes, values, and taken-for-granted cultural patterns to the classroom ecology are critically assessed, is also related to the masculine orientation of the classroom management paradigm. As we shall see when we examine more carefully the key conceptual underpinnings of the technicist approach to teaching, the classroom manager who collects data, monitors student compliance with classroom rules, and determines appropriate technique and procedure does not, in true Cartesian fashion, experience the need for self-reflection.

Technicist Approach

The influence of the technological mode of consciousness, as Raymond Callahan documented in *Education and the Cult of Efficiency* (1962), goes back to the early part of this century, when educators found in Frederick Taylor's time and motion studies a model for thinking about the scientific management of the classroom. A more recent source of influence, however, was Ralph Tyler's *Basic Principles of Curriculum and Instruction*. First published in 1949, Tyler's slender book further strengthened the Cartesian way of "systematically and intelligently" understanding the classroom. For Tyler, "education is a process of changing the behavior patterns of people," which he defined to include thinking and feeling (pp. 5–6). This required both the specification of the behaviors to be changed (to be expressed as behavioral objectives) and a systematic approach to evaluating whether the objectives had been attained. Neither Taylor nor Tyler should be viewed as entirely responsible for the reductionist view that equates learning with a behavior that can be objectively observed; they simply articulated the issues in a manner that crystallized a more generally held conceptual orientation that had been built up in teacher education institutions over previous decades.

What is important for us is the way in which the technological orientation continues as the dominant intellectual framework for thinking about what constitutes the teacher's professional knowledge. The emphasis on behavioral objectives gives special legitimacy to the technological pattern of thinking, while at the same time making the cultural and linguistic characteristics of the classroom appear even more illusive. In a widely used textbook on classroom management, Thomas L. Good and Jere E. Brophy warned that the collection of data on student behavior should not include attempts to "interpret what the behavior means" (1978, p. 37). The data should simply speak for itself; thus the need to remain "objective." Duke is more explicit about whether culture should be viewed as an influence on student behavior. In the National Society for the Study of Education yearbook, *Classroom Management*, he states that "cultural influences serve to confuse more than to clarify the teacher's decision-making functions" (1979, p. 356). Aside from the ambiguity of determining the exact influence of culture on behavior, Duke sees a more sinister ideological issue: "Efforts to explain human behavior in terms of influences external to the individual" (the cultural factor) lead to the "depersonalization of blame," whereby "individual students who misbehave no longer are held responsible for their actions" (p. 359). In his view, the teacher's professionalism would be better served by recognizing how the "long tradition of valuing individuality helps to uphold the image of the autonomous teacher in a self-contained classroom" (p. 358).

Although Doyle's (1986) recent summary of research on classroom organization and management provides evidence of a far more complex and sophisticated understanding of the interactive patterns that characterize a classroom, its emphasis on behavioral management reflects the continuing dominance of the technicist approach to teacher professionalism. This mindset, like a conceptual map that illuminates and hides at the same time, can only take account of explicit forms of knowledge; that is, we can only know that which is observable. The explicit-observable nature of what is to be known makes it amenable to measurement and greater certainty. In turn, this fosters a greater emphasis on reducing classroom interactive patterns to their component parts for the purpose of reconstituting them in a manner that increases rational control and efficiency. These characteristics—a concern with measurement, thinking in terms of component parts, the search for more efficient procedures, the development of techniques that are not context specific—are, according to Peter Berger and colleagues, intrinsic to technological production (1974). Thinking of education as like a process of technological production is clearly revealed in a conceptually limited metaphorical language: education as a "management process," the student as a "product," and behaviors as expressions of "exit skills," "competencies," or "outcomes."

This technicist pattern of thinking, with its machine-like analogues, incorporates key aspects of the Cartesian tradition that reflect the masculine concern with rational control and power. The basic assumptions of this tradition that are absolutely essential for supporting the technicist orientation taken in the classroom management paradigm include (1) a view of the rational process as culturally neutral, (2) a view of language as a conduit, and (3) a view of learning as individually centered. As the body of knowledge we believe essential to the teacher's professional judgment represents a direct challenge to these three key interdependent assumptions, we shall examine them more closely.

THE RATIONAL PROCESS AS CULTURALLY NEUTRAL. The view of the rational process we find reflected in the classroom management paradigm has the characteristic, as Richard Rorty refers to it, of mirroring what is in the external world (1979). Thus behaviors such as nonattendance, negative physical contact, and talking out of turn are activities that can be objectively represented in thought. The relationships between behaviors, such as the teacher's response to disruptive behavior or student questions, are also logically specifiable as objective events. Once the characteristics of the behaviors and relational patterns are known, it is possible to find causal explanations; that is, the teacher's behavior (reprimands, praise, wait time, etc.) can be understood as causally related to a sequence of events that occur in the classroom. This objective understanding is further enhanced by careful observation and the systematic collection of data. Once the data verify the existence of a regular pattern, the task of the classroom manager is to conceptualize a new pattern of relationships, such as designing and announcing consequences for severe misbehavior or instituting a grading system that encourages participation, and to implement these interventions under conditions that allow for further data collection.

This view of the rational process contains several interesting elements. First, it assumes that thinking is independent of psychological and bodily experiences. Self-identity, what Nietzsche (1888/1967), termed "ressentient feelings," memory, and a host of bodily experiences that are part of the person's embeddedness in a physical context can all be kept separate from the rational process. Second, the capacity for thought to be based on a mirror image of external events, an assumption essential for maintaining that knowledge is objective, requires viewing the individual knower as free of cultural influence. This means that the capacity to conceptualize is not influenced by the cognitive mapping processes that some social linguists claim is an aspect of the person's language (Johnson, 1987; Lakoff, 1987). Nor is it influenced by cultural patterns internalized as part of the person's preunderstandings that are brought to moments of decision and reflection, as some contemporary thinkers claim (Gadamer, 1976). Lastly, this view of the rational process requires the acceptance of a naive realism whereby the behaviors of others can be taken at face value, requiring no interpretation of their inner worlds of meaning, intentionality, or unconscious enactment of cultural patterns, such as using a speech rhythm that differs from the taken-for-granted rhythm of the teacher or observer collecting the data.

LANGUAGE AS A CONDUIT. The second key assumption that underpins the classroom management paradigm is that language is a conduit for the transmission of information. As we shall later be discussing what teachers should understand about using a conduit view of language, the comments here will be limited to putting in focus how this view of language helps to buttress a masculine emphasis on objectivity. In essence, the conduit view of language is being used whenever communication is represented as a process of transmitting information. Such typical statements as "the data should be sent to the policy makers," "you will find the information in the library," and "it is very difficult to put that concept into words" suggest a linear, sender-receiver model of communication. Communication is viewed as an exchange of information, with words being viewed either as containers into which meaning is put ("put your ideas into words") or as corresponding to real objects and relations in the world. The power of symbols to represent real entities and relationships, so this view holds, makes it possible to have "factual" communication.

Briefly, this view of language is not only incorrect but is also largely responsible for many of the limitations that characterize the classroom management paradigm. Although it is relatively easy to explain why language should not be viewed as a conduit, it will take a greater effort to account fully for the different dimensions of language that the educational researcher and classroom practitioner need to understand. Indeed, the following chapters are intended to address this area of neglect. The view of language as a conduit is incorrect for the following reasons. First, the relationship between speaker and listener or writer and reader involves interpreting the verbal and written word in terms of the conceptual framework that the participant brings to the event. Communication is a matter not of *extracting* meaning and information from statements but of *constituting* meaning by the participants. The conceptual tools and frames available to the participants shape the communication. This means that identities, values, mood, and culturally ladened interpretative frameworks come into play as part of the ongoing co-construction of meaning (Reddy, 1979). Furthermore, words are only part of communication; context and nonverbal communication are also part of a process that makes the image of a conduit connecting two people appear oversimplistic. While the sender-receiver model of communication suggests rational control over the sending of explicit messages, the contextual and nonverbal dimensions of communication open the door to recognizing the role of implicit understandings, the unconscious influence of cultural patterns, and even the influence of psychological factors.

The last reason for rejecting the conduit view of language, and thus the view of objective knowledge about classroom behavior, is that language is metaphorical. The meaning of words does not come from the *discovery* of objective entities and relationships they correspond to. Instead, through a process of metaphorical thinking, words come to symbolize constructions wherein the new is understood in terms of the familiar; as people make new associations words take on new meanings and thus help to constitute new interpretative schemata. Since we shall later address what teachers should understand about the process of metaphorical thinking as an aspect of the classroom ecology, we shall conclude this discussion by pointing out that metaphors provide the schemes or cognitive models that are the basis of thought. Words are used to perform many functions, but they are not containers into which meaning is put; nor do they represent or correspond to real entities (Eco, 1979). When understood as metaphors, they can be seen as providing a schema for interpretation and understanding that reflects the metaphorical thinking of the past. The word *behavior*, for example, has an experiential dimension (our concept of behavior is indeed related to direct experience with the opaqueness of other people's actions); it also has a social history that encompasses the past intellectual debates that established which analogues were to prevail in applying science to the social domain. To put it another way, language reproduces in thought the metaphorical thinking of the past. This constitutive role of language, along with interpretative involvement of the participants, makes it difficult to sustain the view of language as a conduit for rational and objective communication—a view that is essential to the control-oriented, personally detached Cartesianism of the classroom management–effective teacher literatures.

LEARNING AS INDIVIDUALLY CENTERED. The third cornerstone of Cartesian thinking still held by educators in general, and the advocates of the classroom management paradigm in particular, is an individualistic view of learning and behavior. We agree with Seymour Sarason's observation that explanations "based on the characteristics of individuals may contain a kind of truth, but that truth is obtained at the expense of discerning regularities that persist despite individual variations in behavior and the passage of time" (1982, p. 24). The "regularities" that the metaphor of "individualism" puts out of focus are the cultural patterns (traditions and implicit understandings) that influence the communication processes of the classroom. Feminists interested in how the masculinization of thought led to the idea of objective knowledge, as well as philosophers such as Richard Rorty, note that the invention of mind as the "inner arena" of ideas was solidified in the *Mediations* of Descartes. The view that experience occurs within an autonomous self, and that the process of thought must be purged of traditional ways of understanding if the objectivity of the external world is to be grasped, provided not only the sense of separate individual existence that concerns feminist writers but also a model for thinking of the individual as the basic social and psychological unit. It is important to note that the historical roots of this image of the self-contained individual was formed before the "regularities" in culture and language were recognized.

As we shall attempt to show in later chapters, this view of autonomous individuals as having inner states—thoughts, moods, sensations separate from their past—cannot be sustained if we pay attention to how individuals reenact as part of their natural attitude the cultural patterns of thought, behavior, and communication. We have already touched on how the metaphorical nature of language and thought provides individuals with shared schemes of interpretation that were constituted at an earlier period of time. We have also alluded to the patterns of nonverbal communication (body language, eye contact, the use of personal and social space, etc.) that are learned as part of the taken-for-granted knowledge that is necessary for communicating with other members of the culture. Further support of the argument that the Cartesian view of thought is inadequate as a strictly inner process can be found in Gregory Bateson's (1972) view of mental processes as transactions between the elements that make up the ecology of ongoing relationships. Bateson's perspective shifts the view of mental processes from one that is individually centered to one that emphasizes context, continuities, and interactions.

Implications for Educational Reform

In considering the characteristics of the efforts over the last decade to improve the effectiveness of classroom learning—efforts that range from assertive discipline, to ITIP (instructional theory into practice), to various models of teaching—we find the Cartesian assumptions to be still largely intact. With few exceptions, educational reforms share the Cartesian view of the rational process as culturally neutral, language as a conduit for transmitting information between sender (the teacher) and receivers (the students), and the individualistic view of the learner. What separates the different approaches to improving what goes on in classrooms is procedure. Some tie procedure to behavioral reinforcement, others stress systematic teacher decision making by using classroom research to formulate specific strategies. But they are all teacher centered, oriented toward issues of control and behavioral outcomes, and based on data relating to behavioral patterns.

The limitations of this shared Cartesian orientation can be seen in a summary of the essential elements of instruction derived in modified form from ITIP and used in a teacher education class at a local university. As future teachers, the students were told that the *essential* elements of instruction include the following:

1. Teach to an objective
   a. Formulate an instructional objective
   b. Generate teacher behaviors congruent to intended objectives
   c. Demonstrate use of Bloom's taxonomy
2. Select an objective at the correct level of difficulty
   a. Formulate a task analysis
   b. Use the task analysis as the basis for the diagnostic/prescriptive process
3. Monitor the progress of the students and adjust the learning
   a. Elicit congruent overt behavior from students

    b. Check the observed behavior

    c. Use the task analysis of the objective and/or knowledge of
       the principles of learning to interpret the observed behav-
       ior

4. Use the principles of learning that affect

    a. Motivation

    b. Rate and degree of learning

    c. Transfer

    d. Retention

We are not against being systematic, basing teaching processes on research findings, or using reinforcement—as long as they do not become the exclusive approach to understanding what is occurring in the classroom. What we are concerned about is the nearly uniform silence on the importance of understanding the cultural patterns that influence the manner in which the teacher and students think and communicate. This is the more symbolic dimension of the classroom ecology that is not seen because the Cartesian lenses put in focus only a surface dimension of what can be observed, measured, and routinized. In contrast to the above summary of the essential elements of instruction, we think that the professional knowledge of teachers must be grounded in a more complex understanding of the individual, language, and the rational process that has been fashioned into a male-technicist approach to education. Providing an overview of what constitutes this more complex foundation of professional knowledge is our next task.

BEYOND THE CLASSROOM MANAGEMENT PARADIGM

Institutionalized approaches to education will always require some degree of concern with issues relating to good classroom management procedures. Our interest in reframing how to think about the teacher's professional knowledge should, therefore, not be viewed as a rejection of the teacher's responsibility to make sound judgments about the learning and behavioral processes occurring in the classroom. The issue is thus not that of control but of what the teacher takes into account in making a judgment. As this issue is critical to understanding our arguments that the teacher's professional knowledge is based on the wrong paradigm (i.e., Cartesian), we want to quote two typical statements taken from the classroom management literature:

An assertive teacher is one who clearly and firmly expresses her wants and feelings to the children and is prepared to back up her words with actions. She clearly tells the children what behavior is acceptable and which is unacceptable. The assertive teacher recognizes the fact that she has wants and needs and has the right to get them met in the classroom. She is also aware of her limitations and realizes that she has the right to ask for assistance in her efforts, be it from the principal, parent(s), or peers. (Canter, 1979, p. 30)

In summary, the need to restore order in a classroom is a sign that the mechanisms that establish and sustain order are not working. The repair process itself is complex and risky as are the decisions concerning when and how to intervene. Successful managers appear to be able to decide early whether an act will disrupt order and to intervene in an inconspicuous way to cut off the path toward disorder. In attending to misbehavior and interventions, however, the emphasis remains on the primary vector of action as the fundamental means of holding order in place in classrooms. (Doyle, 1986, p. 422)

The oversimplistic understanding of the classroom embedded in these two statements is, in our view, a factor that contributes to the basic breakdown in classroom communication; and these breakdowns will, in turn, be manifested in behavior that the Cartesian-oriented classroom manager will view as disruptive. This self-perpetuating cycle is furthered as the disruptive behavior leads to stronger and more systematic control procedures. The real issue is to establish what the teacher needs to understand about the dynamics of the classroom, so that the teacher's decisions reflect more of a balance between the empowering potential of the educational process, the need to maintain a classroom environment that facilitates educationally significant communication, and what Nel Noddings (1986) refers to as the teacher's fidelity to the students. The latter, as Noddings explains it, involves a form of care for the student as a person as well as for the quality of relations among the class participants. Control and caring are not opposing terms; but the form of control is transformed by the presence of care. We agree with Noddings's observation that when teachers act as models of caring they also "model a host of other desirable qualities: meticulous preparation, lively presentation, critical thinking, appreciative listening, constructive evaluation, genuine curiosity" (1986, p. 503). But even this concern for confirming teacher-student relationships and an empowering learning experience can be misdirected if the teacher lacks the means of understanding the cultural and linguistic patterns that make up the ecology of the classroom.

The Cultural Complexity of the Classroom

Absent from the statements about the "assertive teacher" and the "mechanisms that establish and sustain order" is an awareness of the student as a cultural being and of how language processes encode culturally specific ways of thinking and acting. In terms of the classroom management paradigm, all the information the teacher needs about the student is disclosed to the objective observer. A simple example that Clifford Geertz uses to make a point about how the nature of culture differs from an involuntary physiological response of the organism seems particularly relevant to illuminating the problem with this view. In borrowing an example from Gilbert Ryle's discussion of "thick description," a phrase that relates very much to the in-depth interpretation of interaction patterns we are proposing as basic to the teacher's professionalism, Geertz (1973) makes the point that the "I-am-a-camera" way of understanding cannot discriminate between the involuntary contraction of the right eyelid and the deliberate eyelid contraction that is meant to impart a particular message to someone else who understands the pattern for encoding the message. An example of the "I-am-a-camera" way of understanding, the classroom management way of viewing behavior and relations between individuals thus ignores how behavior, context, and the observer are part of a complex message exchange that is encoded in culturally dictated patterns.

Contrary to how the teacher is represented in the examples taken from the classroom management paradigm, we think that teachers would be able to discriminate between an eyelid contraction that is an involuntary blink and the wink that is a deliberate act of nonverbal communication, just as they have a taken-for-granted understanding of the meaning of other culturally embedded forms of communication. Teachers, too, are cultural beings who have internalized as part of their natural attitude toward everyday social events the culturally prescribed patterns for how to think and behave. It is the shared nature of these patterns that enables the teacher to recognize when a student is using a wink to send a message to another student; teachers also understand how context is critical to recognizing the wink as a conspiratorial gesture as opposed to an awkward first attempt at flirtation. Our point here is that teachers themselves are more culturally complex than they are represented to be in the classroom manager–teacher effectiveness literature. While their complexity as cultural beings helps us view them as something more than managers, it can also be the reason for miscommunication when they fail to recognize the cultural basis of their own interpretations and the possibility that a student's behavior and thought patterns are grounded in a culturally different symbolic world. When armed with the powerful techniques of behavior reinforcement, teachers who uncritically accept the myth that they are simply basing professional judgments on objective data can do a great deal of psychological and educational damage to students who may, out of necessity, communicate outwardly that they are in compliance with teacher expectations.

We would like to present an example of a white, middle-class teacher who was not aware of how her own cultural orientation led to a misinterpretation of black students' performance. This will help establish that the issues we are dealing with have more serious social and educational implications than the failure to discriminate between a blink and a wink (although anyone who has mistaken the former for the latter may testify to its significance). The example comes from the research carried out by Sarah Michaels and James Collins (1984) in an urban first-grade classroom. The focus of the research was on differences in language styles. The teacher, they found, had a taken-for-granted understanding of the structure and sequencing that constituted the appropriate narrative form that was to be followed during sharing time. This schema fit the literate pattern of discourse: a topic-centered, focused, explicit description of single events with a linear pattern of development.

Michaels and Collins found that white students who followed this pattern of storytelling were reinforced and guided by the interactions of the teacher. The black students, however, did not follow the topic-centered pattern of presentation; they had, instead, a style of discourse that involved implicit associations. They also organized the themes of their stories through the use of paralinguistic cues that were not understood by the teacher. The result was a pattern of interaction that spiraled downward, educationally speaking, as the teacher interrupted the black students in an attempt to get them to state the topic and to connect information together in an explicit and linear manner. Their use of anecdotal associations rather than linear description made it difficult for the teacher to understand what the students were saying, as their accounts did not seem to have beginnings, middles, or ends. In failing to understand what the students were sharing, the teacher, according to Michaels and Collins, would interject questions in a manner that disrupted the students in mid-sentence and threw them off the themes they were developing in their topic-associating style. Later the teacher attempted to get the black children to conform to her implicit schema by emphasizing that appropriate topics for sharing were "really, really very important . . . and sort of different" (p. 120). When it became clear that the emphasis on "very important" did not change the black students' narrative style, the teacher announced a new guideline: sharing would involve telling about only "one thing" (p. 123).

Using the Terms Culture and Language

As this example of cultural misunderstanding is not unique except in the specifics of the situation, we want to return to the basic question of what should constitute the basis of the teacher's professional knowledge. In contrast to Duke's (1979) observation about the vague nature of culture and the general indifference that is shown toward culture by the proponents of the classroom management paradigm, we want to identify those aspects of culture and language that should be part of the teacher's professional education. But before providing an overview of how this cultural-language territory is to be approached in subsequent chapters, we want to clarify how we are using the terms *culture* and *language*. As we view both culture and language semiotically (that is, as involving the encoding of meaning that makes communication possible), it is, in one sense, impossible to separate them. In order to illuminate the distinctive characteristics of the classroom milieu of meaning and pattern, we find it necessary to use the special explanatory power of the term *culture;* in other instances we use the term *language*. The separate use of the terms helps to manage the relation of foreground and background; when one term is used to foreground certain aspects of the milieu of pattern and meaning, the other term remains associated with the background.

CULTURE. Our use of the word *culture* is largely dependent on Clifford Geertz's interpretation. For Geertz, "culture patterns are 'programs'; they provide a template or blueprint for the organization of social and psychological processes" (1973, p. 216). He also refers to culture as "historically transmitted patterns of meaning embodied in symbols . . . by means of which [people] communicate, perpetuate, and develop their knowledge about and attitudes toward life" (p. 89). This view of cultural patterns as derived from the past and serving as the initial basis for understanding the present, relates to an important point made by another anthropologist, Ward Goodenough. As he put it, "no one can treat every sensory experience from moment to moment as if it were unique, for then past experience would be no help in dealing with the present" (1981, p. 63). The issue here is not whether we *should* be dependent; it is the deeper one of recognizing that we are not as individualistic and autonomous as the liberal tradition of thought suggests. We shall later see, as we situate the discussion more in terms of the classroom, that the term *culture* provides a way of understanding how nearly all aspects of human experience are based on taken-for-granted categories of understanding, patterns of social interaction, and prejudices of taste, sound, and color. Goodenough's summary makes this point in a different way. "Culture," he writes, "consists of standards for deciding what is, standards for deciding what can be, standards for deciding how one feels about it, standards for deciding what to do about it, and standards for deciding how to go about doing it" (1981, p. 62).

Pattern, schema, and *template* are some of the terms these anthropologists use to explain how forms of understanding shaped in the distant past are encoded as guides for living in the present. As most of us are not directly aware of these templates for organizing "social and psychological processes," to use Geertz's phrase, we want to qualify the emphasis in the Goodenough statement on how culture helps us in "deciding" what to do in different situations. The process of "deciding" should not be interpreted here as meaning that the individual is consciously aware of how the pattern, or template, influences the thought process and affective states. The teacher who interrupted the black first-grade students because their pattern of discourse did not conform to her own linear and topic-centered pattern, for example, was making many decisions; but it is unlikely that she was aware of how the cultural patterns of her language group were influencing her conscious decision to find a strategy that would help keep errant students on the topic. As in this example, the guiding cultural patterns are seldom part of the person's conscious awareness. Instead, they are experienced by the individual as part of a worldview that is transparent or taken for granted. Edward Hall's (1977) observation that we tend to be unaware of our own cultural patterns as long as the patterns are followed seems relevant here. It points to the fact that most of our cultural knowledge is taken for granted; that is, cultural codes underpin what individuals experience as the normal state of things, and this sense of normality or taken-for-grantedness is often projected as the basis of other people's experience. This is the basis for "culture shock," an experience encountered when taken-for-granted cultural patterns are not followed.

Our proposal to shift teacher education from a primarily Cartesian paradigm to a more culturally and linguistically sensitive framework for understanding the classroom is dependent on the recognition of the point we have just made about how we are largely under the unconscious control of the cultural patterns shared by our language community. Even though we agree with the preponderance of evidence that supports the argument that individuals are unconscious of many of the guiding cultural patterns, we think that it is possible to make explicit some of the patterns that are present in classroom life. We also believe that an understanding of these patterns is essential to understanding part of the basis of miscommunication as well as forms of conceptualization and behavior that may be misjudged as the expression of a lack of intellectual ability or deviant social behavior.

But it must be kept in mind that the taken-for-granted nature of these cultural patterns makes our approach more difficult than that of the classroom management paradigm, wherein the objective nature of observation is taken for granted (which is actually a good example of the guiding influence of a complex cultural tradition). The process of making explicit these hidden cultural patterns is facilitated, in part, by naming them and by developing a theoretical understanding of the relationships between the patterns. This use of language, as feminists have taught us in recent years, provides the conceptual distance from the taken-for-granted nature of classroom experience that is necessary to recognize relationships and characteristics that otherwise would not be evident. Much of the identification of the processes of language and culture that constitute the symbolic medium within which teachers and students interact and negotiate meanings has already been done by anthropologists, social linguists, and others interested in the classroom. Our efforts to broaden the conceptual basis of the teacher's professional knowledge will thus involve a heavy reliance on their work.

LANGUAGE. We also wish to clarify our special use of the term *language* as the basis for our metaphorical image of the classroom as an ecology of relationships. As we indicated earlier, language cannot be separated from culture. This connection can be seen more clearly if we recognize that language, in its broadest sense, is the necessary medium for a culture to be lived and renewed as part of a shared communal life (Halliday, 1978). But here we would like to emphasize more the processes of communication or information exchange that are encoded in culturally specific ways, and to do this we need to focus more specifically on language.

In one sense the sender-receiver model of language embedded in the classroom management paradigm touches on an elementary truth about the communicative function of language. But it oversimplifies the cultural dynamics of communication, since the interactions of teacher and students involve the sharing and negotiation of meanings that relate both to interpersonal relationships and the instructional process. Gregory Bateson's observation seems critical to viewing language as more than a conduit through which information is transmitted:

> Language continually asserts by the syntax of subject and predicate that "things" somehow "have" qualities and attributes. A more precise way of talking would insist that the "things" are produced, are seen as separate from other "things," and are made "real" by their internal relations and by their behavior in relationship with other things and with the speaker. (1980a, p. 67)

Instead of viewing language in the linear manner, whereby communication involves only one side of an interaction (i.e., the information the teacher wants to communicate to students), Bateson urges us to think of language more as a process wherein relationships evolve through the continual feedback of information exchanges. This view of language emphasizes its contextual and interactive nature. To put it in another way that relates more directly to the classroom, language serves to communicate information and, at the same time, as the medium for maintaining and negotiating social relationships.

Although our view of language encompasses the understanding that language provides the conceptual schemes that collectively constitutes a group's view of reality, we want to emphasize the need to view language as more than spoken and written communication. Bateson's more ecological perspective complements this aspect of language but also points beyond it in a way that is particularly fruitful for understanding the multiple levels of message exchanges that characterize a classroom. The use of social space, dress, facial expression, body movement, and voice pitch are all part of an ecology of relationship; and they all are complex, culturally embedded sign systems that must be interpreted by the teacher. Even the design of desks and the layout of classroom physical space can be understood as a coded message system that conveys meaning and must be interpreted. Seating patterns, for example, may communicate implicit beliefs regarding student and teacher roles.

To summarize our use of the term *language*, we are using it in the broadest sense to mean that an activity involves a sign that signifies a meaning or value to another person. What a gesture, tone of voice, or conversational style signifies has to be interpreted by the teacher. And in terms of our view of the teacher's professional knowledge, this involves sorting out the more personal dimensions of what is being communicated from the more culturally prescribed aspects of content and form. It also involves an awareness of the teacher's own culturally prescribed patterns of communicating.

ECOLOGY OF THE CLASSROOM AND PROFESSIONAL DECISION MAKING: AN OVERVIEW OF THEMES

A point we have been making, albeit somewhat indirectly, is that the teacher's professional judgment should be based on a body of knowledge essential to providing classroom instruction. This body of knowledge includes the content areas of the curriculum; an understanding of the physiological, psychological, and cultural influences on the learning process; and an understanding of the cultural and language processes that constitute the dynamic environment of the classroom. Although our main interest here is on illuminating the different aspects of the classroom ecology that must be taken into consideration as part of the teacher's professional decision making, we will at times identify how the cultural and language processes that influence communication in the classroom relate to issues in the content area and to the process of learning itself. Our main concern, however, will be to establish a new conceptual basis for understanding the dynamics of the classroom and to illuminate aspects of the teacher's decision making that have been neglected by the proponents of a more technicist approach. We think that as an understanding of the formative influences of culture and language is deepened, there will be corresponding changes in thinking about the structure of knowledge that makes up the content area of the curriculum and in thinking about the processes of learning—from an individualistic to a more culturally centered view of learning. These developments, however, are outside the immediate focus of this book.

Although the ecology of the classroom could be understood from the perspective of a critical semiotics, where attention is given to cultural conventions or codes that, in turn, generate the signs that serve as the basic unit of communication, we wish to use a language that is more accessible to the classroom teacher. We shall draw on a number of areas of inquiry concerned with different aspects of the culture-language-thought connection that are related to the professional judgments that teachers continually face as they attempt to orchestrate and direct communication processes in the classroom. In one sense these processes, which constitute the symbolic medium of the classroom that the teacher and students must continually interpret and give meaning to, are interrelated. But in order to illuminate different aspects of the classroom ecology, it is necessary to use a vocabulary that gives the alternative perspective of a different theoretical framework. Thus one level of understanding is achieved by using the language derived from the current discourse on metaphor, and another level of understanding comes into focus as we draw from the literature that addresses the function of framing in conversation. Similarly, the dynamics of classroom ecology can be explained in terms of primary socialization; but the use of other theoretical concerns, such as the current interest in the cognitive differences between the printed and spoken word, also helps bring into sharp focus the complexity of the issues that teachers must decide.

Chapter 2 addresses one of the most important, though least understood, characteristics of the classroom, namely, the metaphorical nature of language and thought. We have already discussed how the technicist approach to classroom management is based on a conduit view of language, as well as how this way of thinking about language as a neutral conveyer of information strengthens the notion of objective knowledge. Important educational and political issues, varying from ethnicity to gender, are ignored by this way of understanding. In order to help teachers more fully recognize these issues, as well as base their teaching on a sounder cognitive foundation, we shall summarize recent insights about the central role that metaphor plays in the thought process. The poet Robert Frost warned teachers of the dangers of not understanding the nature of metaphorical thinking. In his essay "Education by Poetry," he wrote:

> [If] you don't know the metaphor in its strength and weaknesses, you don't know how far you may expect to ride it and when it may break down with you. You are not safe in science; you are not safe in history. . . . All metaphor breaks down somewhere. That is the beauty of it. It is touch and go with the metaphor, and until you have lived with it long enough you don't know where it is going. You don't know how much you can get out of it and when it will cease to yield. It is a very living thing. It is life itself. (Cox & Lathem, 1968, p. 33)

Frost is indeed correct about metaphor being fundamental to our view of reality and in suggesting that the teacher's professionalism requires an understanding of how the use of metaphor facilitates a new way of understanding—and when its use is carried to a point at which it creates misunderstanding. This ability is not widely shared by parents and other professionals—though their efforts would be greatly enhanced if they were better attuned to the shaping force of metaphor. But the professionalism of the teacher requires the deepest understanding of the constitutive role of metaphor; as the introduction of new concepts can only be understood in terms of the familiar, teachers cannot claim ignorance or indifference without communicating a willing sense of complicity in professional malpractice.

Our task in Chapter 2 will be to explain the different forms of metaphor (i.e., analogic, iconic, and generative—or root—metaphor) that come into play as the teacher introduces students to both the formal and informal curriculum. We will also explain the connection between metaphorical thinking and the problems of cultural and gender domination that often occur in the classroom. Our main task, however, will be to utilize typical classroom situations in which understanding is being guided by the use of metaphor in order to highlight the educationally significant moments (what Frost refers to as the moments when metaphor expands the ability to understand or when metaphor breaks down) to which teachers need to be particularly alert. We also want to explain how teachers can introduce metaphor into the curriculum in a manner that helps sensitize students to this aspect of their language environment.

Chapter 3 deals with the nonverbal communication that makes the ecology of the classroom a complex environment of message exchanges. Although the dominant culture tends to emphasize the spoken and written word as the primary means of communication, nonverbal forms of communication are important sources of information that may, at times, change how the spoken word is understood. Nonverbal communication in the classroom includes tone of voice, intonation, facial expression, gaze, body movement, interpersonal space, silence, and so forth. Faced with a classroom of students who are continually communicating about their feelings, moods, attitudes, understandings, and expectations, teachers must be able to make prompt assessments of what is being communicated and respond either on an individual or group basis in a manner that maintains a supportive educational environment. Nonverbal communication involves an element of conscious intent and the use of cultural patterns of expression that are often not fully recognized by either the sender or receiver of the message.

A primary purpose of this chapter will be to introduce a vocabulary for identifying the different forms of nonverbal communication that teachers should be able to recognize, provide an overview of the educationally relevant findings that have come from recent research into this area of communication, and identify a number of guidelines that teachers might consider as they attempt to interpret what students are learning and gauge students' willingness to support the direction the educational process is taking.

Chapter 4 provides a theoretical framework for understanding how the teacher's choice of curriculum materials, as well as control over instructional talk, is part of the process of primary socialization (Bowers, 1987a). By drawing on the language of the sociology of knowledge, it is possible to illuminate the dynamics of primary socialization that are under the teacher's control—even when teachers are not consciously aware of their influence on the conceptual development of students who are learning something for the first time. Primary socialization has to do with *how* culture is passed on. It also has to do with *whose* culture is made real and legitimate through the language that is given to students. Culture that is communicated to students largely at a taken-for-granted (tacit) level, such as the way a natural language is learned or the way gender-specific attitudes were shared in the past, has a different educational effect on students than those aspects of culture that are learned at an explicit level. The latter, when combined with a historical perspective, complex vocabulary, and theoretical framework that enable students to represent conceptually the complexity of the issues that are being dealt with, provides the conceptual basis for the competence in communication necessary for democratic decision making. Culture learned at the tacit level represents a form of shared knowledge that is used in context, but it generally exerts an unconscious control over thought and behavior.

An understanding of the dynamics of primary socialization, it can be argued, is really at the heart of the teacher's professional knowledge. In addition to providing an explanation of the process of primary socialization, the chapter will be used to identify the different "moves" in the process that are under the teacher's control: the language that is used to define "what is," the aspects of culture that are to be made explicit or left at a taken-for-granted level, the introduction of a historical perspective that questions the sense of objectivity, and the deep level of awareness that comes with a cross-cultural perspective. We shall also discuss the educational effects that are likely to result when teachers are not attentive to the dynamics of the reality-constructing process they are part of. Classroom decisions leading to a form of primary socialization that limits the ability to think and communicate about socially relevant issues will be discussed. Similarly, we will identify the professional judgments that make socialization a more emancipating process.

Chapter 5 will address a number of classroom issues that can be dealt with more effectively when the teacher understands the process of framing, as well as how the use of solidarity and power affect the learning environment. The multiple levels of communication that are characteristic of the classroom ecology would result in total symbolic noise, like the simultaneous scrambling of TV channels, if it were not for the process of framing. Framing establishes the boundaries and focus of experience that allow for communication to be based on a common footing. Since framing determines what will be attended to, and on what basis, it involves the exercise of control. It also determines the status relationships, as well as other culturally prescribed patterns of behavior, that are appropriate to what is being communicated. Thus the exercise of control at this most basic level of communicative events is influenced by cultural norms; this also means that miscommunication in the classroom has to do not only with improper framing but also, in some instances, with cultural factors that may make the frame incomprehensible to students who do not share the teacher's cultural assumptions.

Framing of communication, especially within the classroom, continually involves teacher-student relationships that move on a continuum from a shared sense of solidarity in a common undertaking to the exercise of power involving status and role distinction. Where the teacher is on this continuum, and the appropriateness to the classroom context of either the expression of solidarity with students or the exercise of power, is critical to whether the teacher is engaging students in educative experiences or performing a custodial role. We will use this chapter to explain not only what teachers should understand about the dynamic nature of framing, and how it relates to classroom relationships of power and solidarity, but also how the teacher's control over the allocation of turn-taking rights, the continuing process of negotiation of classroom processes, and the use of humor influence the learning environment. These are all aspects of communication in the classroom that help illustrate why the professional judgment of the teacher should be based on a sociological and cultural understanding rather than a behavioral model that relies chiefly on reinforcement as the means of control.

Chapter 6 takes up the issue of how the language processes of the classroom can be understood as an ecology of power that advantages certain groups of students over others. Contrary to the classroom management paradigm, which treats the nature of the individual, rational process, and language as culturally neutral, we think it is imperative to ground pedagogical practices, as well as curricular decisions, in a more culturally informed manner. The recognition that not all cultural groups value the same forms of knowledge, and may even diverge in learning styles in ways that reflect differences in cultural views of reality, brings into the open the political nature of the teacher's role. The classroom management paradigm, on the other hand, uses the language of science and technology to hide its political nature—which largely involves imposing a technicist, white, masculine, middle-class set of values and view of knowledge on all students. We thus want to clarify those aspects of the classroom ecology that require a sensitivity to the political nature of curricular decisions, teaching strategies, and approaches to classroom management.

In this chapter we shall utilize the insights of Michel Foucault, the French social philosopher, into the nature of power as a field of asymmetrical relationships. This will provide a more comprehensive approach to understanding the political processes at work in the classroom. Power, as Foucault broadly defines it, involves an "action upon an action" that results in a modification or repression of subsequent thought and behavior. It is often exercised through institutionalized strategies that affect the patterns of social relationships, the means by which identities are constituted and lived out, and the values and views of reality that will be given privileged standing over others. The exercise of power, as Foucault has demonstrated in numerous historical studies of the interconnection of new forms of knowledge and new elites, points to the need for a broader definition of what constitutes a political relationship. As all the chapters deal with the educational implications of the diverse cultural patterns that make up the ecology of most classrooms, we want to use Foucault's way of looking at power (politics) as a way of illuminating two aspects of the classroom that have been largely ignored in the classroom management literature: the consequences of privileging literacy (print) over orality (spoken word) and classroom practices that continue to foster gender-based inequalities. Transmitting culture through the printed word influences consciousness and social relationships in a fundamentally different way than does voice communication. As part of their professional knowledge, teachers need to understand not only the immediate educational issues, such as how the use of the printed word reconstitutes the culture the student is learning about in accordance with a specific thought pattern, but also how each form of communication contributes to the formation of different types of societies. Similarly, teachers need to have a professional knowledge of the many ways in which gender inequalities are perpetuated in the classroom, as well as how the issue of gender relationships is viewed by different cultural groups.

Chapter 7 utilizes the insights derived from our examination of the classroom as an ecology of language processes and cultural patterns as a basis for a culturally responsive approach to supervision and teacher inservice. The field of teacher supervision, we argue, has been dominated by the same tradition of Cartesian thought that has exerted such a profound influence on thinking about effective teaching and classroom management. By viewing the classroom primarily in terms of behaviors that can be measured, supervision has become highly technicist in orientation. Observation of teacher-student behaviors may yield valuable information about certain aspects of the learning environment. But we will argue that this approach to supervision, which is a critical part of teacher socialization, is too narrow. The critical elements of supervision are, in a sense, dictated by the characteristics of a classroom ecology: the mental ecology of the classroom (the ideas and values encoded in the formal and informal curriculum), the teacher's gatekeeper role in primary socialization, and the patterns of nonverbal communication that characterize the ecology of classroom relationships. These classroom characteristics lead to thinking of the role of the supervisor in terms of qualitative fieldwork. The supervisor's task is thus defined in terms of critical description, interpretation, and evaluation—but in a framework that is sensitive to how the patterns of culture and language influence thought and communication. In effect, we argue for a shift from an awareness of behavior to an awareness of how cultural patterns are individualized and communicated in the classroom.

The Afterword, "Educating Teachers for the Twenty-First Century," places the ecology of the classroom within the larger ecology, where cultural practices interact with the natural systems that constitute our habitat. The evidence from scientific studies of "ozone holes," "greenhouse effect," "global warming," "pesticide poisoning," "special extinctions," "acid rain" (to cite just a few of the environmental problems that are receiving media attention) strongly suggests that our culture, as well as others, is based on assumptions that ignore the interdependence of cultural and natural systems. Our assumptions about technological progress, the autonomous individual, and the power of the rational process to create artificial systems that can be substituted for natural systems, as well as the practice of defining our standard of living in terms of levels of consumption (where more is equated with better), do not make sense when we look at the depletion of nonrenewable resources and the other environmental consequences of this cultural orientation. The challenge for the teacher, as a gatekeeper in the cultural transmission process, is to help students rethink those aspects of the culture, those traditions of thought and practice formed in response to an earlier set of social and environmental circumstances, that are based on assumptions that sanction the domination and exploitation of the environment. Other theories of educational reform, we argue, are based on assumptions that do not recognize our interdependence with natural systems. An uncritical acceptance of their guiding metaphors of technology, individual emancipation, and rational self-direction will simply exacerbate the ecological crisis. In the past, we were able to compensate for or ignore the damage caused by what Bateson termed "pathological ideas." Today, the extent of documented ecological damage suggests that the margin for error in our guiding ideologies has all but disappeared.

Our purpose is to help establish a new conceptual foundation for thinking about effective classroom practices, effective in the sense of being justified on sound pedagogical and political grounds. We shall thus incorporate the insights and classroom practices from other paradigms, including classroom management, when they can be reconciled with our more culture- and language-sensitive orientation. We shall also clarify why certain classroom procedures that are presently being promoted represent hidden and, in some cases, not so hidden forms of cultural domination. In addition, we shall be buttressing the argument that the conceptual foundations of teacher professionalism are more properly derived from anthropology, social and cultural linguistics, and sociology than from behaviorism and industrial engineering. Industrial engineering, for example, has not helped teachers recognize Robert Frost's point about extending a metaphor, such as thinking of the student as a "product," beyond its proper limits; nor has behaviorism made them aware that the essence of their own professionalism involves more than behavioral management.

CHAPTER 2

Metaphor, Language, and Thought

"I'm going to do some work," Richard Dodds announces to his seventh-grade shop students, and he proceeds to act out several examples of lifting objects from the floor to the top of his desk. In each case, he emphasizes the effort involved in lifting, then concludes: "So, work has to do with weight or, I'll give it another word, *force*." He writes the word FORCE on the blackboard and underlines it. "So one component of work is that I've got to have some force. I'm going to do some more work."

This time the teacher pushes on his desk, sliding it several feet across the front of the classroom. Again, he claims to have done work. He runs through this example a second time, but asks a student to hold the desk still as he applies pressure to the opposite side. The desk remains in place, and he asks the class:

"Have I done work? No, I haven't. I have to move it somewhere. No matter how hard I try, if I don't move it, I haven't done any work. A second component of work is distance. So, *work*—what we're going to talk about today—equals force times distance." (As he talks, he writes on the board: WORK = FORCE × DISTANCE.) "Work equals force times distance. *That's* the thing that I want us to understand today. Work equals force times distance. We're going to find out ways in the next week to make work a little easier."

At this point in the lesson Richard has moved from his introduction to a formal definition of the type that might be found in an elementary physics textbook. He continues by eliciting examples from his students of "things that save work." A direct reference to the students' science class cues their responses: pulley, lever, wedge, inclined plane, wheel and axle, screw.

The rest of the lesson is devoted to providing students with a concrete demonstration of the mathematical relationship expressed in the definition of WORK = FORCE × DISTANCE. In making this demonstration, Richard uses a wooden model of a wheel and axle that raises and lowers a small bucket on a string. Different-sized wheels are attached to the assembly to show that larger wheels (increased distance) reduce the amount of force required (make the task easier). At the end of the lesson, he tells the students: "I'm going to ask you for homework tonight to give me examples of five things that use a wheel and axle." The reference to "home*work*" reframes the lesson. Homework is a part of the students' everyday experience; it needs no formal definition.

This teacher was attempting to provide students with a conceptual basis for understanding the nature of work. Although knowledgeable about the concepts he was presenting, and skilled in providing concrete examples, he was unaware of the metaphorical nature of the language and thought process in which he was engaging the students. The students were also unaware of being caught up in a network of metaphorical understanding. Teachers of other subjects share the same dependency on the use of metaphor to introduce students to new ideas and ways of understanding. Because of the traditional practice of associating metaphor with what English teachers talk about, as well as several deeply held misconceptions about how language is used as a tool (conduit) of expression and the objective nature of knowledge, many teachers fail to recognize the educational implications of this aspect of the language environment. This lack of understanding, in turn, prevents them from being sensitive to the constitutive role that metaphor plays in the learning process and from knowing in a professional sense when the metaphor breaks down and thus contributes to misunderstanding. In order to make explicit the professional judgments that teachers should be able to make about this aspect of the classroom ecology, we want to explain the connection between metaphor and thought, identify different forms of metaphor that have pedological implications, and establish a basis for recognizing the culturally specific nature of metaphorical thinking. This last area of concern is especially important to teachers who are educating students from different cultural backgrounds, particularly since the inability of students from nondominant cultural backgrounds to understand may have more to do with the use of unfamiliar metaphorical frameworks than with individual intelligence and motivation.

CONCEPTUAL FOUNDATIONS

Our understanding of the connection of language, which we view as metaphorical, and thought must start with Martin Heidegger's insight that the individual is born (what he called our "thrownness") into a social world of existing patterns, relationships, and ways of understanding. Learning the language of this social world involves acquiring this heritage of meaning and patterns for understanding in a manner that becomes part of the individual's natural attitude. In terms of the dominant culture this can be understood in terms of being born into a society that views time as linear and measurable, the printed word as having greater authority than the spoken word, change as progressive, and the individual as autonomous. The process of learning to think and speak the language that encodes the cultural forms of understanding provides the individual a conceptual framework that serves as a basis for understanding new phenomena. As Heidegger put it, "the language already hides in itself a developed way of conceiving" (1927/1962, p. 199).

To put it another way, the language of the culture provides the shared set of preunderstandings that will guide the interpretations the individual makes of new experiences; for the most part these preunderstandings will not be part of what the individual is explicitly aware of. In writing about the differences that separate the dominant white culture from those of Native Americans, Jamake Highwater provides examples that suggest how deeply rooted and hidden these preunderstandings are. The examples also remind us of how a set of cultural preunderstandings can lead to undesirable social and ecological consequences while preventing us, as it were, from recognizing the "developed way of conceiving" that is acquired as part of the process of becoming a member of the culture. To quote Highwater:

> When an English word is descriptive—like the word "wilderness"—I am often appalled by what is implied by the description. After all the forest is not "wild" in the sense that it is something needing to be tamed or controlled or harnessed. For Blackfeet Indians, the forest is the natural state of the world. It is the cities that are wild and seen to need "taming." (1981, p. 5)

As another example of fundamental differences in cultural preunderstandings, Highwater observes:

> For most primal peoples the earth is so marvelous that their connotation of it requires it to be spelled in English with a capital "E." How perplex-

ing it is to discover two English synonyms for Earth—"soil" and "dirt"—used to describe uncleanliness, *soiled* and *dirty*. And how upsetting it is to discover that the word "dirty" in English is also used to depict obscenities. (p. 5)

Before we get into an explanation of how the metaphorical nature of thought can be used to understand what Heidegger means when he says that "language speaks" us as we speak the language, we want to summarize the key points being made here about the nature of language:

1. It is not that thought is reducible to language, but that thought cannot be treated as separate from language, as suggested by Highwater's examples as well as examples that could be taken from the area of gender discrimination.
2. Language makes thought possible while simultaneously constraining it to the conceptual boundaries of the language. This does not mean that the constraints of language, like the example of associating nature with being wild and in need of taming, cannot be made explicit and reconceptualized. But it requires a special effort for individuals to make explicit the taken-for-granted framework of cultural preunderstanding; it also requires a special ability on the teacher's part to facilitate it.
3. Language is *not* a neutral tool for the expression of ideas preformed in the mind of the individual. This view of language, whereby it is used in the instrumental sense of sharing ideas with others, does not take account of its constitutive role. A more accurate way of thinking about language would be to view it as the medium within which the individual interprets and understands, rather than as something external, like a tool, that is selected for achieving a specific and conscious purpose.

One approach to clarifying how the use of language in the classroom "hides within itself a developed way of conceiving" is to consider the metaphorical nature of language as well as the role that metaphor plays in the thought process. Although much of the language of nonverbal communication is metaphorical, we are concerned here with the spoken and written language that is the basis of classroom discourse. The above quotation from Heidegger points to one of the functions of metaphor; namely, of providing a schema for understanding. The teacher's explanation of work that we presented earlier, when accepted by students, provides a schema (interpretative framework or conceptual pattern) for understanding the physical manipulation of objects as examples of work. Other students socialized to a different metaphorical framework for understanding might interpret activity (including mental activity) associated with monetary compensation as work. Another example of an embedded schema can be found in Madeline Hunter's explanation of how the teacher should think about the process of learning:

> While the first decision of teaching is based on the content, the *what* of teaching, the second decision is directed to *student behavior* that makes learning possible, the student's *how* of learning. There are two aspects of a student's learning behavior. One aspect is focused on students' output which validates acquisition of the knowledge or skill. That output must be *perceivable*. (1986, p. 5)

The schema or model here is that of the student as a machine, whereby inputs lead to measurable (observable) outputs. The conceptual coherence of Hunter's statements about the learning process is sustained by this metaphor as an interpretative schema.

There is another function of metaphor that reflects the power of human imagination, which, in turn, gives our language its symbolic openness. The embedded schema, as found in the teacher's explanation of work and Hunter's statement on inputs and outputs, leads to a thought process wherein the present is understood in terms of the accepted (and often unquestioned) thought patterns of the past. But a more critically aware and imaginative aspect of metaphorical thinking can lead to substituting new schemata as a basis of interpretation. Whether metaphor plays a passively conservative or more dynamic role depends on individuals, who must reflect on the adequacy of their conceptual models for expressing the distinctive elements of awareness and understanding.

Originally, metaphor (*metaphora* to the Greeks) meant "to carry over." That is, metaphor is the means of understanding something in terms of something else. The way of understanding, appropriate in one context, is carried over into another context, with the metaphor providing the conceptual scaffolding for understanding new situations. In addition to understanding the new in terms of the familiar, metaphorical thinking enables us to obtain a fresh perspective on situations that are so familiar they have lost their meaning. This process of seeing something in comparison with something else involves the use of imagination—such as understanding a community as a "moral ecology," the planet as a "spaceship," and the indigenous people as

"Indians." Richard Brown's explanation of metaphor, whereby metaphor is "understood as an illustrative device whereby a term from one level or frame of reference is used within a different level or frame" (1978, p. 78), points to the role of imagination in recognizing a basis for comparison; but as the deliberately varied examples suggest, the basis of comparison may be less significant than the differences. Thus in saying that metaphorical thinking has an imaginative dimension, we are not suggesting that the recognition of common elements is always based on profound insight. Thinking of the president as a quarterback, the computer as intelligent, and the student as a machine are examples of misdirected and shallow thinking.

FORMS OF METAPHOR

The need to understand the new in terms of the familiar, and to revitalize the familiar by making associations with new areas of experience, makes the classroom a seedbed of metaphorical thinking. In order to recognize more clearly the decisions that teachers must be able to make in order to insure that metaphorical thinking deepens the students' understanding, rather than providing misleading and confusing schemata for understanding, we want to identify three aspects of metaphorical thinking that exert a particularly profound influence on the process of learning. In effect, we shall be dealing with how language provides the conceptual mapping process that both facilitates and guides understanding.

Analogic Thinking

A common characteristic of communication in the classroom, from the first grade through graduate school, is the use of analogic thinking. Unlike social settings, in which learning is often more context dependent and involves the use of other people as models, learning in schools is characterized by a more abstract approach whereby new concepts and procedures (whatever the content of the curriculum) are introduced through the media of talk and print. As a more abstract form of learning, the new content that the teacher introduces often cannot be understood on its own—unless it is simply memorized. As this is unlikely to involve real understanding, good teachers attempt to provide a foothold for understanding by identifying some area of experience or understanding that is already familiar to the students. The familiar, in possessing common elements with the new idea that is being introduced, serves as a model, or schema, for understanding. For example, in a chapter on infectious diseases students read that "footballs are not the only things that can be passed from person to person. Almost every time you are with people, you pass micro-organisms to each other" (Meeks & Heit, 1982, p. 167). The familiar experience of passing and catching a football becomes the basis of understanding how disease is spread. This process of thinking of the new as being like the familiar is an example of analogic thinking.

The use of analogic thinking to introduce new concepts and pro-cedures is such a common aspect of classroom communication that the process goes largely unnoticed. It is also essential to communica-tion outside the classroom, and even to the advancement of the most esoteric forms of research. For example, in the early work on artificial intelligence the brain was seen *as like* a "neural network," connected by communication lines. And in genetic research, the four nucleic acids—often abbreviated by the letters A, C, G, and T—are viewed *as like* an alphabet. To carry this line of analogic thinking further, the genetic code is thought of *as like* a set of plans and instructions that regulate the growth and metabolism of the organism. Use of analogic thinking in the classroom involves a similar juxtaposition in thought of two domains of experience—the structure of the idea or experience that is to be illuminated through comparison, and the area of previous understanding that provides the model for thinking about what is new and otherwise incomprehensible. In the classroom, to cite ex-amples taken from textbooks, students are taught to think of the body as like a machine that has parts and needs continual maintenance, time as like a unit of value that can be wasted or well spent, and the sun as like a huge ball of glowing gases that gives us heat and light. Observation in any classroom, regardless of subject area, will yield a rich set of examples of the teacher or textbook writer introducing a new concept by attempting to compare or associate it with something students already understand.

Because analogic thinking is so fundamental and natural to new understanding, several key characteristics of the process generally go unnoticed:

1. Analogic thinking involves thinking of something *as if* it is like something else. Often the as-if element of analogic thinking is lost sight of—time then *becomes* money; the body, a machine; and change, progress.
2. Analogic thinking involves comparisons between two domains of experience that have similarities in pattern structure and process.

However, the similarities that are the basis of comparison (e.g., "healthy cities are like boys and girls—they grow bigger and bigger") are often less important than the differences. For example, computer memory cannot replicate the existential dimensions of human memory; the president exercises control over setting the direction of our national priorities in a way that does not correspond to the role of the quarterback; and business practices are not really like warfare, even though business borrows much of its vocabulary from that area of experience.

3. The familiar domain of experience that provides the schema, or model, used to comprehend the new domain of understanding is always distinct to a particular cultural group. Thus money, machines, and competitive quarterbacks, while familiar to the Anglo-white middle class, might not provide a meaningful basis of understanding to the Native American who spells the word earth with a capital "E." As a consequence, analogic thinking must be viewed as utilizing conceptual building blocks that are both historically and culturally specific.

All of these characteristics are important points for any teacher in any classroom. The third, however, has particularly significant implications for the teacher who is sensitive to issues related to the problem of cultural domination of one group by another as well as the pedagogical issue of making a connection between the new and the familiar that facilitates understanding.

Generative Metaphor

In our classroom observations and study of teaching materials we found the presence of another aspect of metaphorical thinking that goes largely unnoticed. But like an invisible hand, it shapes, directs, inhibits, and frames what is being learned. Although this aspect is essentially part of analogic thinking, in that it seeks to explain the new in terms of the familiar, we think it deserves special treatment.

The aspect of metaphorical thinking to be discussed in this section has been given a number of labels: generative metaphors (Schon, 1979), root metaphors (Brown, 1978), and source-domain metaphors (Johnson, 1987). We shall use the terms, as the context of the discussion dictates, as nearly interchangeable. The important point is that all three terms refer to how metaphors may be used by a cultural group as conceptual templates for bringing to human experience a moral and conceptual sense of order. In this sense, generative, or root, metaphors provide the basic framework of a people's conceptual guidance system. If there is a distinction between generative and root metaphor, it is that the latter encodes assumptions about reality deeply rooted in the mythologies and religious beliefs of the past. The ideas of original sin, the universe as operating with a machine-like sense of order, understanding as connected with seeing, and the mind as a computer represent four examples of root metaphors that provide master templates for guiding the organization and interpretation of experience. These examples were deliberately chosen to demonstrate the complexity and multileveled character of this aspect of metaphor. The first two examples represent the most rudimentary of our conceptual and moral templates at different points in the history of Western culture. The cultural assumptions that connect understanding with seeing (vision, enlightenment, perception) rather than hearing coexisted with other master templates. In some instances, root metaphors relate to specific domains of cultural experience, while in other instances they serve to legitimate or undermine the hold of other master templates. The processes whereby the conceptual foundations are established, strengthened, transformed, and overturned are the substance of intellectual and cultural history.

For our purposes it is important to keep in mind that generative metaphors are not thing-like and thus do not have neatly discernible boundaries. But they have a history that can, with some effort, be identified. And they have real consequences in that they exert a powerful influence on our ways of thinking and interacting with one another and with our environment. Because generative metaphors have the potential of both enriching the quality of our lives as well as threatening it (as occurred when we viewed the "wilderness" as hostile and in need of subjugation), we will focus on how the process of understanding is metaphorically constituted. Awareness of this process is, in our opinion, absolutely essential for teachers, as it will enable them to recognize a number of other pedagogically significant decisions that continually arise in the classroom. But whether teachers will be able to discriminate between life-enhancing and life-threatening master templates of understanding is dependent, in part, on their critical understanding of how their cultural traditions relate to the environmental and social issues we now face. This is where a liberal education must complement the teacher's professional understanding of the dynamics of cultural reproduction in the classroom. To put it another way, being able to recognize a generative metaphor is not in itself important if the teacher does not understand why its use in a particular context may be inappropriate. An example of this is the tendency of many educators to view a computer as simply a tool that facilitates the processing of information and the expansion of ideas and thus to equate thinking with the manipulation of data.

One of the functions of a generative metaphor is to provide the conceptual structure, or model, for understanding experience. As Mark Johnson puts it: "In order for us to have meaningful, connected experiences that we can comprehend and reason about, there must be pattern and order to our actions, perceptions, and conceptions. A *schema is a recurrent pattern, shape, regularity in, or of, these ongoing ordering activities*" (1987, p. 29). This statement is important to our discussion of generative metaphors for two reasons. First, it challenges the commonsense view that the information used as the basis of thinking is derived from objective awareness—a problem we touched on earlier. Second, a generative metaphor provides the schema we use (often unconsciously) to conceptualize and bring a sense of order and meaning to our experiences. Thus the nature of the generative metaphor becomes critical to how we understand and act in the world.

Donald Schon provides a good example of how a generative metaphor frames a particular way of thinking about a social problem. During the 1950s, when people were concerned about the problem of urban housing, a group of experts suggested that community housing be understood in terms of a medical model wherein undesirable conditions would be viewed as diseased. The use of the generative metaphor (i.e., a diseased condition) led to the recommendation that health could only be restored by removing the cause of the disease; this meant replacing the existing buildings with an entirely new plan of urban development. In another instance, housing experts used a different generative metaphor, which led to an entirely different response to the problem. Instead of the medical model, which led to thinking of eliminating the "disease" and its causes, the community housing situation was viewed as a natural community; that is, as an ecology of relationships that included positive and negative elements. The response to the problem fostered by this very different generative metaphor led to a policy designed to nurture some existing aspects of community patterns and restructure others. The two different generative metaphors—thinking of a community as diseased and thinking of it as a natural ecology—provided two interpretative frameworks, or schemata, for thinking and responding to the problem. The choice of generative metaphors literally framed what was to be seen and understood—and the actions that were to follow. This example demonstrates that the choice of a different generative metaphor reframes (i.e., provides a different interpretative framework) the pattern of thought.

Another way of thinking about generative metaphors is to introduce Johnson's (1987) notion of a "source-domain." The basic problem in understanding the constitutive role of metaphor in the thought process is to recognize how "certain source-domains get mapped onto certain target-domains" (p. 106). To use the classroom example of the lesson on work at the beginning of the chapter, the target-domain is the new area of experience that needs to be understood. In this case, it is the problem of helping students understand the nature of work. As the teacher put it, "I'm going to do some work"; the rest of the lesson involved the use of a vocabulary drawn from a particular area of understanding, what Johnson terms the "source-domain." In this case the source-domain is the field of physics. The target-domain, to use Johnson's phrase, was the new area of experience that the teacher wanted the students to understand. The source-domain (the conceptual model for explaining mechanical energy) that was "mapped onto" (i.e., used as the schema for understanding) the target-domain thus led to an understanding of work that had to involve more than the expenditure of effort. Work had to involve force and distance. By using the language of physics as the generative metaphor the teacher was able to bring a mathematical precision to the commonsense understanding of work the students brought to the classroom. But the use of physics as the source-domain (generative) metaphor involved a conceptual mapping process that would make it impossible to consider thinking as a form of work or to view personal intent and motivation as important aspects of work. Similarly, other areas of experience, such as breathing, would have to be reconceptualized to fit the schema the teacher introduced for thinking about work in that it involves the movement of oxygen into the lungs. If the teacher had used other generative metaphors, that is, borrowed the conceptual model and accompanying vocabulary from other source-domains of experience, the students would have acquired entirely different ways of thinking about work. These might have included thinking of work as a calling; work as involving activity that produces something that is socially useful, fosters meaningful social relationships, and enhances self-growth (the Buddhist view of work); work as an activity that involves financial compensation and is figured into the gross national product; work as an activity that is understood in terms of another generative metaphor—the white, Western, masculine experience.

Observation in a classroom, regardless of the grade level, yields a steady stream of examples of generative metaphors being used as a basis for understanding some aspect of the culture the student is encountering for the first time or explanations that are sanctioned by the educational establishment. For example, a textbook title such as "The United States and Its Neighbors" utilizes the generative metaphor of relationships among neighbors to frame the student's thinking about the relationships among nations. The choice of other generative metaphors might illuminate the political nature of the relationship among nations, including economic and cultural tensions. In the textbook *Dimensions of Life* (Henderson, 1985), the unit on "Becoming a Fully Functioning Person" utilizes the generative metaphor of a mountain as a schema for students to use in understanding that the most basic level of human existence (base of the mountain) involves the meeting of physical and safety needs. The next higher level (like the stages of ascent up a mountain) are love, acceptance, and esteem needs. At the top, which is visually represented in the text as the peak of the mountain, are self-actualization needs. To avoid the impression that only the soft areas of study, such as the social sciences, depend on the use of generative metaphors to bring a needed sense of conceptual order, we would like to introduce some of the vocabulary used in computing: *bomb, collisions, execute, exploded file, fail safe, purge, coercion, command, crash, target, trap,* and *execution*. The source-domain, or generative, metaphor here is obviously that of the military. Other examples of how a generative metaphor derived from one area of experience provides the conceptual structure for making sense of another area of experience can be seen in such statements as "the body consists of distinct though interconnected parts" (machine is model for thinking about the body), "his criticisms were right on target" (warfare is model for thinking about an argument), and "since the speed of sound is constant through a medium, shorter waves have to travel with a higher frequency to cover the same distance as longer waves with lower frequency" (wave action of water is model for understanding sound).

It is important to take seriously the metaphor Schon uses to describe the function of metaphor: generative metaphors quite literally *generate* a largely ready-made conceptual framework for understanding a new area of experience. Our direct experiences, which range from bodily processes to familiarity with machines, business, sports, war, medicine, and so forth, involve learning complex, patterned ways of thinking (analogues) that are transferred to other domains of experience. When aspects of the new area of experience cannot be fully understood or expressed in terms of the borrowed language schema, then other generative metaphors are introduced or created, along with a new vocabulary that is essential in the conceptual reframing process. We can see this occurring as we shift from thinking of the environment in terms of exploitation to perceiving it in terms of nurturing and interdependency. Teacher education, to cite another example, has moved from the generative metaphor of organic growth, wherein teachers were perceived as nurturing students' natural curiosity, to that of a machine-like production process, with learning now understood in terms of inputs and outputs and students viewed as products of the system. Our own efforts here represent an attempt to overcome the limitations of the technocratically oriented generative metaphor by suggesting that the culture-language-thought ecology provides a more adequate schema for thinking about the deeper dimensions of education as a process of cultural reproduction.

We want to conclude this section by emphasizing the pervasiveness of teacher and student dependence on the use of generative metaphors and the potential inadequacy of thinking of something as a model of something else.

Iconic Metaphor

The use of analogic thinking and generative metaphors occurs primarily in classroom situations in which there is a conscious intent to introduce a way of understanding that previously has not been established for the student. The conscious intent of the teacher or the writer of a textbook (film script, software program, and so forth) is generally focused on the concept of factual information; their use of metaphor to frame a new way of understanding largely occurs, like the earlier use of a gender-oriented language, as part of the cultural-linguistic process that is taken for granted by the participants. It is, in effect, an aspect of understanding that is necessary for recognizing the form and detail of the foreground knowledge that the teacher is consciously attempting to share with students. The connection between the use of analogic thinking and generative metaphors and the introduction of ideas new to students means that much of the classroom discourse will be characterized by these forms of metaphor. There is also, however, another form of metaphor used in the classroom that does not fit the standard view of metaphor as involving a comparative framework for understanding. An examination of any written curricular materials will reveal the use of sentences containing a nonanalogic form of metaphor, or what more directly could be termed "iconic" (image) metaphor. Teacher and student talk is similarly dependent on sentences that are heavily dependent on iconic metaphors.

An interesting thing happens when we have a name for these iconic metaphors: We become aware of them as one of the most common aspects of talking and writing. We also become aware that an important element in the thought process involves the stringing together of images, or mental pictures. For example, the stringing together of iconic metaphors into a mental picture of what the author wants to convey can be seen in the following hypothetical examples: "Jim Beckworth *spent* his *later years running* a *ranch* and *trading post* near the *mountain pass* he *discovered*"; "*Notice* how the nuclear particles *rearrange themselves*"; "For a *long time, our society* was *held together,* even in *periods* of *rapid change,* by a *largely liberal Protestant cultural center* that *sought* to *reconcile* the *claims* of *community* and *individuality.*" The italicized words will be understood by most students and teachers, depending on their cultural background, because the words correspond to background experiences for which they now possess distinct images (mental pictures). The Russian linguist Lev Semenovich Vygotsky summarizes this process of thinking in images: "The primary word is not a straightforward symbol for a concept but rather an image, or picture, a mental sketch of a concept, a short tale about it—indeed, a small work of art. In naming an object by means of such a pictorial concept, man ties it into a group with a large number of other objects" (1962, p. 75). If the background of students includes direct experience (either bodily or culturally) that enables them to associate words (e.g., *rapid change, individuality, long time, rearrange, notice, running, ranch,* and so forth) with a referent, the sentence or string of images (mental pictures) will be meaningful.

In the example that began this chapter, the students who encountered the teacher's opening statement, "I am going to do some work," most likely had an image of work acquired in other settings—when parents had assigned them house- or yardkeeping tasks that involved the experience of work, or when they had listened to the conversations of others that involved the topic of work. In effect, these students possessed, in terms of their perspective, an understanding of what the word *work* meant. The teacher's task was to change the conceptual basis of what would function as a well-established iconic metaphor for most students in the class, and he did this by introducing a new vocabulary that he attempted to ground in experiences students could observe. But the lesson's success was dependent on the shared understanding of what other iconic metaphors referred to.

In order to understand what is pedagogically significant about iconic metaphors, we will focus on examples that have an established and largely accepted sense of meaning; that is, we want to explain the metaphorical nature of the words that are taken for granted in classroom discourse. The examples we will use to bring out the distinctive characteristics of iconic metaphors are such commonly used terms as *progress, intelligence, individualism,* and *work* (an iconic metaphor that was being challenged by the shop teacher).

These iconic metaphors were chosen because they are examples of words with a history that can be more easily traced back to an earlier period of analogic thinking, a time when people were attempting to understand new aspects of experience that were frozen in a language that seemed outmoded. During the time of the French Revolution, for example, intellectuals argued about whether change was progressive and about what constituted evidence of progress. These debates represented the analogic stage of metaphorical thinking, with new ideas about the authority of rational thought and a new view of individualism (two other metaphors that were also being grounded in a new way) providing a new conceptual framework for overturning tradition as the primary authority in people's lives. In effect, the iconic metaphor of "progress" encodes the earlier process of analogic thinking, but this fact is taken for granted by later generations.

More recently, the iconic metaphor of "intelligence," which was given a stable set of meanings early in this century by a group of psychologists who created a test for the "objective" measurement of people's intelligence, has been challenged on the grounds that it is both culturally biased and based on an excessively limited view of intelligent behavior. During the period of time that the word carried the accepted package of understandings established by the perspective that prevailed in the earlier stage of analogic debate, it was used as an iconic metaphor by people who accepted unquestioningly the view that intelligence could be demonstrated in a test situation. The history of the word *individualism* reveals a number of stages in which established meanings were contested, resulting in a new iconic metaphor that would be the conventional basis of thought until it was challenged and reconstituted with a new referent. Individualism has been understood in terms of a series of iconic images that have included, from feudal times to the present, the individual as a subject, citizen, self-expressive, and, now, self-creating. The intellectual and political process of changing the referent of an iconic metaphor can be seen more clearly in terms of our own experience with the image of work. Until recently the use of this iconic metaphor was not problematic; people who worked received monetary compensation that could be figured into the gross national product. People who did not receive compensation were thus not seen as doing work. With the rise of gender consciousness, this iconic metaphor was challenged, and we entered a period of analogic thinking in which the debate still continues about what activities should be associated with our image of work. This analogic phase of thinking, which will involve reconstituting the generative metaphors, will lead to a new and more complex image of what constitutes work. When the process of metaphorical thinking achieves this new stage of consensus, when people can once again use the word without questioning whether the word is associated with the proper area of experience, it will again be used as an iconic metaphor that is strung together in a sentence with other mental pictures.

It is also important to recognize that iconic metaphors are not limited to words. The design of a car, a dress, or a building may be metaphorical in that it suggests a relationship to something else that frames how it is to be understood. The car may suggest efficiency or flight (if we go back to the car designs of the 1950s), the dress may communicate rebellion (as well as group membership), while the building may suggest the rational sense of balance of the Greeks or the clean functionalism of the modern era. Body language is also an example of communicating through iconic metaphor, since certain gestures are associated with anger, detachment, friendliness, and so forth. The student who sits in the back of the room may not have gotten there by chance but may be using the organization of social space and body language to communicate noninterest or resistance. The imaginative function of metaphor, whereby something—a gesture, design, or pattern—suggests something else, also characterizes this domain of nonverbal communication.

In summary, the key points about the political, conceptual, taken-for-granted, and culturally specific nature of iconic metaphors include the following:

1. Iconic metaphors are an outgrowth of either experience in which the referent is personally grounded or a historical process wherein one set of associations prevails over others in a politically contested situation.
2. The iconic metaphor reproduces in thought (encode) the conceptual orientations (including the metaphorical associations) that characterized the earlier historical process. As John Deely puts it, in discussing the nature of a natural language, the iconic metaphor serves as a "carrier of historically structured experiences" (1982, p. 89).
3. Iconic metaphors involve a taken-for-granted stage of language

development, a stage in which the experiential basis of the referent signified by the word (e.g., *divides, links, appreciates,* to use different examples) is not being challenged.

4. The connection between an iconic metaphor and the thought processes and perceptions of the people who represented an earlier period in the development of the language community must always be understood as culturally specific. To put this last point another way, iconic metaphors are culturally specific: Freedom and individualism, for example, have different meanings for Anglo-Americans and the Japanese.

METAPHOR IN THE CLASSROOM

Our task in the previous part of this chapter has been to lay out the conceptual foundations for understanding metaphor as a primary aspect of everyday, ordinary language. It is within this context that metaphor can be seen as far more than simply a poetic device. That is, its common usage brings into focus the conceptual processes through which we acquire cultural beliefs and the implicit patterns of understanding into which we are able to incorporate new experience. This process is particularly important in the classroom, where learning tends to be oriented more toward abstract and context-free ideas. Under such conditions, metaphor is likely to serve as the main anchor in efforts to make sense of the school curriculum.

At this point, we wish to situate the implications of this view firmly within the practical world of day-to-day classroom teaching. Thus we now turn to a somewhat more focused set of questions:

What exactly should teachers understand about the metaphorical nature of language?

How will this understanding contribute to their professional knowledge?

In what ways will it help teachers improve the quality of their instruction?

As noted in Chapter 1, Robert Frost counseled educators that, "All metaphor breaks down somewhere. . . . It is touch and go with the metaphor, and until you have lived with it long enough you don't know where it is going. You don't know how much you can get out of it and when it will cease to yield" (Cox & Lathem, 1968, p. 33). We believe this is sound advice. Yet it can be taken a step further by identifying specific strategies that will help teachers recognize when metaphor may be used constructively and when it leads to miscommunication. We would like to accompany these strategies with a note of caution. They should not be regarded as recipe-like prescriptions for good teaching but rather as solely heuristic considerations. Their application by a particular teacher working with a particular group of students is what Joseph Schwab (1969) has referred to as a "practical art." In other words, these strategies are genuinely useful only to the extent that they augment, not replace, the teacher's insight and judgment.

The first step in identifying these strategies is to return to our earlier distinctions between analogic, generative, and iconic metaphor.

Analogic Metaphor

We begin with analogic metaphor because it is likely to be more easily recognized than other types of metaphorical thought. As noted earlier, analogic metaphor is a form of comparison that underscores the similarities between two domains of experience. Such comparison is pervasive in classroom instruction because it provides a foothold for understanding the unfamiliar in terms of the familiar. Consider, for example, the following statements, taken from the first few pages of a middle school textbook, *Life Science* (Balzer et al., 1983):

"The study of living things can enrich your life." (p. 1)
"Plants trap sunlight for energy." (p. 5)
"This life scientist is looking at a bed of lobsters." (p. 6)
"As life scientists learned more about the tiny organisms, we were able to combat and slow the spread of diseases." (p. 7)
"Scientists then analyze the data and draw conclusions." (p. 10)
"If the hypothesis stands the test of new data, it can become a theory." (p. 11)

In these statements, the words *enrich, trap, bed, combat, draw,* and *stand* all function as analogic metaphors. They work (in the sense that they express meaning) for two reasons. First, there are similarities between the types of experience that each word brings into comparison. Learning (study) is in some way like accumulating such "riches" as money or material goods. What plants do to sunlight is in some ways like what hunters do to their prey. A bed of lobsters is in some ways like a river bed or bed of flowers. Diseases are in some ways like enemies—they can be fought in combat. Second, the source-domain of the implied comparison is likely to be familiar. These analogic metaphors provide the initial conceptual scaffolding because middle school students have had previous experience with riches, beds, traps, combat, drawing, and standing. The teaching strategies that we will consider follow directly from these two characteristics of analogic metaphor.

The first strategy involves developing a sensitivity to what we will metaphorically call the conceptual boundaries of analogic thought. These boundaries encompass the similarities, but not the differences, between the types of experience brought into comparison by an analogic metaphor. To put this another way, analogies bring into focus the similarities between two domains of experience but put out of focus the differences between those domains of experience. This can be illustrated with the term *genetic engineering*. This analogic metaphor brings into focus how changing genetic structures is like engineering. However, it also puts out of focus many of the ethical and political questions that make these two processes substantially different.

A term such as *genetic engineering* may not be problematic for someone who is familiar with the differences that are put out of focus by this metaphor. Specifically, those who already know about the processes brought into comparison are not likely to view the metaphor in its most literal sense. Yet for students being introduced to the concept, the implied comparison is likely to remain tacit, the differences unrecognized, and the term accepted at face value. This impoverishes the students' understanding, and at a later time they may find themselves surprised and unable to see why the process (i.e., genetic engineering) does not conform to their initial expectations.

Teachers who recognize and are sensitive to the conceptual boundaries of analogic metaphors are often able to make these boundaries explicit. Without detracting from the value of analogic thought as a medium through which students may grasp new ideas, they are able to minimize the danger of mistaking metaphors for literal expressions of reality. A second example should help demonstrate this point. Recall the high school English teacher we described in the opening of Chapter 1. In the context of a vocabulary lesson, she explained to her students, "Words are like people; new ones are always being born, others are growing old and dying. But, of course, it's a very slow process." This teacher quite skillfully used an analogic metaphor comparing words with people, bringing into focus the similarity that both words and people change over time. Thus the metaphor introduced a dynamic view of language that holds far-reaching implications for how students view the nature of words. Yet in the same breath, the teacher also alerted her students to at least one major difference between the two domains of experience (life and language) that were compared. In this instance, the students were brought to sophisticated understanding in a dual sense: They were both introduced to a perspective they might not have considered before and reminded that this perspective holds certain limitations.

Recognizing the conceptual boundaries of metaphorical thought is a strategy that we will further develop in considering the generative and iconic forms of metaphor. However, the characteristics of analogic thinking suggest a second strategy that will contribute to the teacher's professional knowledge. This strategy involves recognizing the appropriateness of an analogic metaphor as it relates to the students' cultural experience. As noted earlier, analogic metaphors are meaningful only when their source-domains (e.g., engineering, riches, beds, traps) are familiar. If a student is unable to match up the source-domain with shared prior experience, the metaphor will not make sense and the idea or concept that the teacher is trying to communicate will remain inaccessible. In this situation, the metaphor becomes a source of miscommunication, confusion, and possible resentment.

The appropriateness of analogic metaphors is an issue that brings into focus the student's cultural experience as it relates to ethnicity, age, gender, and class. This point can be made clear by providing an example. In introducing a certain type of plant, a middle school biology teacher commented to her students, "We think of these as weeds; you can sometimes find 'em growing in your front lawn, where they're about as welcome as a person's first gray hair." The source-domain of this analogic metaphor is the process of growing old. From a phenomenological perspective, it may not be the most effective metaphor the teacher might have selected, because middle school students are not likely to have had firsthand experience with the source-domain, that is, one's first gray hair.

Yet, more to the point, there is an implicit cultural assumption in how the gray hair metaphor is intended to work. The aging process, or source-domain, is used to typify a negative and unwelcome experience. The dominant culture in which the teacher participates highly values youth (being young), or at least its appearance, and most Anglo students will understand this, having heard their parents and other elders bemoan the physical signs of age. Yet not all cultures share these norms. On the contrary, some cultures associate aging (and its physical manifestations) with positive values (respect, wisdom, veneration), and the process is welcomed, not scorned. Students raised in such a culture may miss the point of the metaphor. The effect is the same as if the teacher were speaking a different language.

The cultural assumptions that underpin analogic thought are also related to gender. The implications of this can be seen in source-domains that relate to cultural distinctions between masculine and feminine experience. Consider, for example, analogic computing terms, some of which were mentioned earlier in this chapter:

Bomb	Information revolution
Command	Pilot
Crash	Purge
Data capture	Range
Escape	Target
Execute	Thrashing
Exploded file	Track
Fail safe	

These terms suggest a military source-domain, one which may be culturally less accessible for female than for male students. When such terms are used to introduce concepts that are a part of the school curriculum, they serve to reproduce cultural biases that tacitly reinforce stereotypes and exclude certain groups from fully participating in classroom life.

Teachers who recognize the cultural dimensions of analogic metaphor can work to promote greater curricular accessibility in two ways. First, they can make source-domains explicit, thereby calling attention to the cultural perspectives embedded within analogic expressions. Second, they can provide alternative metaphors that balance and integrate a diversity of perspectives. Again, we will return to these strategies in considering other forms of metaphorical thought. At this point we only wish to emphasize that an understanding of metaphor in the classroom must be coupled with teachers' insights into their own and their students' cultural experience.

Generative Metaphor

Analogic and generative metaphors function in similar ways. Both bring into comparison and highlight the similarities between two or more domains of experience. Thus we will be dealing with the same processes but at a somewhat deeper level of understanding. The term *generative* simply calls our attention to a particular feature of metaphorical language—its ability to generate broad conceptual frameworks that lend order and coherence to how we make sense of common, everyday experience. Considered in this light, the teaching strategies previously identified take on renewed importance. As before, we will develop questions of basic understanding that relate to the conceptual boundaries of metaphorical thought as well as questions of effective communication that relate to the appropriateness of metaphors to the cultural background of students.

Recall that our first strategy relies on a high degree of sensitivity to the conceptual boundaries of metaphor. In the case of generative metaphors, these boundaries are particularly difficult to recognize, because the boundaries are not clearly demarcated and the metaphors themselves are often not stated explicitly. Instead, they are implied in how we describe certain dimensions of experience. This point can be illustrated by returning to a generative metaphor that we have already considered, that is, the conduit view of language. As Michael Reddy (1979) notes, the conduit metaphor is represented in the common expressions that we have adopted in order to describe communication processes. When a classroom teacher explains that the answer to a specific question can be found *in* the textbook or that students should include their thesis *in* the first paragraph of their essays, the preposition *in* is used as a metaphor. It implies that ideas are like physical objects; they can be placed in a textbook or paragraph. When teachers comment that we get ideas from reading a story or that we must struggle to get across a complicated idea, the verb *to get* is also used in this metaphorical sense to suggest that ideas, like physical objects, are transmitted from person to person. To further illustrate this view, consider the following sentence, taken from a handout given to a class of high school students: "For many years nutritionists have been lecturing about the deficiencies in our national diet, but the audience has been very small and little information ever filtered through to the larger middle segment of our populations."

In this illustration, the implied view of communication involves experts (nutritionists) who possess information that they hope to deliver like so many bushels of corn. All of these examples depend on an implied metaphor—language as a conduit—that generates a coherent view of how communication works. This view runs something like the following. First, the process is linear; it begins with a sender who formulates an idea and puts this idea into words. Second, the words (message) are then delivered to a receiver. And finally, the receiver unpacks the message in the words provided by the sender. In making this view explicit, we are in a better position to identify its conceptual boundaries. Throughout the process, for instance, the sender remains unaffected. Language itself is seen simply as a tool—something that the sender makes use of after formulating an idea. In short, these conceptual boundaries exclude any opportunity for recognizing how language influences the sender's original idea.

Classroom teachers do not rely solely on a conduit metaphor for understanding and explaining how communication works. The teacher in Chapter 1 who told her students that "words are like people" was challenging this view by introducing an alternative metaphor. The development of such alternative metaphors can serve as an effective strategy for helping students gain new insight into the nature of their experience. At what point it makes sense to employ this strategy again depends on the teacher's sensitivity to the conceptual boundaries of metaphorical expressions and how they shape the students' ability to recognize cultural patterns of thought.

The inability of certain generative metaphors to provide a strong basis for understanding complex issues may be signaled in the classroom by the students' intuitive reaction at particular points in a discussion, lecture, or demonstration. This can be illustrated by using another example. Carolyn Hayward is a young math and chemistry teacher at a suburban high school. Her schedule includes a fourth-period chemistry class with an enrollment of eighteen students. It is still early in the school year, and Carolyn's topic for today's lesson is chemical research. Specifically, she hopes to relate chemistry to the students' everyday experience and introduce relevant "social issues" through class discussion. She begins her lesson with the following comments:

> "OK, today we're going to continue talking about the reasons why we're studying chemistry. And you might recall that last week we talked about the fact that if we knew something about chemistry or about science, then we could make better decisions about our environment, especially with the issue of toxic waste being something that's very important. The main focus of our discussion today is going to be: What are the benefits and what are the costs of chemical research? Let's start by thinking of some of the benefits. What are the benefits we get from chemical research?"

Carolyn's voice is tentative, and she looks out to her students for signs that they understand her question. After a brief pause, a student offers the first response: "Medicine—people's lives last longer and they're more healthy in their old age." With Carolyn's encouragement, other examples quickly follow: plastics, clothing, fertilizers, preservatives. Carolyn writes these on the chalkboard under the heading PRODUCTS. She is now visibly more confident that their discussion is off to a good start. Turning again toward the class, she sums up, "OK, medicine, clothes, plastic containers; they're all examples of products, and one of the benefits of these products is convenience. They make our lives easier. Now, what about the costs?" A student points to the chalkboard in responding, "Some of these could be both benefits and costs. I mean products could also be wastes. They could be dangerous." Carolyn acknowledges the student's comments, and asks, "What are the costs of waste that are dangerous to the environment?" The classroom becomes quiet, and the students who have been following the discussion look puzzled. Carolyn rephrases her question, "What is the balance here?" More silence. "I don't know," a student finally responds, "it's kind of a hard question. I think it depends on, ah, how you feel about the benefits and the, ah, costs. You know, things like that are hard to put a dollar value on." Carolyn nods her head, "Right. Some of these wastes are harmful to the environment; they're hard to get rid of. So the costs that we're looking at are contamination of our water and ground and our atmosphere." The student restates his point, "But it's really hard to put a dollar value on it." Carolyn again nods her head, "Yes, so we're looking at a balance here between the benefits and costs of the risks involved." The student shakes his head. Neither he nor Carolyn seems satisfied that they have understood each other. Nevertheless, Carolyn takes a deep breath and moves on.

In this example, the teacher used a number of generative metaphors in order to focus the class discussion. In particular, the metaphor of "cost" was used to refer to environmental pollution. This metaphor generated a framework for understanding pollution as "a price we pay" for convenient products. This brought into focus a process that in certain ways is similar to economic exchange. That is, we give up one thing (money) in order to gain another (goods or services). The conceptual boundaries of this metaphor are suggested by the differences between the two domains of experience that the metaphor brings into comparison. For example, people do not possess the environment ("our water and ground and our atmosphere") in the same sense that they possess an amount of money. In other words, the person-environment relationship is not simply one of ownership. In part, this is why the metaphor quickly broke down. As a student indicated, "It's kind of a hard question . . . things like that are hard to put a dollar value on." Yet Carolyn responded by sticking with the metaphor, referring back to the notions of cost and balance. As long as Carolyn stayed within the conceptual boundaries of the cost metaphor, while her student moved beyond this framework, their communication remained blocked.

When a generative metaphor breaks down, teachers face a number of options. First, like Carolyn, they may choose to forge ahead to a new topic. Doing so keeps the conceptual boundaries of the metaphor at a tacit level, and this may lead to further miscommunication in the future. Second, teachers may decide to make the conceptual boundaries of the metaphor explicit. In the case above, Carolyn might have begun this process by following the lead of her student in asking why something like pollution is difficult to place a dollar value on. This tactic serves to clarify the basis of their understanding and help students develop a sensitivity to the nonliteral nature of metaphorical thought. Third, teachers may introduce alternative metaphors that allow the topic or concept under consideration to be reframed. Carolyn, for example, could have turned from the cost metaphor in order to describe pollution as a form of plunder. This metaphor generates ethical and political issues that may be difficult to recognize from the perspective of cost-benefit analysis. Still more examples could be offered that might help students come to grips with environmental pollution as a multifaceted and complex issue. Yet the point we wish to emphasize is that alternative metaphors shift the conceptual boundaries of how an issue may be understood, thus providing new points of access for students to enter into discussion.

The options available to teachers, such as those suggested above, underscore the importance of developing a sensitivity to the conceptual boundaries of metaphors that shape classroom instruction. This sensitivity provides the grounds on which teachers can judge when a metaphor is likely to break down and block rather than facilitate student learning. There is, however, another set of considerations that we believe contribute to effective classroom communication. These considerations focus on the appropriateness, as opposed to the adequacy, of generative metaphors. The former can only be determined in relation to the student's cultural experiences. What cultural groups bring with them to the classroom shapes how the source-domains of specific metaphors are understood. This point again calls attention to issues of ethnicity, gender, class, age, and so forth. As before, we will use an example in order to illustrate these considerations within the context of classroom teaching.

Tom Sanders is a high school social studies teacher. His sixth-period "Contemporary Issues" class has an enrollment of twenty-two students. At the beginning of Friday's class, a boy slips into his chair and calls out, "What are we doing today, Tom?" "Talking about how the government controls your life," the teacher replies with a conspiratorial smile. He then turns to the class, raising his voice, "I want to get back today to talking about government authority in regulating and trying to control the private sector—business and industry." Tom continues with a few introductory comments and then asks the class for specific examples of "government intervention." Various students generate a list that includes taxes, OSHA, affirmative action, minimum wage laws, airline safety inspections by the FAA, and trade tariffs. Tom picks up on the minimum wage example noting, "This is one that affects a lot of you. If they raise the minimum wage—I read yesterday that they're planning to—will it make it easier or more difficult for you to get summer jobs?" Discussion on this issue continues for some time, with about one-third of the students volunteering comments. Finally, Tom calls on a student who has remained quiet throughout the class, "Carol, what do you think?" "I'm not sure," she responds hesitantly. Tom continues, "Let's try something else. If we look back at all these examples, these regulations are meant to protect certain people, aren't they?" Carol nods her head, pauses, and then remarks, "I was thinking about child labor laws and the factory conditions we studied in history. . . ." Her comments launch their discussion off in a direction that provides greater balance to the lesson as a whole.

In this brief example, Tom began class discussion with the generative metaphor of authority, a source-domain that is grounded in conventional conceptions of individual power and control. This implicitly generated a largely masculine perspective on the relationship between government and private enterprise by bringing into focus separation (us against them) as opposed to interdependence. When the teacher switched the metaphor to one of protection, he introduced a quite different perspective on the nature of the relationship under consideration. The protection metaphor is grounded in a source-domain that is less dependent on dominant masculine patterns of understanding. In this respect, it served to provide alternate points of access into the discussion.

A conclusion that may be drawn from these considerations is that every generative metaphor represents various cultural biases. This does not mean that classroom teachers should or can avoid the use of metaphorical language. Rather, this issue is how appropriate particular metaphors are in relation to the students' life experiences. Appropriate metaphors provide a basis for understanding new concepts and relationships. Inappropriate metaphors restrict such understanding and function inadvertently to exclude certain groups from fully participating in class activities.

Iconic Metaphor

Like analogic and generative metaphors, iconic metaphors provide culturally and historically grounded patterns of understanding. They are also commonplace and largely taken for granted in ordinary, everyday language. Yet, unlike the metaphors considered in the two previous sections, iconic metaphors have reached a level of acceptance wherein analogic or comparative functions no longer dominate their use. Instead, iconic metaphors rely on a direct association between words and images. For example, when we use such words as *individual, work, nature, freedom, language, community,* an image or collection of images stands behind each word. These words become associated with images by the ways and contexts in which they are used. "Iconic," in this respect, signifies the conventionally accepted mental pictures, or schema, that have stabilized over time.

These images are a product of a word's history within a language community and have their origins in the politics of an earlier stage of analogic thinking in which one set of comparisons prevailed over others. They are learned through a socialization process that we will consider more fully in subsequent chapters. At this point, we will focus on iconic metaphor as one part of this socialization process. In the classroom, iconic metaphor depends not only on how a word is used in various physical and social contexts but also on its use in relation to other words. In making these associations, teachers and texts actively seek to modify images as a primary function of communication. Instruction, from this perspective, can be viewed as an image-reinforcing process.

As images are built up and acquired, they establish the conceptual boundaries for how we think about particular concepts, values, and relationships. In other words, the images suggested by the use of iconic metaphors function in much the same way as source-domains operate in the analogic and generative forms of metaphor, but the schemata they provide as a basis of understanding does not involve comparisons. Earlier we focused on source-domains as a way of developing greater sensitivity to the conceptual boundaries of metaphorical expressions. Here we will focus on images, but our strategy is basically the same. Our central concern is to foster an awareness of how metaphors influence patterns of understanding. Foremost, this involves special attention to recognizing the conceptual boundaries of a metaphor. If these boundaries remain at a tacit level of understanding, teachers and students have no basis for determining the adequacy of images developed through ongoing instruction. An example will help illustrate this point.

One of the high school English teachers we observed, Gordon Lombard, began a lesson with the following comments to his class:

> "Today you can have the first ten minutes to study your vocabulary. Does everybody have this week's list? Now, before you get started, I want to give you a way to learn these words. Let's see, start with the first word, *trudge*. Now what does that mean? Oh yes, to walk or march slowly forward. Now go on to the second word, *filly*, a young female horse. Then back to the first word again, *trudge*, to walk or march forward, and *filly*, a young female horse. Now you can go on to the third word, *barbarian*. What does *barbarian* mean? Well, let's see, one of those types who lacks artistic or literary culture. Now back to *filly*, a young female horse, and *trudge*, to walk or march forward. Then *filly* again, a young female horse, and back to *barbarian*, one lacking in artistic or literary culture. With each new word, go all the way back to the beginning and then work forward again. This is how I did it when I was a student. It's easy and it works; I guarantee it."

In this example, Gordon used a variety of iconic metaphors. Yet, what lent his explanation a sense of coherence was its focus on the learning process itself. That is, the procedure he described is a procedure for learning. As the procedure is developed, it becomes a context for understanding what it means to learn. In particular, this context reinforces an image of learning as a linear and systematic process. The task of each student was to match up vocabulary words with definitions in a prespecified sequence of repetition. This is a step-by-step process aimed at total recall of each word-definition pair. In short, learning is achieved through rote memorization.

The point we wish to emphasize is that the teacher in this example was not using language simply as a conduit for sending a particular message to his students. Rather, he was constructing an image connected with a metaphorical understanding of what it means to learn. Bringing this image forward, as we have done here, allows us an opportunity to recognize its conceptual boundaries and, more important, how the iconic metaphor "to learn" reproduces in current thought the pattern of thinking that characterized the historical period in which it was originally formed. In our example, the boundaries being reinforced were quite narrow. They excluded, for example, the students' motivation and personal interests as well as the cultural and social dimensions of learning. In other words, once we move beyond instances of learning that solely involve rote memorization, the image, or schema, being reinforced quickly becomes an inadequate depiction of how people learn. This is the point at which the metaphor breaks down.

We have, thus far, considered this example in terms of adequacy. By making explicit the image suggested by the iconic metaphor, a teacher gains a necessary framework for asking how the image itself stacks up against educational criteria:

Where is this image likely to lead myself and my students?
How will it shape our understanding?
What are its limitations?

Again, these are questions of how adequately the image serves instructional purposes. Yet once an image is made explicit, we may also consider its appropriateness in relation to the cultural experience of students. This raises a different set of questions for the teacher to consider:

Whose image is this?
How far back in our history do we have to go to find its origins?
Is it accessible to all my students, or might it tacitly exclude certain groups?

Addressing questions of metaphorical appropriateness will, as before, require us to move away from a conduit view of language. Our interest in doing so is to consider the historical and cultural dimensions of metaphorical images. Returning to the previous example, we can now examine the image of learning that this teacher reinforced within at least its immediate historical context. In part, this image reflects an approach taken by early educational psychologists who were interested in understanding memory as the capacity of an individual to make mental connections between various objects in the environment. The relevance of this capacity to learning would seem straightforward. That is, here memory is viewed as our ability to connect, for example, words with their definitions, names with faces, dates with events in history, and so forth. Strengthening these connections calls for repetition, drill, and practice. This is, we might also note, a largely rational, Western, and masculine orientation to understanding how people learn. In a culturally diverse classroom, not all students are likely to share such an orientation, and those who do not are at a distinct disadvantage. They are likely to find the teacher's intentions difficult to understand or his explanation irrelevant to how they viewed the task at hand.

Recognizing that iconic metaphors are historically and culturally grounded ("information cells" that are handed down from the past) should alert us to the possibilities for miscommunication when different cultural groups use the same word or term to reference fundamentally different images. Examples of this are common in cross-cultural situations. Murray Wax and his colleagues (1964) illustrate a typical example in describing an ethnographic study of Native American education. They report that some of the Sioux parents they interviewed criticized the federal schools in their study because the teachers there "don't teach the children *competition*" (p. 54). The researchers were intrigued by this complaint because it ran counter to their understanding of this cultural group. When they asked what was meant by *competition*, they soon realized that the parents were using the word to mean something quite different from its accepted meaning in the dominant Anglo culture. Specifically, the Sioux notion of competition did not imply rivalry or one person gaining at the expense of another; that is, the word was not associated with an image of a contest between students. Rather, it involved a relationship between teacher and students in which the teacher challenges the students and models excellence in an effort to motivate them.

In this example, the anthropologists' sensitivity to culturally grounded patterns of understanding allowed them to exercise caution in interpreting how an iconic metaphor was being used. In other words, they knew when to ask for more information that would help bring forward the cultural images of "competition." This, we believe, holds an important lesson for classroom teachers. Like anthropologists, their professional skills must include "knowing when to ask." Muriel Saville-Troike (1978) has addressed this issue in the context of bilingual education, identifying teaching strategies that foster cultural sensitivity. In many respects, the role she advocates is the exact opposite of that typically prescribed for teachers. More often than not we think of teaching in terms of answering rather than asking questions. What we have tried to suggest through various examples is that this image (iconic metaphor) of teaching often serves to undermine effective classroom communication.

At this point it should be clear that the process of making iconic metaphors explicit is not quite as analytic as we have portrayed it in earlier illustrations. Rather, it depends on the teacher's ability to operate in a receptive mode that is characterized by intuition as well as logical analysis. This can be illustrated in practical terms by going back once again to our example of the teacher who began his lesson with an explanation of how to study a vocabulary list. Stepping back from his role as information giver, at least temporarily, this teacher faces a number of options. He might, for instance, decide to begin not with explaining his strategy for learning the words but rather by asking the students to share any ideas of their own. Given this task, how should we go about it? This pedagogical move would, of course, reinforce a quite different image of what it means to learn. It is an image that helps bring into focus the cooperative dimensions of learning, and it is likely to provide greater access for students to participate in developing a shared image of the process. This shift toward a more receptive stance on the part of the teacher would also provide an opportunity for him to gain insight into how both individuals and cultural groups make sense of their classroom experience. The teacher also needs to recognize when an iconic metaphor needs to be put in its historical and cultural context by asking, "Where did we get that image?" "What were the issues being confronted when that image, or schema, became the new norm of understanding?" This receptiveness to the students' experience and awareness of how iconic metaphors reproduce past ways of understanding involve a sensitivity to when the teacher and students are speaking the language and when, to paraphrase Heidegger, language is speaking them.

In this chapter, we have focused on the metaphorical nature of language and on how various types of metaphor reproduce cultural patterns of thought. We have given particular attention to ways in which classroom teachers can secure a greater sensitivity to how this process operates and to their intentional or unintentional participation in developing the patterns of understanding that underpin daily instruction. Teachers, nevertheless, communicate with their students in many ways that extend beyond written and verbal forms of language. The use of space, gestures, tone of voice, and so forth all play into the ecology of the classroom. Thus in the following chapter it is necessary to broaden our discussion to include these nonverbal forms of communication as well as how they interact with spoken and written language.

CHAPTER 3

Nonverbal Communication

The approach to teaching suggested by the classroom management literature stresses the importance of preplanning, systematic follow-through, and strict adherence to rules set by the teacher. It is very much a picture of the teacher who is fully aware of what is happening in the classroom, who exercises rational control over the dynamics of student interaction. This view of the teacher, however, is brought into question by the literature on nonverbal communication. According to the estimate of Raymond Birdwhistell, a pioneer in the study of kinesics, or body movement, 65 percent of the communication process is related to nonverbal behavior that occurs below the level of conscious awareness (DeLong, 1981). If this estimate holds for the typical classroom, or even misses by a good margin, it means that a significant amount of classroom communication is not explicitly recognized by teachers and thus is not part of their rationally based classroom management procedures.

Although we do not share the technicist orientation of translating all knowledge about classroom processes into rationalized procedures, we do believe that it is essential for teachers to obtain an improved understanding of the nonverbal patterns of communication that occur in the classroom. This understanding may be transformed by the Cartesian-minded into new procedures for managing the classroom; we would hope, however, that it will contribute to illuminating the narrowness of this approach and to providing an informed basis for recognizing the complex interplay between cultural pattern, communication, and what students learn. As we shall explain later in this chapter, we think that an understanding of nonverbal communication provides the basis for a whole series of pedagogically significant decisions that are sensitive to the way in which the student's cultural heritage influences understanding and communicating. We also think that understanding this aspect of the classroom ecology will help teachers recognize what is actually occurring as they interact with students.

The conduit view of language, which we challenged in the previous chapter with the arguments about the metaphorical nature of language providing the schema for understanding, has also had an undesirable influence on the education of teachers. Like most people in our society who have been educated to view language as a tool of expression, those who manage our teacher education programs have perpetuated a view of language that is associated almost exclusively with the spoken and printed word. There are many cultural and historical reasons for this overly narrow view of language. But one that has been particularly influential is the association of knowledge with explicit awareness and the belief that this knowledge is intentionally communicated to others. On the surface the spoken and written word appears as the natural means of communicating this knowledge to others, particularly since there is an element of awareness and conscious intent in the mental process of choosing words to express thoughts. But as we pointed out in the previous chapter, this view of the person as being in control of a specific body of explicit knowledge does not account for the play of metaphor, nor does it account for Bateson's point that face-to-face communication involves a metalevel at which there is communication about how the spoken word should be interpreted. To make this point another way, the conduit view of transmitting information puts out of focus all the nonverbal communication that frames how the message is to be received.

HIDDEN PATTERNS OF COMMUNICATION

"In all mammals," Bateson writes, "the organs of sense become also organs for the transmission of messages about relationships" (1972, p. 370). Metacommunication—that is, communication about what is being communicated—involves changes in body posture, pitch of voice, use of longer or shorter pauses, change in gaze, laughter, spatial distances, and so forth. These are only part of the "vocabulary" of nonverbal communication used to establish a fuller sense of the context and the nature of the interpersonal relationship within which verbal messages are shared and interpreted. People who are impaired physically or who come from a cultural background that utilizes unfamiliar patterns for coding messages about the verbal message are often misunderstood. As an example of the former, Bateson observes that "a blind man makes us uncomfortable, not because he cannot see . . . but because he does not transmit to us through the movement of his eyes the messages we expect and need so we may know and be sure of the state of our relationship to him" (1972, p. 370). In face-to-face interaction, the maintaining of eye contact, rolling backward of the eyes, shift of gaze at a critical moment, and blank stare each represents part of a complex message that is being communicated about the relationship. These messages are often a more trustworthy guide to understanding the relationship than the content of the verbal message. For example, a stranger who moves physically into our culturally prescribed zone of intimate space will likely be viewed as aggressive or too pushy and forward—regardless of what is being said.

Metacommunication may be intentional, such as a wink to an accomplice who is participating in a bout of teasing with a third person. Another example is the gentle touch, while saying something that may be difficult for the other person to accept, that changes how the verbal message will be received. But not all messages about the verbal message are intentionally (consciously) communicated. While trying not to communicate a deep sense of anger toward students of what is perceived as a violation of trust, the teacher, for example, may continue to speak in a normal tone and rhythm of voice but inadvertently communicate the real inner state of feelings with a blanched face or a rigid body posture. Regardless of whether the metacommunication is partly on the conscious level, or mostly done unconsciously, it represents a pattern of expressive behavior shared by other members of the cultural group. Were it not a shared pattern, the message might go entirely unnoted or might be perceived as communicating something entirely different. The expressive facial movements that we interpret as a smile, which is a positive signal in the dominant Western culture about the meaning of a relationship, may mean embarrassment in another culture or, in still another culture, a warning that unless tension is reduced hostility or attack will follow (Birdwhistell, 1970).

When we take into account the vital importance of metacommunication as a source of supplemental messages, and the extent to which the ecology of the classroom is constituted by multiple and ongoing messages about the shifting state of interpersonal relationships between students, as well as between students and teacher, we see the teacher being confronted with a whole new set of issues to address. If the students and teacher shared identical patterns of nonverbal communication, the problem of miscommunicating would be greatly reduced. This would not necessarily mean a state of harmony in the classroom, but it would result in a more accurate assessment of the actual state of interpersonal relationships. Few classrooms are characterized by such monoculture. Differences in gender, age, social class, and ethnicity increase the possibility of misunderstanding, as a variety of communication patterns come into play. The challenge confronting teachers, as they attempt to orchestrate the myriad nonverbal channels of communication, is to interpret the ongoing metacommunication, often encoded in unfamiliar cultural patterns, and to make corresponding adjustments in their pedagogy and curriculum.

In a presidential address to the Council on Anthropology and Education, Courtney B. Cazden observed that only two instances had come to her attention of systematic attempts to involve educational anthropologists in changing teacher strategies to take account of the cultural differences among students (1983). Although we think there has been a more informal process of infiltration, whereby ethnographic studies of classrooms have yielded insights into cultural differences that have helped individual teachers fine-tune their approach to teaching, approaches to teacher education have generally ignored the cultural and linguistic pluralism that increasingly characterize American classrooms. Cazden's criticism was meant to cut two ways, directed both at ethnographers who were content with explaining "educational failure without showing how it can be reversed" (1983, p. 36) and teacher education programs that ignored the implications of the ethnographer's findings. The importance of Cazden's statement to our task is twofold. First, her acknowledgement of the gulf that separates the professional education of teachers from a vital source of knowledge about cultural differences serves as a cautionary warning that what we are attempting here must be viewed as helping to lay the conceptual foundations for a new approach in teacher education. Second, we believe that a more systematic approach to the "mutual calibration and reciprocity," to use Frederick Erickson's phrase (1982b, p. 173), that is necessary for educational success in multicultural classrooms must involve long-term collaboration between educational anthropologists and teacher educators. Our efforts in the rest of this chapter thus must be viewed as introductory to this process.

Before we address the pedagogical implications of nonverbal communication in the classroom, it is necessary to identify the general categories used to study the dimensions of interpersonal communication. These categories—proxemics, kinesics, and paralanguage—should not be taken to mean that people switch, as they would a television set, from one channel to the next. Unlike the metaphor of the television, nonverbal communication occurs simultaneously, with all the channels of communication being integrated and synchronized with what the speaker intends to accomplish with the spoken word. At least that is what occurs when communication goes smoothly. There are slip-ups, of course, when the use of space, body language, tone of voice, and so forth contradicts or qualifies the verbal message in unintended ways. Apologies, expressions of "that's not what I meant" (Tannen, 1986b), and disrupted personal relations attest to the difficulty of integrating the channels of communication with the verbal message, and with the evolving social context, into clear, meaningful, and satisfying exchanges with others.

Proxemics

In a chapter entitled "Space Speaks," Edward Hall, one of the early researchers on how space is used as part of the language system of a culture, writes that "spatial changes give tone to a communication, accent it, and at times even overrides the spoken word. The flow and shift of distance between people as they interact with each other is part and parcel of the communication process" (1959, p. 160). The use of social space can be viewed as a marvelous multiple message system that both communicates the attitudes that speakers intend toward each other and provides for the reenactment, and thus the reinforcement, of cultural patterns and norms that extend back in time. As mentioned earlier, conscious intent and unconscious reenactment of cultural patterns cannot be neatly separated; viewing them as simultaneous, complementary, and part of the person's natural attitude probably is more accurate—even though this mix of explicit and implicit knowledge is a source of frustration to people who want to organize everything on a rational basis and to believe that we are completely autonomous individuals.

This fusing of culturally prescribed pattern and deliberate communication about the meaning of the relationship can be seen in how the individual, in choosing to communicate certain information to others (e.g., emotional feelings, facts about a product, reciprocation of a greeting), will change the pattern of social spacing to fit the nature of the message. Intimate conversation is undermined if shouted from across the room, just as status and role relationships may begin to disintegrate as the spatial distance is reduced to the more personal zone of conversation. The sustaining of role and status differences, as well as the topics of conversation, is dependent on the spacing patterns between speakers. As Hall points out, there are some topics that are difficult to talk about if the proper social spacing is not adhered to.

Hall's study of proxemics (social spacing patterns) led to the identification of four distinct zones of spatial distance and the forms of social activity and message exchange that are appropriate to each zone. Differences in cultural group will, of course, lead to variations in how spatial distance, social relations, and message interrelate. Thus Hall's examples must be seen as specific to the white, middle-class group who lived in the northeastern states where he carried out his research (1969).

The four distinct zones of space can be viewed as part of the cultural coding process that is used to signal the nature of the social relationship. Interaction at an intimate distance (six to eighteen inches) brings an enlarged awareness of the other's physical features (which, in turn, are used to communicate nuances in the evolving relationship); it is the distance for expressing affection, comfort, and protection. Hall found that personal distance has two dimensions: a close phase (eighteen to thirty inches), which allows easy body contact, such as touching, and a far phase (thirty to forty-eight inches), which allows for subjects of personal interest to be communicated without raising the voice. The distance people adopt in relation to each other signals the nature of their relationship. As Hall notes, people who are dating or married can stay within their partner's close personal zone, but an outsider cannot move into this zone without prompting basic questions about the status of the relationship. Social distance (four to seven feet), which involves changes in physiological awareness and tone of voice, is the spacing used for impersonal business and casual social gatherings. The last spacing pattern, public distance, appears to have a close phase (twelve to twenty-five feet) and a far phase (beyond twenty-five feet), both of which involve a more formal form of communication in which gesture, body stance, and tempo and tone of voice must be altered to convey a desired impression to a listening public (Hall, 1969).

Hall's studies of spacing patterns in other cultures illustrate that these patterns vary, depending on the cultural group. Even within the dominant culture, special circumstances—such as people on a bus, subway, or elevator who must stand in the close personal or even intimate spatial distance—create exceptions in which spatial patterns are not viewed as communicating a new message about the relationship. During these temporary lapses, when people are in the wrong space, so to speak, bodies are held rigid and, even though there may be physical contact, eye gaze is usually averted. Other variables, such as the level of anxiety individuals feel about their own performance or toward others, will influence spacing patterns. Students who received praise, for example, were observed sitting closer to the person who praised them than students who were introverted and anxious about their relationship (Sommer, 1969). The use of space may also communicate important transitions in relationships or activities. In one classroom it was observed that the teacher would sit at the desk when eliciting ideas or talking with students in a manner that attained the level of dialogue; but when giving directions or information or assuming a more directive role, the teacher stood at the center of the room. Thus the space that the teacher occupied signaled a transition between types of communication and social relationships.

Spatial distance alone is seldom the only channel used to communicate about the nature of a relationship. Talking to another person while sitting behind a large desk or standing and directing your comments to a seated person may alter the sense of status (power) relationship and completely override the message of spatial distance. The use of voice and eye gaze can also influence spatial relations. By the projection of a loud, authoritative voice over the entire classroom, the islands of personal and even intimate space that bond students together in group work can be transformed back into the social distance that signals the activities are once again under the teacher's control. Similarly, the use of eye contact on the part of the teacher, or the gaze that reaches across the room, changes the spatial patterns and thus the type of communication that is appropriate. Space does indeed speak about the ongoing process of interpersonal behavior, but body movement and voice patterns are also part of the metacommunication process.

Kinesics

Kinesics, which is more popularly known as body language, is another vital part of the multichannel message system that supplements and frames how the spoken word is to be interpreted. Conversation, as John Gumperz (1977) points out, is always situated in a semiotically rich context that provides the participants the cues necessary for assessing the other's intentions and meanings. Facial expression, eye gaze, hand movement, and body positioning are as integral to the communication process as is verbal communication. In his early studies of body gestures as an aspect of communication, Ray Birdwhistell concluded that the "kinesics has forms which are astonishingly like words in a language" (1970, p. 80). What he meant here is that body movement and gesture involve patterns that are understood by members of a language community as communicating or signaling a specific message, such as averting eye contact when embarrassed or thrusting the head forward and pointing with the finger when angry.

Body gestures, as researchers have found, are synchronized with speaking; that is, they are essential to reinforcing the spoken message and, at the same time, providing a rhythmic quality that binds the participants together. Birdwhistell views gestures as adding depth to how the interplay of signals are to be interpreted. They also add a sense of continuity that ties the discrete verbal message together into a unified sense of experience. Knowing what the other is communicating is not just an intellectual affair, like thinking about the other person's verbal messages. The contextual cues communicated through body gestures help create the ambiance, or mood, of the situation and bring into play a message exchange system rooted in the unconscious knowledge acquired as a member of the cultural group. To put this another way, the cultural patterns used to express this parallel and synchronized language system may trigger a deeper sense of meaning and response pattern than is recognized by the widely held view that individuals are in conscious control of the thoughts and actions they communicate to others. As an example, such body gestures as sitting more on the forward edge of the chair or putting on one's coat signal to the other person a readiness to break off the conversation. The cues connect with the knowledge already encoded in the taken-for-granted patterns, and these patterns, in turn, dictate what constitutes an appropriate response—unless, of course, a speaker chooses to ignore the metamessages. Although conscious intent is an important aspect of communication, much of the communication process is embedded in patterns that do their work below the level of awareness. Within the ongoing process of communication, our awareness of these patterns usually occurs when there is a breakdown—such as the partner in a serious conversation who glances at her watch or begins to observe other people who are passing by.

The body, as a "vehicle of communication" (to use Mary Douglas' phrase), is part of the social system that is reenacted and thus sustained through communication. As Douglas puts it, "the exchanges which are being communicated constitute the social system" (1978, p. 299). In order to recognize how versatile the body is as a vehicle of communication we might ask the question, "What communicates?" The answer includes the eyes, facial expression (smiles, frowns, grimaces, etc.), body posture and rhythm—including position and use of hands, arms, legs, and head. Moreover, the synchronization of these different dimensions of body communication generally involves adjustments for changes in social context. For example, the body language—to use the popularized phrase—that accompanies listening behavior that involves a friend is very different from the listening behavior that involves the opposition political candidate or a superior

who is "talking down." In a subsequent section dealing with pedagogical and curricular issues we shall provide a number of examples
of how these patterns of nonverbal communication affect the educational influence of verbal communication.

For now we wish to emphasize that while people may individ-
ualize the reenactment of these patterns, they are, for the most part,
dependent on socially acquired patterns of expression. While individual meaning and intent are still a vital, though perhaps less dominant, aspect of nonverbal communication, we must keep in mind
Birdwhistell's observation that researchers "have been unable to discover any single facial expression, stance, or body position which
conveys an *identical* meaning in all societies . . . the methods of organizing body motion into communicative behavior by various societies
may be as variable as the structures of the languages of these societies" (1970, p. 81; emphasis added). But this does not mean that communication cannot occur across cultural boundaries or that the
boundaries, in some areas of experience, are always maintained.
Rather it points to the need for teachers to better understand the cultural basis of both communication and miscommunication.

Prosody

When we add prosody (what Bateson termed "paralanguage") to the
other channels of communication we have already identified as critically important sources of cues about how the spoken word is to be
interpreted, it is possible to see an added dimension in the subtlety
and information richness that characterize effective communication.
By the same token, as we shall see in the section on classroom practices, this subtlety can be a source of miscommunication, confusion,
incorrect judgments, and educational failure. Like the other forms of
metacommunication, prosody is largely formulaic. But when the
teacher or other participant in spoken interactions is accustomed to
different formulaic patterns, the subtlety of the paralinguistic cues is
likely to be missed or, even worse, misinterpreted.

According to John Gumperz, prosody involves the signals or cues
expressed through changes in voice tone and rhythm. This includes
the raising and lowering of pitch, as well as rhythmic acceleration and
deceleration of cadence, that tell the listener what is being stressed in
verbal communication. Gumperz gives the example of the West Indian bus driver in London who, in announcing "exact change,
please," said *please* with extra loudness, in a higher pitch, and with
falling intonation. The "please" was also separated from the "exact

change" part of the statement by a longer pause. To the passengers, the prosody of the bus driver—use of pitch, tone, and rhythm pattern—led them to interpret his "exact change, please" as a command. As Gumperz reports, a passenger exited the bus muttering, "Why do these people have to be so rude and threatening about it" (1977, p. 199). This example, which also helps to illuminate how a social status system relates to who is perceived as having the right to use various prosodic patterns, demonstrates how prosodic cues determine what gets chunked together in a speech event as a distinct bit of information. Gumperz notes that "exact change, please" could have been uttered as a single chunk. The pause, changes in loudness and pitch register, and falling intonation created two separate information units ("exact change" and "please"), with the latter being given more emphasis than seemed appropriate to the status-conscious passengers. Two additional examples given by Gumperz may help in understanding the role of prosody in signaling how the different parts of the information communicated through the spoken word are to be interpreted. In the example of "I am giving a paper," it is the word *paper* that will be stressed by members of the dominant Anglo-white language community; while in the statement "I'm canceling my paper," the word *canceling* will be emphasized by the prosodic cues of tone, pitch, and changes in rhythm.

Another function of prosody is to provide the cues that signal when the participants may change their role from listener to speaker. When we take account of the multiple channels of communication that constitute the information-rich ecology of face-to-face communication, what R. P. McDermott describes as people "being environments for each other" (1976, p. 28), a critical issue becomes that of recognizing when to enter into the conversation in a manner that does not interrupt the speaker—who may misinterpret excessive enthusiasm or a bad sense of timing as a challenge that the rest of what was to be said was not worth hearing. The pauses that follow vocalizations and utterances serve, in part, to signal whether the speaker expects to continue or gives up to the listener the right to speak. The allocation of speaking turns, as well as the tempo of speaking, is rhythmic and suggests the importance of timing in binding speakers together. As Ron Scollon observes, "Speakers time their entrances into the flow of conversation according to the tempo set by the previous speakers. After entering into that rhythm, speakers often accelerate or retard their tempo to establish what is in effect a new tempo" (1982, p. 340). The rhythmic nature of speech, which is synchronized with rhythmic kinesic patterns, gives special importance to the pauses that separate vocalization into units. It is through this prosodic cue that speakers signal intent about whether they plan to continue; it is also the case that the pauses may be interpreted by the speaking partner as the opportunity to take the floor. In this ongoing process of negotiating speaking turns, timing is all-important.

The length of the pauses that punctuate the flow of verbal communication is important for several other reasons that should concern educators. The first is that research (Siegman, 1979) dealing with speakers in interview situations suggests that when a speaker felt stress and anxiety longer pauses would be taken. Conversely, when the interviewee felt the warmth and encouragement of the interviewer, there were fewer long pauses that might suggest lack of fluency, intelligence, and competency. A second study of how people who take longer pauses in speaking are viewed found that among members of mainstream culture, people who took short pauses tended to view themselves as "warmhearted," "easygoing," "cooperative," "attentive to people"; while the people in the study who took longer pauses than their conversational partners viewed themselves as "reserved," "detached," "critical," "distrustful," "rigid," "indolent," and "undependable" (reported in Scollon, 1985, p. 25). This stereotyping, which in mainstream culture is associated with the "silent type," also carries over to viewing members of other cultural groups who have a different timing pattern as either "pushy and aggressive" (in the case of quick talkers) or as dull, slow, uncooperative, and distrustful (in the case of slow talkers). Conversational silence, according to Scollon, is seen within mainstream culture as an indicator of undesirable attributes, because silence is generally associated with incompetence, while "smooth talk is taken as the natural state of a smoothly running cognitive and interactional" person (1985, p. 26).

Aside from the stereotyping associated with differences in timing, one last point needs to be brought out: People who view themselves as possessing positive attributes have been found to take the floor more often and to hold it longer than their slower-speaking partners. The problems of stereotyping and social control become especially problematic when members of a nonmainstream cultural group view silence as having a different meaning. According to Scollon, the Athabaskans of Northern Alberta view *quiet* as "a term for knowledge, control, cooperation, attention to others, and a socially productive attitude" (1985, p. 27). In concluding this section of the discussion it is important to remember Mary Douglas's comment that communication reproduces the power relationships within the social system and that the prosodic cues, including the way in which silence is interpreted, may be the most significant part of the message exchange.

CULTURAL DIFFERENCES IN LEARNING STYLES

In her widely read book, *Mastery Teaching*, Madeline Hunter states that "teaching is now defined as a *constant stream of professional decisions made before, during, and after interaction with the student; decisions which, when implemented, increase the probability of learning*" (1986, p. 3; emphasis in original). We fully agree with her understanding of teaching as an ongoing interactive process and the teacher's professional knowledge as properly including the ability to recognize how the interaction patterns of the classroom influence the learning process. But we part company with her, and the other technicist approaches to classroom management, over two fundamental issues. The first has to do with what we see as the need to view students' behavior, in part, as the expression of patterns learned through membership within their primary culture. The second has to do with the belief that teachers' professional judgment should include a knowledge of how their own cultural patterns may both obstruct students' ability to learn and influence their own judgments about students' performance. Without a deep understanding of the differences in cultural patterns—in thought and communication (which includes behavior)—the teacher is likely to use the techniques of classroom control in a manner that may further reinforce inequalities of knowledge and skill acquisition. This is a concern of Courtney Cazden's that we share; we also share her sensitivity to how easy it is to introduce teachers to information on cultural differences that, because of its shallow nature, further contributes to stereotyping and thus differential treatment (1988).

Ethnographic research in classrooms provides a wealth of evidence on cultural differences in learning styles and in patterns of discourse and social interaction—what Susan Philips calls the "participation structures" of the invisible culture (1983, p. 79). The differences should not be viewed as evidence that members of one cultural group are intellectually superior; nor should they be abstracted from the reality of the modern world, which displays an increasing intermixing and layering of cultural patterns. Rather, the differences further underscore the incorrectness of the Cartesian model of the rational teacher using language as a conduit to provide the factual knowledge students are to use as the basis of individual thought.

The range of learning styles and participant structures is indeed overwhelming, particularly when we consider that the diversity of cultural groups in America can be understood as encompassing—in addition to complex variations among black, Hispanic, Native American, Asian, Hawaiian, European, and Middle Eastern populations—differences that cut across gender and age groupings. It can even be argued that the oral tradition characteristic of the experience of all children is culturally distinct from the thought processes and participation structures that characterize the literacy-oriented culture of the classroom (Ong, 1982; Scollon & Scollon, 1985).

As suggested in the previous chapter, differences in cultural styles of learning can, in part, be understood in terms of differences in metaphorical frameworks that reflect the traditional practices of cultural groups. But they also reflect important differences in both the ecology of information exchanges specific to each cultural group and what is perceived as constituting important information. Examples from classroom ethnographers will help to demonstrate this range of variation.

In her classic study of the cultural differences that separate the Anglo (cultural mainstream) teacher from the Warm Spring Indian students, Susan Philips found variations in cultural patterns that undermine successful communication and learning. The "cultural incongruity" of styles involved a teacher who brought to the reservation classroom the mainstream cultural assumptions about individualism (being "naturally" competitive and self-responsible), a linear-sequential pattern of thinking, and a mechanistic sense of time. By organizing the patterns of classroom social interaction in accordance with these taken-for-granted assumptions, the teacher exercised control over pacing the lesson, calling upon individuals to respond, and organizing all the activities in the classroom. But in contrast to the classroom situation, where a single adult was responsible for their behavior, the Indian students were accustomed to being raised by a number of people. Moreover, when their behavior was out of line with the expectations of their primary culture, they were accustomed to being held accountable as a group; that is, punishment was shared by the group of children. This sense of group responsibility was further strengthened by patterns of social interaction that were noncoercive in nature (Philips, 1983).

In contrast to the "participant structures" of the mainstream classroom, the students were not accustomed to obtaining permission to speak, much less from a single source of control. Nor did the competitive atmosphere or the sequential pattern of student response that the teacher expected fit the students' sense of normal behavior. The patterns of social interaction among the Indian students—involving more use of "the visual and tactile channels of communication" (Philips, 1983, p. 102)—were equally disorienting to the teacher, particularly when it resulted in students paying more attention to each other than to the teacher's directions.

Other studies of how differences in cultural assumptions and patterns influence the learning process have replicated Philips's findings of "cultural incongruity" (Erickson & Mohatt, 1982; Heath, 1982, 1983; Scollon & Scollon, 1984). The Scollons, for example, found that Athabaskan children were accustomed to making their own sense of a story (which they viewed as possessing a four-part structure) while carefully attending to the sense that others would give it. In the context of the classroom, where the teacher expects a form of learning that attends to the abstract details of the story, the nonfocused interaction patterns of the Athabaskan student would be seen incorrectly as "incompetence, insecurity, hostility, or at best shallow understanding" (1984, p. 195). Shirley Brice Heath's study of language patterns that characterized black children in a southeastern part of the country she named "Trackton" provides insight into another dimension of cultural incongruity; in this case, how basic differences in discourse styles and accompanying cognitive patterns are critical to whether the experiences of the classroom lead to success or failure. The white teacher, accustomed to asking questions that required factual, out-of-context answers, was told by a Trackton third-grade boy, "Ain't nobody can talk about things being about theirselves!" (1982, p. 105). Heath's study of language socialization among the black children of Trackton revealed patterns of unusual richness and complexity, but patterns structurally different from those encountered in a more typical classroom that reflected the discourse and cognitive style of mainstream white culture. The third-grader, in protesting the abstractness of the knowledge the teacher's question was intended to elicit, recognized that the teacher and students operated in separate domains of understanding. The teacher's questions, as Heath observes, "were unfamiliar in their frequency, purposes, and types, and in the domains of content knowledge and skill display they assumed on the part of students" (1982, p. 123).

It is possible to identify numerous other examples of differences in cultural patterns of learning and social interaction among students that point to the importance of teachers' possessing a body of knowledge that would enable them to respond to Cazden's basic question, "How is instruction differentiated?" (1988, p. 82). The problems of dealing with cultural incongruity in the classroom range from adapting reading lessons for Hawaiian children in a manner that incorporates the *talk story* style of the primary culture (Au & Jordon, 1981), to realizing how Anglo socializing patterns impose individualistic values on Hispanic students (Warren, 1982), to perceiving how differences between black English and standard English can affect a student's understanding of quantitative relations (Orr, .987). The recent interest in gender differences in cognitive style and patterns of social interaction (Belenky, Clinchy, Goldberger, & Tarule, 1986; Keller, 1987) adds yet another dimension to the problem of adapting pedagogical and curricular decisions to the cultural diversity that characterizes the classroom. A case can even be made that the age difference that separates the teacher from students, even where both share the same primary culture, involves the use of metaphorical frameworks of understanding that may leave students in a disadvantaged position in the learning process.

Our main point in providing this brief overview of cultural differences is to emphasize that learning styles cannot be separated from the patterns of metacommunication that, in some instances, are specific to a cultural group and, in other instances, are shared—but expressed in ways that reflect personal interpretations. To put it another way, the teacher who is sensitive to the cultural differences among students must be able to recognize how a cultural group uses its own metacommunication patterns to share information as well as to differentiate the important from the unimportant. Again, we return to the problem of basing professional decisions on pattern recognition—the taken-for-granted cultural patterns of students and teacher alike.

CLASSROOM IMPLICATIONS

In the following discussion of the classroom implications of the three dimensions of metacommunication—proxemics, kinesics, and prosody—we want to stress the importance of taking seriously two points of caution. The first has to do with the problem of stereotyping, wherein the teacher, in recognizing a pattern in a student's style of thought and social interaction that is associated with an identifiable cultural group, attributes to the student the other characteristics popularly associated with the primary cultural group. The stereotyping lies in seeing neither the distinctness of the student nor how this distinctness may include an integration of cultural styles. A student with a discourse style associated with the patterns taught in the home and reinforced in the larger community may also have internalized values, as well as patterns of thought and interaction, of the dominant culture. The blurring of cultural genres, to paraphrase Clifford Geertz, is part of the reality of our modern, media-intensive society.

Another form of stereotyping lies in viewing a student as a culture-free individual; the attempt to view a student as an individual often masks an assumption that everybody is basically the same— that is, everybody shares the patterns taken for granted by members of the dominant culture. Stereotyping always involves generalizing from fragmentary evidence; in this case, it is a matter of recognizing neither the distinctness of a student's patterns nor how these patterns express membership in a cultural group. Viewing girls as individuals, and thus as sharing the masculine-oriented cultural baggage associated with the dominant cultural view of individualism, is an example of this form of stereotyping. It is the reverse of such stereotyped images of girls as being unable to do well at mathematics, but it is no less detrimental to the educational process. In terms of both types of stereotyping, the remedy is to avoid formulaic responses based on a limited perception of attributes—skin color, accent, gender, noncompetitiveness, dressy, style of discourse, and so forth. Stated more positively, the antidote is to attend closely both to what students communicate and how they communicate it to others, to learn to discriminate between the individualized element in a shared cultural pattern (including the dominant culture) and what represents the influence of the student's primary culture, and to recognize the functional nature of the student's attributes within the primary culture. This "ethnographic monitoring," to use Dell Hymes's phrase (1981), is one of the preliminary, as well as ongoing, tasks that is basic to the teacher's professional judgment.

The second cautionary point has to do with the danger of reducing an understanding of the metacommunication patterns in the classroom to a technique that can be applied in a variety of contexts. Within the dominant culture, where the Cartesian emphasis on transforming knowledge into technique and deemphasizing the importance of context are still strong, there is a tendency to view knowledge as something that can be packaged as a set of social techniques and applied in a variety of context. Knowledge from the teacher's ethnographic monitoring of students may lead to utilizing classroom practices that have been informed by both earlier observations and trial-and-error classroom practices; but if reduced to a set of standard practices and made available in a way that eliminates the need for teachers to do their own ethnographic monitoring, the techniques will likely lead to discriminatory practices. With this warning in mind, we want to suggest that the classroom recommendations associated with the following discussion of metacommunication be treated as a starting point in developing greater professional sensitivity to an aspect of classroom ecology that has often been inadequately understood.

Proxemics

Careful orchestration of activities in the classroom is basic to a successful learning environment. On this point we find ourselves in agreement with those who have studied the problem of classroom organization and management (Doyle, 1986; Good & Brophy, 1978). But making rules clear, enforcing them consistently, and reinforcing educationally appropriate behavior will not by themselves facilitate learning if the teacher ignores the messages communicated through the language of space. As one dimension of metacommunication, the use of social space involves sending a message about how the relationship between teacher and students is to be interpreted. Differences in cultural coding patterns, as well as variations in whether the student consciously uses social space to communicate a specific message to others or is unconsciously enacting cultural patterns, make attention to this aspect of the classroom ecology an ongoing responsibility of the teacher. There are, fortunately, a few guidelines, suggested by recent research, that teachers can follow as they interpret the use of social space as a form of nonverbal communication.

The use of space in the classroom appears to parallel Hall's findings on the connection between zones of spatial distance and forms of involvement in the communication process. The greater the spatial distance between teacher and students, what Hall would categorize as "public distance," the more students become passive listeners and the teacher's talk becomes a lecture. As the teacher physically moves closer to the students, communication becomes more of a two-way process. This distance, which may range from the "social zone" to the "far phase of the personal zone," enables eye contact to become an important aspect of participant involvement, thus making students feel that they are personally being engaged. It also introduces into the relationship a sense of friendliness and caring. Standing closer to nonparticipating students can have the effect of involving them, since they will be drawn into the complex information exchanges that characterize the field of metacommunication—eye contact, changes in rhythm of voice and body movement, and so forth. They are also more likely to be drawn into the verbal communication. If nothing else, reducing the social space will engage the student's attention. On the other hand, the student who is less confident about participating in the ongoing discussion may feel an increased sense of anxiety if the teacher reduces the spatial distance. As the Scollons note, the use of social space involves the expression of power; that is, space is used to communicate who is exercising control in the relationship (1986). The person who is standing expresses power in a way not expressed by the person who is seated, and the person who establishes the distance at which communication is to occur defines the initial bases of the relationship. To recall Hall's point, teachers who stand behind the desk, with students separated by a distance of more than seven feet, must raise their voice, and this is generally accompanied by changes in body language that communicate a dominant position in the relationship.

We would like to cite two examples of how a teacher can consciously utilize social space as a way of signaling important messages to students. The first example involves a teacher who sits at her desk (closely situated in relation to students) when eliciting ideas from students and when engaging them in a discussion that often became a genuine dialogue. However, when giving directions or otherwise assuming a more directive role, the teacher stands at the center of the room. We have observed other teachers who signal the transition from a mutual discussion to a more directive and hierarchical relationship by positioning themselves behind their desk. This transition may also be communicated by moving to the front of the classroom.

The second example also demonstrates an awareness of how the use of social space influences the learning environment. "OK, I'm going to ask you to work on your own today," the teacher announces. "Either read or study your spelling, but please work quietly." The students open their notebooks or paperback novels and bend their heads over their desks. The teacher picks up his role book, sits down in a swivel chair with casters, and pushes himself down the first row of desks, stopping to talk briefly with each individual student. Because the student desks are set front-to-back with no space in between, the teacher must maneuver his chair to the side of each student so they are sitting shoulder-to-shoulder rather than directly face-to-face. The oblique positioning helps make their interaction less of a confrontation. Also, the fact that the teacher is sitting down, physically on an equal level with the students, relaxes their talk.

Students may also use social space to communicate about their relationship to what is occurring in the classroom. Taking a seat at the back of the room or on the periphery of the class, which allows quick access to the door, communicates to the observant teacher the message of noninvolvement. Just as the dynamics of standing further from the students leads to talking *at* the students, sitting on the edge of the participatory triangle that extends across the front row and through the center of the class allows the student to assume the stance of nonengaged observer. But for students who situate themselves on the periphery, there are educational consequences that are not always understood or fully anticipated. In his study of the "ecology of participation," Robert Sommer (1969) found that the social location of students is critical to their degree of involvement in the educational process. Students in the front rows, where eye contact can be established, participate more than students in the back rows. Similarly, participation is greater for students sitting in the center rows than for those occupying the outside rows. He also found that when seating is organized around a table a few students talk more, while in row seating more students are involved in the interchange.

A caveat must be given with regard to any discussion of how the proxemic patterns of the classroom can be orchestrated by the teacher. The following example of how a teacher used the patterns of classroom spatial relations to reinforce successful achievement may be effective with students who share the dominant cultural values pertaining to the nature of individualism and competitiveness. When students wish to share information (other than brief comments) with the class as a whole, the teacher asks them to come to the front of the room, although the line-of-sight openness of the classroom does not require this positioning for students to be easily heard and seen. Students in this class often work in pairs on activities that require them to make something, do an "experiment," put together a puzzle, and so forth. When a pair of students have done well on an activity, the teacher often invites them to the front of the room to show the class their success. Again, the line-of-sight openness of the room does not require this, but the front center of the classroom has taken on a tacitly recognized status as a focal point for the students' attention.

Using the front of the classroom to reinforce individual achievement or to signal important classroom events also involves the reenactment of another pattern taken for granted within the dominant culture. This involves the dominant role of the teacher in directing the activities of the classroom; in terms of the proxemic patterns of the classroom, this was expressed in the way the teacher calls out to the students, regardless of where they are seated. This calling out, or projecting the teacher's voice (control) over the farthest reaches of the classroom, has the effect of spotlighting the activities of individual students or working groups. Although the classroom management literature suggests that this is an appropriate and effective strategy, research on the use of these cultural patterns with students from different cultural backgrounds strongly suggests the opposite conclusion (Erickson & Mohatt, 1982).

In her study of the participant structures used by teachers from the dominant Anglo culture with Warm Springs Indian students, Susan Philips found cultural miscommunication, unresponsiveness, and frustration on both sides. The cultural patterns taken for granted by the Anglo teacher included standing in front of the classroom to implement classroom management procedures. This use of space to communicate control reinforced the other elements of what Philips identified as the participant structures that dictated the patterns of student involvement: organizing students into small groups in which speaking turns were allocated in a sequential order; one-to-one involvement with the teacher based on a first-come, first-served principle; and individual seatwork in which the book was treated as the primary source of learning (Philips, 1983). The teacher's use of social space reflected the dominant cultural assumptions about the linear and abstract nature of learning, individualism, and the role of adults that did not fit the cultural patterns of the Warm Springs Indians. Philips found that students were unresponsive to the teacher's strategy of calling out to them as individuals who would have to respond in front of the entire group. They were also found to be less accustomed to following the direction of a single adult and to limiting communication to the verbal and written channels. A teacher who had adapted to the cultural patterns of the students was quoted by Philips as saying, "I spend as little time in front of the class as possible" (1972, p. 382). Similarly, instead of spotlighting individual achievement (e.g., directing questions to individuals, assigning individual reports, and announcing individual achievement to the entire class), the teacher used participant structures that fostered group projects and allowed students to move about so they could approach her with questions no one else could hear.

The use of research to develop a more culturally congruent pedagogy, as carried out by anthropologists and linguists associated with the Kamehameha Early Education Program (KEEP), yielded similar insights into the spatial patterns that seemed most effective with Hawaiian children. Recognizing that the organization and use of space in the classroom must reflect the cultural patterns of communication experienced by the students in the home and primary community led to abandoning a spatial organization that differentiated between students' attending to their own learning tasks and responding to teacher direction. In building on the discourse style that Hawaiian children learn from adults, the class space was organized into learning centers in which students could interact in interpreting and structuring the learning event. This arrangement of space, with students rotating to different learning centers within the room and the teacher interacting directly with groups of students, also replicated the Hawaiian pattern of children having multiple caretakers. Group rather than individual seatwork thus allowed for "high rates of peer interaction, frequent scanning of other children's errors, and offering and soliciting peer help" (Vogt, Jordon, & Tharp, 1987, p. 280). In the dominant culture, by contrast, the classroom space is organized in a manner that reinforces the perception that these forms of student interaction are expressions of cheating.

The attempt of the KEEP researchers to introduce what they had discovered about effective learning environments for Hawaiian students to other minority cultural groups, in this case the Rough Rock Demonstration School on the Navajo Reservation, alerts us to the danger of generalizing from one cultural group to another. The introduction of the spatial patterns (learning centers) that had proven so effective in fostering cooperative interaction among Hawaiian students created unanticipated problems in the Navajo classroom. While the grouping together of four or five boys and girls produced the maximum interaction among Hawaiian students, the mixing of sexes went against basic Navajo cultural norms. The Navajo students worked only in groups of two or three of the same sex, responding best—like the Hawaiian students—when the teacher's questions were directed to the group rather than to individuals. There were other differences, too, such as the Navajo students' preference for relating text to personal experience by dealing with the story as a complete unit rather than approaching it in terms of segmented units developed in a linear fashion, as was more characteristic of the Hawaiian students' cognitive style (Vogt et al., 1987).

Given the wide cultural variation in how social space is used to frame relationships and to facilitate patterns of thought and social interaction, it is important to keep in mind a few principles that should guide the teacher's judgment. The first relates to the absolute necessity of recognizing spatial patterns as an aspect of classroom communication that is generally not made explicit. Though it is seldom openly acknowledged, the messages are generally understood and responded to at the cultural level of implicit understanding rather than at the conscious level. The teacher needs to observe how, with different students, spatial patterns influence student involvement and the content of what can be discussed. Observation of the consequences that follow from making gradual changes in the spatial patterns, as well as discussing with students patterns that appear to contribute to more passivity on their part, will help to integrate more effectively the multiple channels of communication that make up the classroom ecology.

The second principle relates to the need for careful observation of how the students' use of social space *may* reflect the patterns of their primary culture. A culturally sensitive pedagogy requires that the students not be viewed simply as autonomous individuals, as this view of the individual often carries with it the cultural assumptions of the dominant Anglo society. Because the study of the students' primary culture is a complex and difficult task, particularly when teachers—like most everybody else—have difficulty in recognizing their own taken-for-granted cultural patterns, it would be helpful to involve members of the minority culture as well as anthropologists as part of teacher professional development programs. The inservices should also deal with how the spatial patterns of the dominant culture influence the learning environment.

Kinesics

Before highlighting the implications for teaching, let us summarize the role that kinesics, or body language, plays in supplementing the verbal message. The use of the body, including gaze and facial expression, adds additional information to the spoken word. It can confirm the message, qualify it in important yet subtle ways, add new information that perhaps should remain unspoken, and signal important distinctions in social status. Although this dimension of communication is unsuited for expressing linearly organized abstract ideas, it combines context and cultural patterns into complex and subtle messages about feelings and attitudes. Because it integrates social context, cultural patterns that are taken for granted and thus often not seen, with the more conscious aspects of verbal communication, it is difficult to create a fixed list of patterns that teachers can use as a guide to interpreting the kinesic messages in the classroom. But the importance of attending to this aspect of classroom communication cannot be overestimated.

For some time researchers have known that the face, particularly facial expression, is one of the earliest and more important source of communication in the child's development. By the age of three weeks, infants will focus their eyes on the face of their caregiver; the face continues to be the preferred source of information about the nature of social relationships (Izard, 1979). Facial expression communicates feelings; it is also an important source of information about the status of an ongoing conversation. It can add to the rhythm and general ambience of the verbal relationship; it can also lead to terminating conversations in a more or less permanent manner.

Researchers who have studied this aspect of nonverbal communication have found, contrary to the folk knowledge about the teacher establishing control by not smiling until December, that the teacher's facial expression has a great deal to do with student attitudes and degree of involvement in the learning process. With certain groups of students, including those of the dominant Western cultural groups, it has been found that good teachers show varied facial expression, move toward students in order to engage them more directly in conversation, use head nodding to signal attentiveness to what students were saying, smile frequently, and use humor to lighten the atmosphere and create group solidarity (Smith, 1984; Wolfgang, 1979).

To reiterate a point made earlier about metacommunication, the smile, for many cultural groups, is a powerful message about the nature of the interpersonal relationship. When the teacher smiles in a natural and relaxed manner, establishes eye contact with students engaged in the conversational event, and nods his or her head in the rhythmic pattern that has been established, the students are going to feel that their contributions are being taken seriously by the teacher and that they are being confirmed on a more personal level. Smiling communicates warmth, support, and the other values associated with a nonthreatening environment. But it does not, by itself, insure a positive learning environment, particularly if the other aspects of the communication send a contradictory message to the student. An example is the teacher who used all the right nonverbal communication patterns: direct eye contact, head nodding, raised eyebrows, and so forth. The students, however, felt challenged in this situation because the type of questions the teacher posed, and the tone of voice used to communicate them, were seen as questioning their credibility: "Are you sure about that?" "Who told you that?" "Why do you say that?"

The gaze of the teacher both yields important information that supplements the auditory channel of communication and signals to students that they are being observed. The latter may be an important control strategy, depending on how facial expression is coordinated with the glance toward the student who is deviating from a classroom norm. Being seen is often a reminder of what the shared expectations are, and the "cold stare" may communicate more information than the student is prepared to deal with. The use of the eyes also serves to signal information about interpersonal attitudes and even the character of the participants. In terms of mainstream culture, students are expected to maintain eye contact with the person they are talking with; looking away while talking is often interpreted to mean a flaw in the speaker's character that may range from being dishonest to being weak and uncaring. The use of eye contact is important in other ways. For example, Exline, Gray, and Schuette (1965) found that people look more at people they like. In terms of the classroom, eye contact is established more with students who are liked by the teacher and considered more academically gifted. Studies of what contributes to effective teaching behavior have found that classroom disruptions increase whenever the average amount of teacher eye contact with the class declines.

These findings underscore the importance of the teacher's need to be self-monitoring in regard to how the use of gaze and eye contact contribute to a cycle wherein the more able students receive more of the teacher's attention and the less able students tend to be ignored, thus further undermining their chance of development. The teacher, without totally avoiding the more able students, should work at giving the less able students more attention: looking at them and establishing eye contact. This is important for several pedagogically significant reasons. In addition to the mainstream cultural belief that gaze (accompanied by appropriate facial expression) establishes a positive social bond, the shift in gaze has been found to be important to coordinating the timing and synchronization of speech. For example, it was found that if one speaker does not look up at the end of an utterance, there is, in terms of mainstream culture, a longer pause before the other replies. The wearing of dark glasses, which conceal what the eyes are doing, was found to disrupt the normal synchronizing pattern associated with fluent speech.

Two other points of importance for understanding how the teacher's gaze and use of eye contact may influence students' performance need to be brought out. The first is that dialogues involve more gaze than monologues—the absence of eye contact diminishes the exchange of information essential for signaling and synchronizing the allocation of speaking turns. Second, it has been found that the speaker tends to look more at the listener during fluent speech than during hesitant speech (Kendon, 1967). Although hesitancy in speech may, in some instances, reflect the speaker's cognitive process (the pause to gather thought together before launching on), it can also be seen as the outcome of nonparticipatory social relationship. The expression of hesitancy, in turn, may be seen by the teacher as a sign that students do not really have a grasp of what they are talking about or that they lack the ability to express it fluently.

The classroom implications of these findings are important indeed. The connection between teacher gaze and student fluency, as well as the signals given about the nature of the social relationship, suggest that the student's performance is, in part, an expression of an interactive process, a process in which the teacher's attitudes and cultural style are critical factors. Unexamined bias relating to social class, gender, and cultural group—not to mention body type and personality—relates directly to Mary Douglas's observation about communication reproducing the stratification patterns of a social system. Unless teachers are aware of the hidden assumptions that influence this aspect of classroom metacommunication, they may not recognize how differential treatment influences the nurturing and expression of the students' abilities.

Kinesic communication in the classroom also involves the use of the body (positioning and rhythm of hands, head, torso) as a channel of communication. To put it another way, the body can be viewed as a fluid text that is read as part of the message system. Ekman and Friesan (1967) suggest that posture is used to convey a more general attitude toward the other person, while facial expression is used to communicate more specific emotional responses. In terms of classroom communication, the students' body posture and movement (as well as that of the teacher) signal their willingness to talk, their attitude and feelings toward others, and how they perceive status differences. Although observers of the body as a semiotic system have suggested that body posture can be used to convey specific messages (Mehrabian's 1969 study suggests that a forward-leaning posture communicates a positive regard for the other person), we want to emphasize again the importance of recognizing culture as an important aspect of the body as a message system—as is also the case with facial expression, gaze, and eye contact.

The importance of culture as a powerful source of influence on kinesic patterns, and thus a contributing factor to miscommunication within the classroom as well as elsewhere, can be seen in Frederick Erickson's (1979) study of intercultural communication, where blacks were viewed as inattentive and a white counselor was perceived by the blacks as demeaning. The white counselor kept saying the same thing over and over—and thus appeared to be "talking down."

Among other findings about differences in cultural styles of communication, Erickson found that the white counselor interpreted the kinesic responses of the black students to mean inattention. In effect, head nodding, gaze, eye contact, and body posture did not correspond to the dominant white cultural pattern. The body language of the blacks continually elicited from the white counselor a repetition of what had previously been said, which contributed to a rising sense of frustration on both sides. One difference in the two kinesic patterns related to the tendency of white speakers to look only occasionally at the listener and, when in the role of listener, to look continuously at the speaker. In contrast, the pattern of black students, when in the role of speaker, was to look continuously at the listener and when in the role of listener, to look at the speaker only intermittently. As Erickson notes, the white pattern was to signal listening behavior in gross and more explicit ways, while the black kinesic patterns were more subtle and indirect. The repetitious explanations, which followed from the perception that the black students were not listening, were not found in white-white or in black-black encounters, but only in white-black encounters.

Other examples of cultural differences in kinesic patterns were found in Philips's (1983) study of intercultural communication in the Warm Springs Indian classroom. The listening behavior of the Indian students involved different patterns of gaze and eye contact (more diverted away when the teacher was talking) as well as body movement (less nodding in agreement with the teacher and more physical interaction with each other while the teacher was talking), with the result that the Anglo teacher often viewed them as disruptive and unattentive. Studies that have yielded insights into the differences in kinesic patterns among other cultural groups—Hawaiian-American (Au & Jordon, 1981), Italian-American (Erickson, 1982a), Athabaskan (Scollon & Scollon, 1981), and so forth—again raise the issue of teachers being able to adapt to patterns of communication, including the kinesic, that reflect a sensitivity to the student's primary cultural affiliation. Aaron Wolfgang (1979), who has studied the process of multicultural education in Canada, recommends that the teacher's own body language should communicate patience, caring, and respect for the students. In addition to letting students know they are being listened to—with confirming head nodding, eye contact, smiling, and relaxed body posture—teachers need to recognize how their own culture has influenced both their own kinesic patterns and their expectations of students. A culturally sensitive style of teaching requires what few other professions do; namely, a knowledge of cultural patterns that underlie the different channels of communication. This includes a knowledge of the teacher's own cultural patterns and assumptions.

Prosody

Changes in tone and rhythm, as well as use of pauses that accompany speech, are, as we indicated earlier, an important supplementary source of information about how to interpret what is being said. Prosodic cues help the listener recognize what is being emphasized, status distinctions that are being acknowledged between speaker and listener, and the attitudes and mood of the speaker. Since many of the prosodic patterns—tone, change in pitch, chunking together of words, pauses, and so forth—are formulaic, they may not be recognized as the expression of a culturally influenced pattern by either the speaker or listener. This is where the problem arises for the teacher who is attempting to treat all students fairly in the classroom; that is, to teach in a manner that is responsive to the cultural patterns students have acquired as part of their primary socialization.

The prosodic patterns that are part of the teacher's taken-for-granted culture may become the basis for misunderstanding the content and intent of what the student is attempting to say; they may also provide the "evidence" for the teacher's judgment about the student's academic ability. For example, a student who comes from a cultural background where the overlapping of talk is a common occurrence—that is, where the listener begins to talk before the speaker finishes—may be perceived by the teacher accustomed to a different synchronization pattern as impolite and overaggressive. Similarly, the student who speaks softly and utilizes longer pauses between utterances may be viewed by the teacher as academically less able and perhaps poorly motivated. Within the dominant Anglo culture, as Scollon notes, there is a shared assumption that "speech will be fluent except where slowed or interrupted by various intervening factors" (1985, p. 24). Scollon further notes that the faster speaker (in terms of both pace of conversation and utilization of shorter pauses) tends to view the slower speaking partner in more negative terms: taciturn, distrustful, indolent, uncooperative, unresponsive. This assigning of attributes appears to occur between speakers who are members of the dominant cultural group; it also occurs when speakers from the dominant culture interact with speakers from minority cultural groups. The latter situation is especially problematic because some minority cultures have a different attitude toward silence; in contrast to the dominant culture, where silence is viewed as a "malfunction," they view silence as the expression of knowledge, control, respect, and a socially productive attitude (Scollon, 1985, p. 27). The irony is that these students will likely be judged as academically slow and uncooperative by teachers conditioned to the prosodic patterns of mainstream culture. This difference carries over into what Susan Philips refers to as "back channel verbalization," wherein the Anglo teacher encourages verbal excitation among students (1983, p. 105). The changing pitch and intensity of student voices, as well as increase in tempo, are generally interpreted within the mainstream culture as evidence of student involvement in the lesson. Philips observed that the teacher's encouragement of verbal excitation among Warm Spring Indian students created a double-bind for the students; as they met the expected standards of the teacher they violated the norms of their own community.

Speech tempo is also critical to who will be included or excluded from the ongoing classroom conversation. Tempo, as Scollon observes, is an important aspect of the contextualization cues that regulate the allocation of speaking turns. On the surface it seems that the turn-taking game of conversation, in both teacher-student and student-student interaction, is one of the easier and more natural social skills. How does the student know when the teacher has finished talking? When the teacher pauses? When there is a change in tone? Deborah Tannen, in discussing the process of conversational turn-taking, puts in perspective the dynamics that we are all caught up in but seldom recognize:

> In the midst of a conversation, you don't take time to puzzle this out. You sense when I am finished, or about to make a point, or chatting aimlessly, based on your years of experience talking to people. When our habits are similar, there's no problem. What you sense and what you feel are similar. But if our habits are different, you may start to talk before I'm finished—in other words, interrupt—or fail to take your turn when I *am* finished—leading me to observe that you're not paying attention or have nothing to say. (1986, pp. 47–48)

The dynamics of determining speaking turns are dependent, in part, on cultural patterns (what Tannen refers to here as "habits") that influence the speaking partner's ability to "read" the contextual cues—which means correctly interpreting the speaker's use of prosodic cues to signal when a change in speaking turns can take place—without fostering the misunderstandings that result from inadvertent interruptions or failure to maintain the rhythm of the conversation. Viewed from another angle, the prosodic cues can be viewed as part of the micropolitics that determines which speaking partner will control both the content and direction of the conversation. The person who speaks first, and most often, will be able to dominate the relationship by controlling which aspects of social reality are talked about. This point has two important implications for teachers who are attempting to create a classroom atmosphere in which the students' thoughts and voices are encouraged.

The first implication has to do with the teacher's adopting a role that provides a sense of balance in the classroom by preventing students who possess both a faster tempo and a blindness to the prosodic and other metacommunication cues of the slower-paced students from dominating class discussions. This role is often difficult for teachers, as the faster-paced student fits the stereotypical view of the more capable and motivated student. In a sense teachers need to go against the grain of their cultural "habits" by slowing down the pace and attending closely to the slower-paced students' metacommunication about the relationships that are unfolding in the classroom.

A very practical suggestion, grounded in more than twenty years of research into the micropolitics of classroom conversations, was made by Mary Budd Rowe. In studying the wait time of teachers—the time between asking a question of students and following up with another question or giving the answer to the question—Rowe found that the normal pattern of wait time was one second or less. By observing the educational effects of teachers who increased the wait time to three seconds, Rowe (1986) found a number of consequences that relate directly to the problem of having a few students, through their verbal quickness, dominate the classroom conversation. The findings also relate to improving the quality of the students' intellectual involvement. Following are a few of her findings about the consequences of having the teacher set a slower tempo (three-second wait time):

1. The length of student responses increases between 300 percent and 700 percent.
2. More inferences are supported by evidence and logical argument.
3. The number of questions asked by students increases.
4. Student-student exchanges increase and teacher-centered "show-and-tell" behavior decreases.
5. Failures to respond decrease.

6. Disciplinary moves decrease.
7. The variety of students participating voluntarily in discussions increases, as does the number of unsolicited but appropriate contributions by students.

Rowe also found that increasing the wait time after asking a question, and after the student's response, had the following positive consequences for the teacher:

1. A greater flexibility in responding to student comments and increased fluency, that is, fewer discourse errors
2. A change in the number and kind of questions asked
3. An improvement in the expectation for certain students

One of the problems that Rowe encountered in helping teachers overcome the verbal patterns that prevented a three-second wait time brings out how students are able to read the teacher's prosodic cues for preferred performance. In dealing with a teacher's habit of repeating part or all of what a student had just said (this problem of mimicry Rowe found to be widespread and a contributing factor to the one-second wait time tempo), Rowe reports the following student response: " 'Mrs. B., how come you are not repeating things anymore?' Before she could reply, another student answered the question. 'I know. She knows that we can tell from the tone of her voice which answers she likes and which she doesn't, and we can stop thinking' " (p. 46).

Although we all respond, in our culturally influenced ways, to the messages that are metacommunicated, this student was able to make explicit the message in the teacher's prosodic style and to explain its consequences for student learning. In effect, this student's insight is a model of what we are proposing in this chapter about the need for the teacher's professional judgment to be based more strongly on an awareness of the interconnections among culture, patterns of metacommunication, and student learning.

CHAPTER 4

The Teacher's Role in Primary Socialization

In recent years a variety of teaching models have been identified, ranging from the nondirective, facilitating approach of the followers of Carl Rogers to the "mastery teaching" of Madeline Hunter. With the continuing concern about the need to identify the procedures of truly effective teaching, it is likely that new names and teaching strategies will emerge. The ability to assess the conceptual underpinnings of innovations in classroom practice, as well as their actual effectiveness, is an essential aspect of the teacher's professional responsibility. Our purpose in this chapter is to provide a conceptual framework for understanding that the procedure for teaching a lesson is embedded in a complex ecology of relationships, and that within these relationships the teacher plays a critically important gatekeeper role. Before addressing the larger issue of professional decision making that surrounds the more basic elements of instruction, we wish to reiterate a basic point of misunderstanding that characterizes most explanations about the nature of teaching.

As we indicated in Chapter 1, most thinking about the processes of teaching and learning is based on assumptions that are deeply rooted in a Western, masculine tradition of thought. Although one important assumption (i.e., that we know something only when we are able to express it in the form of verbal or written statements) goes back to Socrates, the other key assumptions can more properly be traced back to René Descartes, the seventeenth-century French philosopher who exerted such a profound influence on what we now take for granted as a modern and Western way of thinking.

Descartes strengthened the Socratic-Platonic tradition of viewing knowledge as capable of being made explicit by arguing that ideas represent the mental activity of the individual; that is, Descartes viewed clear and distinct ideas as being uninfluenced by the individual's past—including the influence of culture, language, and bodily experiences. This emphasis on the individual as a rational being, autonomous from all outside influences, was essential to establishing other characteristics of what has come to be known as a Cartesian way of thinking. The view of the rational process as occurring in the mind of the historically and cultural autonomous individual required, in turn, that statements (i.e., the use of language) be viewed as accurately representing the individual's thought. To put it another way, the individual's clear and distinct thoughts could be communicated to others *through* language; this meant viewing language itself as a neutral conduit through which ideas could be sent from one rational individual to another.

The legacy of this Cartesian tradition, supplemented by other thinkers of this period—Bacon, Locke, Hobbes, Newton—is still the dominant way of thinking in most areas of education. For example, Madeline Hunter's technique of organizing a lesson in terms of "objectives," "anticipatory set," "input and modeling," and so forth involves the procedural pattern of thinking that is such a distinctive characteristic of Cartesian rationalism; it also represents the student as a culturally autonomous individual who uses language to communicate, in conduit fashion, ideas about the objective reality of the external world to the teacher, who is supposed to make an equally objective judgment about the student's performance.

Because we mentioned the other extreme of organizing a learning experience—the nondirective approach of Rogers that characterized many "open classrooms" of the 1960s and early 1970s—it is important to point out that this nontechnicist approach also embodied the basic assumptions of Cartesian thought. Although the nondirective approach to teaching stressed the importance of the affective domain—emotions, authentic feelings, and other internal states—as critically important aspects of supportive learning environments, it nevertheless retained the Cartesian view of the individual as autonomous (that is, free of historical and cultural influence), the reflective process of the individual as an "inner" experience, and language as a neutral carrier of the individual's ideas and feelings (the latter element being distinctly non-Cartesian).

Our reason for reminding the reader of the historical roots of the cultural orientation that underlies a wide range of current thinking about both the way in which learning occurs and the role of the teacher in guiding the process more effectively is to urge a radical (in the sense of dealing with the most fundamental issues) rethinking of the teacher's role in the learning process. But first we need to provide an alternative to the Cartesian way of thinking about the nature of knowledge, language, and the individual. If we do not revise our thinking about these basic questions, we will simply end up with another in the long series of teaching techniques that have perpetuated the cultural dominance of the Western mindset (with its masculine gender orientation) and contributed to the disruption of the ecosystem (Bordo, 1987; Merchant, 1980). These small errors in how we think add up in ways that change the scale of our collective mistakes; at the most basic level of social renewal, where cultural templates are being passed on to youth, it is important for teachers to understand clearly how all the participants in the teaching-learning process are interconnected.

The previous chapters dealing with the metaphorical nature of thought and the processes of metacommunication in the classroom represent a challenge to the Cartesian position of identifying thought processes as occurring exclusively in the head of the student and knowledge with what people are explicitly aware of. Metaphor and metacommunication point to an entirely different way of understanding the interconnections among culture, language, and thought—and, in turn, what is involved in teaching a lesson. Our discussions of the role of metaphor in providing a framework of understanding and the patterns of communication that frame how the verbal communication is to be interpreted both point to the pervasiveness of nonexplicit forms of knowledge and to the ways in which these cultural patterns have been internalized at a taken-for-granted level. It is therefore essential that we adopt a view of the student that puts in focus the interconnectedness, rather than the separateness that characterizes the dualisms of Cartesian thinking: mind as separate from the body, rational thought as separate from the world that is to be understood, and the reflective individual as separate from the influence of tradition and culture. We can see more clearly the transformation in thinking we are urging here if we compare the two different orientations. The teacher's task in terms of the Cartesian paradigm is to guide and assess the intellectual performance of the student (that is the ideal—when student behavior problems are not the major concern). What we are proposing is that the teacher has a responsibility for assessing the quality of intelligence encoded in the cultural resources—the language systems that make up the multiple channels of communication in the classroom—that are given to students as the basis of what they are to think about. From this non-Cartesian perspective, what we previously understood as individual intelligence may be more accurately viewed as the level of intelligence encoded in the ecology of ideas that make up the mental milieu within which the student is situated—such as the sexist way of thinking embedded in the language, patterns of social interaction, and techniques that for centuries guided the unwary student's way of thinking.

FOUNDATIONS OF A NEW PARADIGM

It is possible to associate a name with this radically different way of thinking about intelligence and the interconnectedness of the individual with the larger cultural-biotic ecology. As an anthropologist, biologist, and contributor to a number of other disciplines ranging from social linguistics to psychiatry, Gregory Bateson (1904–1980) has given us a different basis for thinking about (and possibly healing) the interconnectedness of the mind and nature, the person and the larger aggregate—which includes both culture and the natural ecosystems. Some of his key ideas, which we shall present here as essential for rethinking the nature of the instructional process, are supported by the findings of anthropologists and social linguists. In a sense, his ideas help us reinterpret aspects of the older belief system—with its assumptions about individual autonomy, the culture-free nature of the rational process, and so forth—that have essentially been undermined by the insights and findings of cultural anthropologists and social linguists. In contrast to the Cartesian view of students as acting upon clear and distinct ideas that they have formulated (based, of course, on data), Bateson suggests that the evidence of daily experience leads to a radically different view of the mental process.

We would like to explain several of his key ideas and then relate them to the teacher's role in the process of primary socialization that goes on as students are introduced to thinking about new areas of their culture. The mental process, as he views it, involves the individual as part of a larger aggregate of interacting elements. What is important about these interactions is that they involve information exchanges; and it is the totality of these information exchanges that make up the mental process (the mind, or state of intelligence) of the system of which the individual is only a part. The system, which may be primarily cultural, biological, and (more correctly) cultural-biological, involves the cybernetic principle of information feedback, which serves to regulate the patterns of behavior within the system. These information exchanges are, for Bateson, the basic mental units. The following statement makes particularly clear the view that mental activity (information exchanges) is a characteristic of an entire system rather than the activity of an individual acting in a material and non-intelligent universe: "The total self-corrective unit which processes information or, as I say, 'thinks' and 'acts' and 'decides,' is a *system* whose boundaries do not at all coincide with the boundaries either of the body or of what is popularly called the 'self' or consciousness" (1972, p. 319). Several other statements may help further clarify our understanding of the mental activity as encoded in the message exchanges that make up a system or ecology. "The individual mind is immanent," he writes, "but not only in the body. It is immanent also in the pathways and messages outside the body" (1972, p. 461). And in his last essays, he states that "a given mind is likely to be a component or subsystem in some larger and more complex mind, as an individual cell may be a component in an organism, or a person may be a component in a community" (Bateson & Bateson, 1987, p. 19).

An example that Bateson gives of how individuals adapt their thought process and behavior to what is being communicated in the information exchanges among the interacting elements of a system has to do with the act of cutting down a tree:

> Consider a man felling a tree with an axe. Each stroke of the axe is modified or corrected, according to the shape of the cut face of the tree left by the previous stroke. This self-corrective (i.e., mental) process is brought about by a total system, tree-eyes-brain-muscles-axe-stroke-tree; and it is this total system that has the characteristics of immanent mind. More correctly, we should spell the matter out as: (differences in tree)-(differences in retina)-(differences in brain)-(differences in muscles)-(differences in movement of axe)-(differences in tree), etc. What is transmitted around the circuit is transforms of differences. And as noted above, a difference which makes a difference is an *idea* or unit of information. (1972, pp. 317–318)

What we were describing about the process of metacommunication in the classroom—the information exchanges communicated through the kinesic and prosodic patterns of the participants—could also be used as an example of how the individual is a component within a larger message exchange system. But Bateson does not view all parts of the system as processing on the same level the information exchanged that allows the different elements to be interactive. In terms of the example of units of information being exchanged in the ongoing and continually adjusted process of cutting the tree, the individual must be viewed as processing the information in a more complicated (i.e., culturally influenced and symbolic) manner.

Three other points about Bateson's view of mind need to be

brought out before we return to the teacher's role in the process of primary socialization. In contrast to the Cartesian view of knowledge as being explicit in nature (something that can be accurately measured and evaluated), Bateson states that "most of the mental process is unconscious" (1972, p. 463). What he means here is that the information exchanges, like the nonverbal patterns discussed in the previous chapter, are processed at a taken-for-granted level because the "appropriate" response has been encoded in the learned cultural patterns. Second, he challenges the view that human intelligence is of a higher order and thus should be used to bring the natural environment under rational control. "In no system which shows mental characteristics," he observed, "can any part have unilateral control over the whole. In other words, the mental characteristics of the system are immanent, not in some part, but in the system as a whole" (1972, p. 317). Third, the basic unit of survival is not the individual but

> organism plus environment. We are learning by bitter experience that the organism which destroys its environment destroys itself. If, now, we correct the Darwinian unit of survival to include the environment and the interaction between organism and environment, a very strange and surprising identity emerges: the unit of evolutionary survival turns out to be identical with the unit of mind. (1972, p. 483)

He is, of course, using a longer timeframe than we often associate with the immediate behavior of the individual.

In pulling together into book form Bateson's last essays and notes, his daughter, Mary Catherine Bateson, made an observation that we must all keep in mind as we attempt to relate his ideas to the educational process. "The mental landscape in which Gregory moved is, to most of us, a foreign one, as foreign as the ways of thought we might have to explore in the study of a culture with different premises from our own." Although an established anthropologist in her own right, and thus accustomed to working within different conceptual frameworks, she admitted that her father's post-Cartesian way of thinking presented a special challenge. As she put it, "I have consciously to shift gears when I want to work in Gregory's frame of reference" (Bateson & Bateson, 1987, p. 184). His view of social and ecological systems as possessing mental characteristics goes against the grain of our commonsense understanding that intelligence is a function of the brain and perhaps computers—depending on how loose a definition of *intelligence* we want to use. And in deviating from the conventional wisdom reinforced through the multiple pathways of communication that make up everyday experience, we are inclined either to consider him as talking nonsense or ourselves as unintelligent. It is, indeed, difficult to grasp, much less extend, the implications of thinking about information, in the most elementary sense of an idea, as a "difference that makes a difference" and of there being a "determinative *memory* in even the simplest cybernet circuit" that characterizes human interaction as well as a social/natural system (1972, p. 316).

The challenge here is not to prejudge either Bateson or ourselves; rather it is to explore whether the explanatory power of his most basic ideas helps us escape the Cartesian orientation that prevents us from understanding the patterns that connect us to each other and to the natural ecosystems. We would like to begin this effort, this exercise in thinking against the grain of commonsense understanding, by relating his idea that it is the system (the aggregate of interacting elements), rather than the autonomous and reflective individual, that must be understood as possessing "mental characteristics." The classroom can be viewed as such a system, and the language processes—verbal and nonverbal—can be viewed as the pathways through which information is transmitted back and forth, leading to a continual process of adjustment in the thought and behavior of the participants in the system. At the prosodic level, a longer than normally expected pause represents a "difference that makes a difference"; that is, it may be seen as signaling information about the speaker's attitude that will, in turn, lead to an altered response on the listener's part. The averting of eye contact or the edge to the tone of voice may be the information that sets in motion a whole series of events that threaten to disrupt the previous basis of an interpersonal relationship.

Intelligence and Language

Since our focus in this chapter is on the dynamics of how the teacher controls the socialization of students to the stock of knowledge that we know as culture, we want to explore how the verbal (and written) language of the classroom can be understood as constituting part of the mental characteristics of the social system within which students function. In effect, we want to examine the interconnection between the students' thought processes and the "determinative memory" that is encoded in the language used to transmit the culture to students. The level and type of intelligence embedded in the communication processes may in some instances contribute to students' thinking and acting in ways that are detrimental to both themselves and the system with which they are interdependent. To put this another way, the intelligence of students (whether it reaches its fullest expression and contributes to a better adaptation among themselves, culture, and natural ecology systems) is dependent, from Bateson's perspective, on the pattern of intelligence encoded in the communication (semiotic) systems that make up the culture.

This way of viewing intelligence, when related to the classroom, can be most easily understood in terms of how the metaphorical nature of language encodes ways of understanding that are made available to students when they are learning something new. Intelligence, in Bateson's sense of information, is also embedded in the language patterns that make up the nonverbal communication in the classroom; in addition, the architectural space and other artifacts in the classroom—chairs, desks, computers, chalk, books, and so forth— embody mental activities that were carried out by others, at an earlier time and in response to a different ecology of relationships, concerns, and intentionalities. But here we would like to focus specifically on how the metaphorical characteristics of spoken and written language can be understood as the "determinative *memory*" of the culture and thus as constituting the mental characteristics of the social-cultural system we know as the classroom.

When we use everyday examples, Bateson's point that the information exchanges should be understood as mental characteristics of the social-cultural system appears to be common sense, and the Cartesian notion of intelligence as the internal (subjective) thought process of individuals—which we still subscribe to when thinking about teaching strategies and student evaluation—begins to appear to be a strange way of thinking. The examples we would like to use of how language encodes the thought processes of others, who were in turn influenced by the level of understanding of their cultural milieu, have to do with the way in which language encodes mental schemata for maintaining complex gender distinctions, a view of technology as a neutral tool, a view of the individual as a rationally autonomous and self-directing being, and a view of modernization that equates change with progress and tradition with that which is outmoded and limiting. Each of these examples has become the focus of attention in recent years, thus making it easier to recognize that the intelligence (i.e., coded information representing earlier patterns of thought) embedded in the schema distorted our ability to make sense of other information flowing through the pathways of everyday experience. For centuries in the West, the metaphor "man" provided a schema of understanding that highlighted and privileged the qualities of rationality, power, and authority; whereas the metaphor "woman" encoded a different set of attributes—emotionalism, intuition, weakness, and potential wildness. Similarly, the metaphor "technology" encoded the schema of earlier generations, who thought of it as somehow both a neutral tool and the manifestation of progress. The metaphor "individual," as we are demonstrating through numerous examples, put out of focus relationships and interdependencies by providing a schema that represented the person as a distinct moral and rational entity. "Modern," "tradition," "computers," "science," "genetic engineering," "love," and so forth are also metaphors that reflect the state of understanding ("mind," in Bateson's sense) of earlier generations who succeeded in encoding their way of thinking into the language.

As we suggested in Chapter 2, the language "thinks" the teacher and students as they use it to express their insights into the relationships and patterns of their own experience. Bateson's point about mental activity (information exchanges) being the life of a system must also be understood in a temporal sense, whereby past ways of understanding that improved people's ability to respond to the contingencies of their environment may now serve as restraints on understanding our current situation. To put this another way, the level of intelligence presently encoded in the language may cause people to respond, in terms of a new set of relationships, in ways that do not take into account critically important new forms of information. Thinking of the computer as a neutral tool that we control for our purposes and perceiving the natural environment as something that we can manage in terms of human needs are two examples of relying on forms of encoded intelligence that are no longer adequate. Similarly, any teacher who still believes that "intelligence," that distinct metaphor given us by an earlier generation of psychologists, can be objectively measured is relying on a pattern of thought that is now outmoded in an increasingly self-conscious and assertive multicultural world.

One of the implications of recognizing that thought (or mind, or intelligence—whatever term one wishes to use here to designate how language encodes a schema for understanding) is communicated through all the message exchanges and pathways—spoken and written word, kinesics, prosody, artifacts in the classroom—is that the way of thinking may be detrimental to the long-term survival of the system. Students possessing the potential to imagine new relationships, and to respond insightfully to the complexity of their environment, may be educated (given a language that encodes outmoded forms of thinking) to think and act in ways that do not take account of the message exchanges that are actually taking place. Bateson provides an example of what he calls an ecology of bad ideas; the example is important because it brings us back to the central concern of this chapter, namely, the teacher's responsibility for the ecology of ideas that make up the curriculum.

> There is an ecology of bad ideas, just as there is an ecology of weeds, and it is characteristic of the system that basic error propagates itself. It branches out like a rooted parasite through the tissues of life, and everything gets into a rather peculiar mess. When you narrow down your epistemology and act on the premise "What interests me is me, or my organization, or my species," you chop off consideration of other loops of the loop structure. You decide that you want to get rid of the by-products of human life and that Lake Erie will be a good place to put them. You forget that the eco-mental system called Lake Erie is a part of *your* wider eco-mental system—that if Lake Erie is driven insane, its insanity is incorporated in the larger system of *your* thought and experience. (1972, p. 484)

The classroom has been the setting where a number of ecologies of bad ideas have been passed on to students who, in turn, used these ideas as templates for guiding their adult lives. Sexism pervaded the classroom curriculum for hundreds of years, ranging from the use of a masculine metaphorical language in science classes (Keller, 1987) to the use of pronouns that helped sustain the status and role-allocation system that operated in the larger society. The ecology of ideas and values that assured students that experts possess the power to dominate, and even transcend, the forces of nature is a second example. A third example of an ecology of bad ideas that currently exists in many classrooms relates to the way in which students are taught to think about the computer as a neutral tool that expands their mental capabilities (Bowers, 1988). Other examples could easily be cited of how the conceptual frameworks given students prevents them from decoding the message exchanges that characterize their social and environmental relationships. The point that is critical for teachers to consider has to do with the problem of not being consciously aware of much of the culture—patterns of thought, social interaction, and technological activity—that is communicated and unconsciously internalized by students. This problem relates directly to Bateson's point, which anthropologists have also brought to our attention, that "most of the mental process is unconscious." Anthropologists, such as Clifford Geertz and Ward Goodenough, tend to use a somewhat different set of metaphors to make the same point. Goodenough, for example, writes that "to learn the language—that is, to learn to use its vocabulary acceptably—is indispensable for learning the cultural forms its vocabulary encodes" (1981, p. 66). Geertz identifies an equally broad range of mental processes that we reenact without being explicitly aware of them—from our definitions and representations of wealth to our patterns of social greeting.

Although the cultural patterns are recognizable on an operational level (i.e., knowing what the pattern requires in terms of an appropriate social response), it is often difficult to be aware of them as culturally unique or to recognize the assumptions (the thought processes of the past encoded in the current pattern) on which they are based. It is often necessary to get outside one's own cultural framework in order to recognize how much of the culture is taken for granted. Highwater's (1981) observation about how traditional people view the forest as a natural state (as opposed to a wilderness) and the earth as sacred and thus not to be associated with uncleanliness, the Scollons' (1984) description of how the Northern Athabaskan oral tradition involves telling stories in four parts, and the Michaels and Collins (1984) research on classroom discourse showing that black first-graders did not conform to the white teacher's topic-centered and linear style of narrative are just a few of the examples that could be cited as illuminating the otherwise hidden assumptions of the dominant culture. Learning about the information-coding processes of another culture—often understood on the level of such differences as taste, sound, attitudes toward time, and patterns of social interaction—also leads to making explicit taken-for-granted aspects of one's own culture.

Communicative Competence

The problem of making explicit the taken-for-granted nature of cultural patterns and underlying assumptions, when students do not have the opportunity to obtain a perspective on their own culture from the vantage point of another culture, will be a major concern of this chapter. Before addressing the practical issues related to this part of the "symbolic management" process that goes on in the classroom, we want to bring another set of issues into focus; namely, how the dynamics of the cultural transmission process in the classroom influences the student's growth in communicative competence. Communicative competence, within a democratic political framework, is related to Bateson's insight that the unit of survival is not the individual, but "organism plus environment." Introducing the issue of communicative competence into our discussion is also essential to acknowledging that the educational process is inherently political and that the teacher's pattern of thinking (ideology) will be an important factor in determining whether the culture is learned by students in a manner that leads them to view the "self" as the basic unit of survival and progress or to recognize the interdependence of "self," culture, and the ecosystem.

Communicative competence, as we are using the term here (Bowers, 1987b), refers to the political capacity to participate in a group decision-making process. When the culture is learned primarily at the taken-for-granted level, such as the way sexist attitudes were passed on to generations of students, individuals will lack an awareness that aspects of the belief system and social practice are problematic. Politically, these individuals are likely to resist challenges to what is experienced as normal. And if individuals are able to recognize that aspects of the belief system prevent certain problems from being addressed, they will not be able to articulate the issues in an effective way unless they have a basis for understanding them. The ability to find the words and interpretative frameworks for expressing an alternative way of thinking is strengthened by a different pattern of learning: what Bateson terms "deutero-learning" (1972, p. 249). Unlike most problem solving, wherein the cultural patterns learned by the individual largely dictate the solution, deutero-learning involves becoming aware of the cultural patterns and reconceptualizing them in a manner that takes into account the new contextual elements. The phrase *cultural literacy,* as first articulated in *Cultural Literacy for Freedom* (Bowers, 1974), provides a somewhat different way of understanding the form of learning Bateson associates with deutero-learning, or "learning to learn." Cultural literacy means the ability to recognize (make explicit) and reconceptualize the taken-for-granted cultural patterns that would otherwise dictate thought and social action.

We have many examples of this form of learning, the most recent and prominent having to do with making explicit racist and sexist attitudes. There is also increasing evidence that the taken-for-granted cultural patterns that have dominated the workplace, our approach to agriculture, and relationships to the environment are also beginning to be questioned in a manner that fits Bateson's idea of deutero-learning. The important issue here, however, has to do with whether the cultural transmission process in the classroom fosters this ability to think critically about the appropriateness of the mental patterns that have been handed down from the past. A form of communicative competence that helps to renew, in a democratic way, the guiding ecology of ideas is dependent, in large part, on the patterns of learning reinforced in the classroom. Students taught to think of themselves as autonomous individuals, while being conditioned passively to accept the taken-for-granted cultural patterns, will be less able as adults to be open to understanding anyone who questions socially and ecologically inappropriate cultural practices. Instead, they are more likely to be guided by the "determinative *memory*" encoded in the language given them by society as a guide to normal thinking. In their inability to add to the process of negotiating more adequate cultural practices, they will be politically passive or reactionary. Students who encounter a different form of cultural transmission, one displaying the characteristics we will describe in the following section on alternative classroom practice, will more likely possess the conceptual foundations that will enable them to put experience into words, and words into the kind of conceptual framework necessary for discriminating between needed change and worthwhile continuities. To put it in Bateson's terms, they will possess the conceptual means for participating in the more complex information exchange that occurs as we attempt to adjust our cultural patterns to the carrying capacity of the ecosystem; and they will be able to participate in a way that contributes to the solution rather than perpetuates the patterns that are part of the problem.

THE CLASSROOM AS AN ECOLOGY OF IDEAS

There is a wide range of opinion on what constitutes good teaching. But few experts on the education of teachers cite Confucius, Jesus, or Gandhi as model teachers; instead, the experts concern themselves with providing a broad range of principles, procedures, and techniques for the classroom teacher to follow. Good and Brophy, for example, claim that *"Teachers Must Understand that the Crucial Aspects of Teaching Are Task Presentation, Diagnosis, Remediation, and Enrichment"* (1978, p. 92; emphasis in original). Another widely acclaimed leader in teacher education, Madeline Hunter, states that "regardless of who or what is being taught, all teaching decisions fall into three categories: (1) What content to teach, (2) What the student will do to learn and to demonstrate learning has occurred, and (3) What the teacher will do to facilitate the acquisition of that learning" (1986, p. 3). Others, ranging from Hilda Taba's (1962) inductive thinking model to Jerome Bruner's (1966) concept attainment to William Gordon's (1966) synectics, have stressed the importance of teaching strategies based on explicitly stated assumptions about the nature of how learning occurs and the individual-social goals to be attained. Even the behaviorists, such as Randy Sprick (1986), have provided an elaborate set of procedures for teachers to use in maintaining classroom discipline and proper motivation.

Although a case can be made that the teacher's professional knowledge should be sufficiently inclusive of this entire range of teaching models, we think there is a deeper dimension to the process of teaching that has largely been ignored. We present it here not as an alternative to these other models, but as foundational in the sense that it will enable the teacher to make more critical judgments about when various teaching strategies are appropriate and how they should be modified. This deeper dimension of the process of teaching can be seen in the fact that regardless of the teaching strategy or set of disciplinary procedures, there is an interactive process involving the transmission and mediation of culture. The ideological orientation of a particular teaching strategy or set of disciplinary procedures simply alters how this transmission process will be mediated, and thus what aspects of the culture will be emphasized and reinforced. Whether it is a lesson to be taught, or a behavior to be modified and redirected in a way that fits the teacher's definition of "appropriate" or "good," the basic relationships in the classroom have to do with the interactive relationships among culture, language processes, and the thought patterns of all the participants. It is at this level that teaching can be understood as a process of "managing," if we can use this metaphor as a way of emphasizing that the stress on behavior has led to ignoring the mental-symbolic dimension of teaching and learning. What is being "managed," or orchestrated, if we can use a metaphor more in harmony with our post-Cartesian approach, is the symbolic environment that provides the basis of student thought in those areas of cultural experience that are being encountered for the first time.

The instructional process is only one aspect of the learning process that goes on in the classroom. As we indicated earlier, the classroom is an ecology of mind. Not only does it involve the mental processes embedded in the physical artifacts that surround the students (desks, chalkboards, styles of dress, books, the design of the room itself, etc.); it also involves the multiple channels of communication through which information (in Bateson's sense) is shared and transformed. The metaphorical language of nonverbal communication patterns, as well as the spoken and written variety, represents only one layer of the classroom ecology. The conceptual frameworks (ideology) of the people who produce the textbooks, software programs, and films are also a critically important aspect of this mental ecology. The teacher and students, giving individualized expression to explicit and implicit patterns of thought and feeling acquired in encounters with earlier, and perhaps different, mental ecologies, are also key participants. In order to move the discussion in the direction of identifying the critically important professional judgments that teachers must be prepared to make in terms of teaching, we would like to treat these other aspects of the classroom ecology as part of the larger context within which the teaching and learning of the lesson is to be understood. As we indicated earlier, these background communication processes have a significant influence on how the student responds to the instructional process. We would also like the reader to keep in mind that the processes we are identifying as part of primary socialization occur regardless of the type of teaching or behavioral control strategy that is used.

Teacher as Gatekeeper

Regardless of whether we take our examples of instruction from the first grade or a graduate-level class, the instructional process involves "primary socialization." This phrase, which we have taken from Peter Berger and Thomas Luckmann (1967), is being given a somewhat different meaning than they intended. While they used it to designate the child's encounters with the behavioral norms and thought patterns that constitute the social world, we think that the element of dependency and vulnerability is present any time a person (child or adult) encounters for the first time a new dimension of the social-cultural world and is dependent upon the explanations and modeling of another person who has already been socialized to this area of experience. Thus we will use the term here to designate "first-time" encounters with some area of culture: how to think about the nature of time, what is involved in reading, what a fact is, what constitutes expert knowledge, the meaning of computer literacy, the implications of poststructuralism, what art and faith are, and so forth. Primary socialization also encompasses learning the social norms used by members of the society to communicate about relationships, the domains of visual awareness, the uses of technology, and so forth.

In effect, all that constitutes the culture of a people involves first-time encounters for individuals who are dependent on the guidance of others. Obviously, the four-year old child will be dependent on the explanations and modeling of how to think and act toward the new area of cultural experience in a way different from the adult who brings an increasingly complex set of background experiences and ways of understanding to these first-time encounters. But adults, in learning how to think about the computer, statistics, or routines of a new job, are still dependent on significant others who pass on, through language and behavior, the way of understanding that reflects their own prior socialization. Personal doubts, insights, critical reflection, misinterpretation, and incomprehension are all elements of primary socialization when the person who knows attempts to share this social knowledge with the person who does not. Although not a deterministic process, the relationship between the significant other and the person undergoing primary socialization, as well as what the participants bring in terms of background knowledge and attitudes, may cause it to move toward the social determinism end of the continuum.

The process of primary socialization in the classroom is somewhat different from what occurs in what we like to refer to as the real world. Outside the classroom primary socialization is more dependent on contextual cues and social modeling and less on abstract explanations. Second, when a person is learning the thought patterns and behavioral expectations associated with learning a new job, applying for a loan, or functioning as a hospital patient, there are genuine risks involved in asking questions that the significant other (the person who performs the gatekeeper role of admitting the uninitiated into the social stock of knowledge) cannot or is unwilling to answer. Although varied, the risks usually involve denial of access to the social opportunities being sought; and the person who has confused primary socialization to the task or situation at hand with the kind of primary socialization that occurs in some classrooms will often be labeled as incompetent or as having a poor attitude. The basic differences that separate the way primary socialization occurs in some classrooms from the way it occurs in most areas of adult social, economic, and political life point to the potential of the school as a unique institution for providing the conceptual basis of cultural renewal. As with issue of social determinism, the fulfilling of this potential is dependent on a number of variables—including the teacher's ability to understand and, when appropriate, change the dynamics of primary socialization.

We shall use the metaphorical image of the gatekeeper to suggest the crucial role the teacher plays in determining whether the dynamics of primary socialization will be a source of empowerment or a limiting experience. In a sense all significant others are gatekeepers in that they influence which aspects of the culture—ideas, values, social practices, technology, and so forth—will be made available to the individual who is having a first-time experience. But the gatekeeper role of the teacher is more complex and can have a more profound influence on students' development. What makes the teacher's role as a gatekeeper particularly distinctive is the range of the students' cultural exposure that will be mediated by the teacher's pattern of thinking and taken-for-granted beliefs, as well as by what the teacher has not thought about. In effect, students encounter the teacher's representation of the culture, including the selection of curriculum materials, interpretations that reflect the teacher's own past socialization, and biases that are reflected in the legitimation of student responses. How this gatekeeper role is played out in terms of the process of primary socialization in the classroom will, in many instances, influence whether the student acquires the conceptual basis for communicative competence or is further submerged in the cultural ecology of taken-for-granted beliefs. The latter is not always undesirable: The critical issue has to do with whether the ecology of ideas being learned at the taken-for-granted level contributes to the long-term well-being of the "organism plus environment."

Defining "What Is"

At the most basic level of primary socialization, the teacher's gatekeeper role involves making available to the student the language that will serve as the initial basis for thinking about the area of culture that is being encountered for the first time at the conceptual level. Students will have encountered many of the cultural patterns before coming to school and will have learned the patterns of interaction at a preconscious level of understanding—what we are identifying as taken-for-granted knowledge. Examples include the patterns of thought and social activities that characterize the everyday social routines of home and society with which the child interacts. In these social settings the child encounters the patterns that regulate work, eating, time, and so forth. While the child acquires the language that allows for participation in these social activities as a member of the group, this generally involves a language framework that is limited to communicating about the taken-for-granted patterns. As Bateson points out, most of this knowledge and language is acquired and used at an unconscious level of awareness. For example, in acquiring the cultural patterns that regulate the use of time, the child has probably learned that play occurs in certain spaces and work ("clean up your room"), in others. But this level of primary socialization does not provide a basis for thinking *about* the nature of these activities. The preschool, and much of the out-of-school, learning is contextual. In the classroom the teacher is engaged in a process of primary socialization whereby the student is acquiring the conceptual basis—language and theory frameworks for understanding relationships—essential for thinking about work, time, community, computers, science, art, competition, and so forth. Since this form of learning is often removed from the context of experience, the explanatory power of this form of understanding, as well as the ability to communicate it to others, is dependent on the complexity of the language and theory frameworks that are made available by the significant other—that is, parent, teacher, author of textbook or software program, TV personality, and so forth.

The teaching of a lesson represents an aspect of classroom socialization where the teacher's gatekeeping role can be clearly seen. One aspect of the lesson is that the words and concepts made available by the teacher establish the boundaries of what is to be thought about; they also provide the schema, or interpretative framework, for how the part of the culture that is being introduced is to be understood. In Bateson's sense, when students acquire an explanation of how to think about something (e.g., how to "tell" time, what science is, the causes of World War II, the cause of disease), they are, in effect, acquiring the way of thinking encoded in the language that is made available by the decisions of the teacher. Examples of how the language reproduces the thought processes of others can be seen in the following textbook examples. In reading these examples it is important to keep in mind some important variables: students who are learning about something for the first time, the possibility that the teacher's taken-for-granted understanding matches the textbook explanation, and the special sense of authority that the printed word has in the experience of both students and the teacher.

The examples can be taken from any level of the formal educational process and involve any subject; only the variables may change—with significant consequences for how the process of primary socialization is played out. We have chosen at random several textbooks and would like to have them considered in terms of a scenario wherein (1) the teacher's taken-for-granted beliefs largely correspond to the textbook explanations, (2) the students regard the teacher as a significant other (i.e., view the teacher as a source of authority), and (3) the students have not acquired, in a formal way, the language for thinking about this area of cultural experience. In short, consider the influence of these textbook explanations, as well as the teacher's decision-making responsibilities, in terms of students who are in a dependent relationship.

In a high school textbook, *Understanding Economics*, students encounter the following explanation about the nature of choice: "Everyone faces the problem of scarcity. Consequently, all individuals must make *choices*. In fact, some economists define *economics* as the science of choice" (Miller & Pulsinelli, 1983, p. 5). This statement, taken out of the context of the entire book, might seem a trivial example. But since the authors fail to provide students the vocabulary and conceptual frameworks for understanding how choice is always influenced by cultural beliefs and patterns, it serves as a good example of how a first-time explanation provides the conceptual scaffolding for subsequent thought about an area of human activity. The first words and concepts made available to students provide them, in effect, with a specific conceptual orientation. In this case the conceptual orientation reflects the Western view of individuals as autonomous beings who make choices based on what they think and value. For students whose primary socialization to other aspects of the culture are based on the same set of assumptions about the autonomous individual who is free of cultural influence, this explanation is more likely to be accepted as authoritative.

A second example is taken from an elementary textbook, *Science: Understanding Your Environment*. That it is taken from a 1975 publication is not the important issue here. Rather, the issue that deserves consideration has to do with the incompleteness of the explanation; that is, the withholding of the conceptual means for understanding the actual complexity of the problem that students are being asked to consider. In a section of "Conserving Natural Resources" the students read the following:

> There are two kinds of natural resources. One kind is said to be renewable. A *renewable resource* can be replaced. The trees in a forest are an example of a renewable resource. Only the full-grown trees are cut for logs. If new trees are planted and cared for, the forest will be renewed. The other kind of natural resource is non-renewable. Once a *non-renewable resource* is used, it cannot be replaced. Coal, oil, and natural gas are non-renewable resources. It took millions of years for these resources to develop. There is only so much of each one in the earth. They do not form nearly as quickly as they are used. (Mallinson, Mallinson, Brown, & Smallwood, 1975, p. 13)

Using Bateson's terms, this explanation involves the use of a vocabulary that encodes the mental ecology of generations of people who reflected a specific cultural orientation to thinking about the environment: It is *our* environment, and our resources should be "managed wisely," as the authors put it. While leaving the student with misinformation about how effective management can insure the future of our renewable resources, the textbook avoids any explanation of how cultural values and practices contribute to the problem. The vocabulary for thinking about economic, political, moral aspects of the problem is simply not made available to students.

Since any textbook, software program, or teacher explanation could be used as an example of how the vocabulary of primary socialization sets the boundaries and conceptual orientation of the students' initial way of understanding, we have chosen as a third example a textbook that introduces students to how they should think about choosing values:

> In order to have a true value, you must be able to choose freely from alternatives. You cannot choose a value if there is only one option. For example, your parents insist that you learn to play the piano and that you practice an hour daily. If you had no choice in deciding to play an instrument or in choosing which instrument to play, then you will probably not develop a true value. Thus, if a value has been imposed on you by others, it will guide your behavior only superficially. The value will cease when you are not under the influence of those who imposed the value on you (you will probably not continue to play the piano as an adult). A value must be chosen. (Henderson, 1985, p. 34)

For students who have not explicitly thought about the nature and source of values, this explanation gives them the vocabulary for making sense of an important and possibly confusing aspect of their lives—confusing in the sense of their being unable to recognize a clear demarcation line between their own values and those of the people (parents, peers, TV personalities, and so on) with whom they interact. The schema of understanding contained in this explanation provides clear conceptual guidance in viewing authentic values as freely chosen and imposed values as sources of constraint. It also provides a way of thinking of the self as autonomous and self-directing. In effect, this explanation, or any number of others taken from teacher talk, peers, textbooks, software programs, or film (when students are hearing something for the first time), involves socializing students to think in ways that reproduce other people's pattern of thinking. The language provides the connecting link in this process by sharing with the uninitiated student the "determinative memory" of other people's taken-for-granted way of thinking, as well as the new patterns of thought that reflect an attempt to address current issues.

This brings us to the question of how the teacher's gatekeeper role might be played out in a way that contributes to a more empowering form of primary socialization. Regardless of subject area or grade level, the teacher exerts control over two key relationships; and we want to summarize them here in a way that will put in focus professional judgments that teachers must be able to recognize and exercise. The first has to do with the dependence of thought and communication on language. As we pointed out in Chapter 2, the student does not create thought *sui generis* and then put it into words that will, in turn, be communicated to others. The social linguist M. A. K. Halliday summarized the interdependent relationship among thought, language, and context when he wrote, "as a child learns language, he also learns *through* language. . . . This process, like other semiotic processes, is controlled and regulated by the code; and so, in the course of it, the child himself also takes over the coding orientation" (1978, p. 125). What he means by a coding orientation that directs thought according to specific and often unrecognized patterns is demonstrated in his own writing style, where the masculine pronoun is used to designate the person. In effect, his own insights are embedded and framed in a deeper conceptual orientation that escaped his attention because it was so much a part of his natural attitude. Although language provides the schema for organizing thought in a socially congruent manner, it does not entirely determine it. The metaphorical nature of thought and the capacity for critical reflection make it possible for many students to see new relationships that are not part of the way of understanding encoded in the language given to them. This interactive relationship does not mean that students start out from a position of empowerment; rather, it is an achievement that comes through testing the explanatory power of the language provided by significant others against their own experience and way of understanding. The possibility of this achievement is significantly undermined when the process of primary socialization does not provide the basic vocabulary for differentiating the flow of experience into thought. To put this another way, without a beginning language framework, thought and communication become difficult achievements—if not impossibilities. At the same time, the initial language framework, such as socialization to the gender-specific language in the discourse of science (Keller, 1985; Longino & Doell, 1987), provides a conceptual orientation that will align the thought of the student to the traditional thought pathways of the society; the unexplored areas of experiences that fall outside the conceptual boundaries of the received language may never be thought or articulated.

The thought-language connection cannot really be discussed

without touching on the second key relationship over which teachers exert an influence, often at an unconscious level. This has to do with the way in which the pattern of thinking embedded in the language often binds the student to outmoded ways of thinking. The textbook explanation about "managing" nonrenewable resources (which emphasizes nature rather than the culture as being problematic) repeats the way of thinking found in Francis Bacon's observations that nature must be "bound into service," put "in constraint," and "molded" through rational understanding and control (quoted in Keller, 1987, p. 242). Similarly, Johannes Kepler (1571–1630) helped establish the workings of a machine as the root metaphor for understanding the universe. As he put it in 1605 in a letter to a friend, "My aim is to show that the celestial machine is to be likened not to a divine organism, but to a clockwork" (quoted in Merchant, 1980, pp. 128–129). This same mechanistic pattern of thought, formed centuries ago as a reaction to what was then perceived as outmoded Aristotelian thinking, is reproduced in a current health textbook's explanation of bones and muscles: "Puppets are moved by strings. They move only when someone decides to pull the strings. What makes your body move? How do muscles and bones work together to move your body?" And in an explanation of the body, students are presented with pictures of how the different functions of a car must be properly cared for, along with the statement: "A car is made up of many complex parts. Each part of a car must function if the car is to run well" (Meeks & Heit, 1982, pp. 102 and 88–89). The subsequent chapters establish that the body is like a car, a machine with many interacting parts that requires the diagnosis and care of experts.

The ecology of ideas (the information threads that make up the warp and woof of our current cultural patterns) to which the student is being introduced may involve, in some instances, acquiring a schema of understanding that was a progressive way of thinking in earlier centuries but totally inappropriate for the current problems faced by the culture. The current effort to eliminate the gender bias in the language of the classroom, a bias that appeared as a progressive development in human thought in the sixteenth and seventeenth centuries, is an example of updating the ecology of ideas that is to be the basis of the student's thought process. There are two other professional judgments that teachers need to recognize as they mediate the process of primary socialization.

COMPLEXITY OF LANGUAGE CODE. Teachers need to become sensitive to their gatekeeper role in the language acquisition process. It is their decisions about curriculum sources and classroom discussions that will determine whether, in this most critical phase of primary socialization, students will be given a limited or complex language code for thinking about the new domain of cultural experience. A limited language code (vocabulary and interpretative framework for understanding relationships) often results in the student's internalizing the factual information or pattern of thought used by others for explaining some aspect of experience. In effect, knowledge transmitted through a limited language code can be reproduced conceptually by students, but it will have little explanatory power in terms of illuminating the relationships that characterize the context of the students' experience. The determination of whether the language framework made available to students is limited (and limiting) involves asking whether the curriculum sources and classroom discussions provide students with the conceptual basis for thinking about the relationship between their own experience in the cultural-natural ecology and the issues that are the focal point of the lesson. If the vocabulary and interpretative framework simply introduce students to the expert's (author, filmmaker, writer of software programs) way of thinking, and if the teacher makes no attempt to supplement the process with other sources and to provide opportunities for the students' own voices to be heard, the teacher has crossed a critical line and could be said to be guilty of professional malfeasance.

Examples of classroom socialization that leaves students with a way of thinking that simplifies the ecology of ideas and relationships that make up everyday experiences are too numerous for complete documentation. What adults do *not* understand about the nature of culture (their own as well as that of other people)—the political and reality-constituting nature of language, the nature of tradition, the nonneutrality of technology, the science-culture connection, and the alternatives to the alienating patterns of work that we seem locked into (to cite a few examples)—suggests that somewhere in the formal education process their teachers were not able to function adequately in their gatekeeper role. The process of supplementing curriculum sources is not difficult, and it does not require that the teacher be an expert. It does require, however, that the teacher recognize that students are carriers of culture and that in the right environment their voices can be heard and further empowered as they find within the ecology of ideas that makes up their community the words and concepts to express themselves. As a model of how to supplement the process of primary socialization, consider the case of a teacher who is using a textbook, *Understanding Economics* (Miller & Pulsinelli, 1983), as the primary curriculum source. The textbook provides students with the language framework of the professional economist: supply and demand, inflation, business cycle, fiscal policy, monetary policy, and so forth. But it does not provide the words and concepts that students need to understand the economic circumstances of their own lives, not to mention the social, political, cultural, and technological forces that impinge on them. Surprisingly enough, this textbook, which is sophisticated in its treatment of economic theory, does not mention *work*, even though it is one of the most basic elements of economic activity. The teacher, as gatekeeper, needs to provide access to other perspectives—those of students, members of the community, social and economic theorists—that will provide a more complete language and conceptual framework. In other instances the gatekeeper role might involve inviting the storytellers who are the bearers of the traditional knowledge of the different cultural groups that make up the community, helping students situate ideas in terms of cultural context and actual social practices, and, in some instances, encouraging students to explore how the abstract representatives of culture relate to the context of their own lives.

LANGUAGE AS POLITICAL GUIDANCE SYSTEM. The gatekeeper role involves making a professional judgment about the adequacy of the schema (model of thinking) embedded in the language made available to students. Although we have not explicitly mentioned the political nature of the teacher's gatekeeper role, the previous discussion about whether primary socialization leaves students with a limited or complex language framework touches on the political nature of the teacher's role (as well as that of anyone who is in the role of significant other). Making a professional judgment about the adequacy (to use a metaphor that can be bent to so many interpretations) of the schema that is being given students as their initial basis of thought simply brings the political issue into the open, where the teacher's responsibilities can be addressed. As Claus Mueller observes, language provides a conceptual guidance system that can also be understood as a political guidance system (1973). The connection between language and people's thought and behavioral patterns can be seen in how a sexist language framework, which was formerly part of the school curriculum, reinforced the ecology of ideas and social practices that privileged men in all areas of cultural life—economic, political, and social. Other examples include the curricula that reinforce, in the process of teaching other content, the assumption that language is a conduit for the expression of individual ideas, that technology is like a neutral tool, that literacy represents progress over an oral tradition, that being free and responsible means escaping the bonds of tradition, and so forth. We cannot think or communicate without some form of language; and this dependence on language involves acquiring (as we discussed in Chapter 2) the particular conceptual pattern encoded in the language—the "determinative memory" of the language community. If we keep in mind that the conceptual map provided by the language is not the territory, as Alfred Korzybiski reminds us (reported in Bateson, 1972), it is then possible to see that different conceptual maps (language frameworks) will guide what individuals are aware of and how they will respond to it. This involves the most basic expression of power and control, and it is political through and through.

Most teachers are now sensitive to language frameworks that reproduce sexist and racist ways of thinking; but they are not usually aware of the schemata made available in the other areas of primary socialization they control: for example, the body is more complicated than a machine in that it is influenced by culture and the individual's way of thinking; values are not simply chosen but are acquired at a tacit level through language and using other people as analogues; and, at least in the Northwest, new trees are cut years before they reach maturity. The ecology of ideas that enable the cultural-natural habitat to exist as a mutually self-correcting system is threatened when the teacher presents to students the vocabulary and conceptual frameworks that encode the assumptions of earlier generations who viewed progress as unlimited—even when it resulted in the depletion of nonrenewable resources. Students who are socialized to an "ecology of bad ideas," particularly when the newly acquired schema for understanding prevents taking account of the information exchanges that characterize current relationships, are not likely to develop the form of communicative competence that will help solve our current cultural-environmental problems. Wendell Berry puts the teacher's responsibility for determining the adequacy of the schemata made available to students in the following way:

> The definitive relationships in the universe are thus not competitive, but interdependent. And from a human point of view they are analogical. We can build one system only within another. We can have agriculture only within nature, and culture only within agriculture. At certain critical points these systems have to conform to one another or destroy one another. (1986, p. 47)

Implicit/Explicit Knowledge

Anthropologists would agree with Bateson's observation that most of our knowledge is experienced and utilized at an unconscious level. Edward Hall refers to the total communication framework that makes up a culture—its patterns of time, space, materials, work, nonverbal communication, and so forth—as the "cultural unconscious" (1977, p. 43). There are a variety of terms used to describe this form of knowledge that we often become aware of only when others (generally people from other cultures) do not follow the patterns: taken-for-granted beliefs, natural attitude, tacit knowledge. Our Cartesian orientation, with its emphasis on explicit knowledge that can be observed and measured, has strengthened the tendency not to recognize the unconscious patterns that guide social interaction and make life generally predictable. Aspects of metaphorical thinking and meta-communication patterns raised in previous chapters are difficult to recognize in our own experience because they are such a natural aspect of experience that they are taken for granted. As we take knowledge for granted, the patterns guide thought and behavior; when forced to deviate from them, there is often a sense of being threatened or a feeling of uncertainty and disorientation. The patterns that regulate how we greet others, drive down the road, organize letters into words and words into sentences, utilize and measure time, eat our food, and so forth represent a passive form of knowledge.

Mary Douglas views this taken-for-granted knowledge as performing an important function:

> Some information is treated as self-evident. The logical steps by which other knowledge has to be justified are not required. This kind of information, never being made explicit, furnishes the stable background on which more coherent meanings are based. It is referred to obliquely as a set of known truths about the earth, the weight and powers of objects, the physiology of humans, and so on. . . . It provides the necessary unexamined assumptions upon which ordinary discourse takes place. Its stability is an illusion, for a large part of discourse is dedicated to creating, revising and obliquely affirming this implicit background, without ever directing explicit attention upon it. When the background of assumptions upholds what is verbally explicit, meanings come across loud and clear. Through these implicit channels of meaning, human society itself is achieved, clarity and speed of clue-reading ensured. In the elusive exchange between explicit and implicit meanings a perceived-to-be-regular universe establishes itself precariously, shifts, topples and sets itself up again. (1975, pp. 3–4)

If all the background knowledge that is taken for granted were made explicit at the same time, there would be total confusion about which aspects needed special attention. The stability and taken-for-granted nature of cultural patterns allowed for gender-specific concerns to be addressed, to cite a recent example. The interplay between implicit and explicit knowledge carries across all areas of social life, including the process of primary socialization that occurs in the classroom as the teacher introduces students to new areas of cultural knowledge. The gatekeeper role of the teacher involves decisions about how much of the background assumptions (shared implicit knowledge) will be made explicit as part of the classroom discussion. Even when teachers are not aware of this aspect of their gatekeeper role, they are engaged, as a natural aspect of communicating with students, in illuminating the culturally hidden or in further reinforcing the hidden nature of the cultural patterns.

When teachers emphasize the factual and objective nature of knowledge, through the vocabulary they make available to students, and use objective tests, primary socialization is more likely to obscure from view the background cultural assumptions. For example, treating historical events as factual and emphasizing dates, places, and events is likely further to reinforce the dominant cultural assumptions that underlie the Christian dating system (should students be aware that other cultures have different calendars?) and what is seen as constituting the historically significant. Primary socialization to any area of the curriculum—how to think about (or do) art, stories as having three parts, economics as divorced from moral concerns and political relationships, the source of values, the role of experts—involves explicit knowledge that teacher and students are attending to. It also involves background knowledge—taken-for-granted assumptions and patterns of thought—that frames how the explicit knowledge will be understood. For example, the task of making explicit the sexist attitudes toward thinking about social roles, the nature of work, personal attributes, and so forth was carried out against a background set of taken-for-granted assumptions about the nature of individualism, personal autonomy, the progressive nature of change, and, until recently, the neutral nature of technology and the scientific method.

The teacher's gatekeeper role, which involves knowing when to make explicit the implicit aspect of cultural belief and practice, is especially difficult, but as we said earlier, decisions about this aspect of primary socialization are inescapable. The difficulty is related, in part, to the general problem that Hall identified as the "cultural unconscious." "What is known least well and is therefore in the poorest position to be studied," he writes, "is what is closest to oneself. . . . These are the unconscious patterns that control one's life" (1977, p. 45). The difficulty is increased by the Cartesian orientation of teacher education programs and the university curriculum in general, both of which reinforce the dominant cultural orientation toward observable and measurable forms of knowledge. For students such as the first-graders who did not conform to the teacher's taken-for-granted patterns of topic-centered, linear development of a story, acquiring the conceptual foundations for thinking about some area of the shared cultural experience (or the more abstract culture of the dominant group) can be a perilous experience. In such situations the causes of the teacher's blindness to implicit assumptions and thought patterns does not much matter. The background knowledge will have the same binding effect on students' thought processes and sense of self, unless, of course, they are grounded in a different set of background assumptions, such as the authority of group norms over individual achievement that Philips (1972) observed in the Warm Springs Indian classrooms. In these situations the teacher's judgments may reflect the unexamined cultural bias of the controlling background assumptions.

Not all of this background knowledge should or can be made explicit. The problem for the student arises when the teacher's taken-for-granted beliefs correspond to the taken-for-granted beliefs of the person who writes the textbook or computer software program. The patterns that regulate thought and behavior—like the interplay between spoken and nonverbal communication patterns or the assumptions that underlie how we think about art, do science, or perform on the athletic field—are so integral to the experience itself that they go unnoticed. Many of the patterns that make up the ecology of mind within which the individual participates serve positive and necessary functions. They are, in fact, substantive traditions that are continued because they provide the templates for dealing with basic human problems in a culturally coherent way. But not all the taken-for-granted knowledge of a cultural group remains useful. In terms of the dominant cultural group, many of the taken-for-granted assumptions were formulated centuries ago, when people were confronting an entirely different set of challenges and interpreted these challenges in terms of a belief system that they had acquired from even earlier times. We have become aware of some of this background knowledge and, in the process of making it explicit, have been able to reformulate it. Examples of areas in which the background knowledge handed down from the past is being made explicit and seriously reconsidered include the privileged status given to the masculine way of thinking, the depletion of nonrenewable resources, and the emphasis on the autonomous, self-directing individual.

One aspect of the teacher's professional judgment is to recognize the educational moment in the process of primary socialization when the taken-for-granted beliefs of students or the author need to be made explicit and reflected upon by the entire class. Teachers also need to monitor their own thought patterns, as many have done with regard to sexist and racist attitudes, to insure that their own cultural blindness does not prevent students from recognizing cultural patterns that may now be ecologically and culturally problematic. This need for professional alertness to an aspect of the cultural transmission process can involve paying special attention to taken-for-granted ways of thinking embedded in the curriculum or in the student's thought patterns. The computer simulation program *Oregon Trail* (Minnesota Educational Computing Consortium, 1985) is typical of how factual information is embedded in a complex mosaic of cultural assumptions that are likely to have a greater impact on the students than the names, dates, and events that will easily be forgotten. As an exercise in primary socialization, the students are given a story line (that they are playing the role of pioneers on their way to the Oregon Territory), a certain amount of information that is to guide their decisions, and a visual animation of the contingencies they face and the consequences of their simulated decision making as nineteenth-century pioneers. The dangers of bandits, swollen rivers, and inhospitable open spaces make the trek to Oregon a real challenge for the students. But the simulation also involves socialization to taken-for-granted beliefs of the dominant cultural group. The vocabulary—*pioneer, Oregon Territory, bandits* (*thieves* in a later version)—frames the student's way of thinking in accordance with the interpretative framework of the pioneers, who viewed themselves as carriers of civilization in an unclaimed wilderness. In fact, the term *pioneer* carries in it the assumption of being the first person or group that prepared the way for others. Similarly, the terms *bandits* and *thieves*, used to refer to those who attacked the pioneers, are not likely to be understood by students undergoing primary socialization as native peoples struggling to preserve their way of life and territory from the invading forces. The simulation program reinforces other background assumptions shared by the dominant culture, including attitudes toward time as something that should not be wasted, life as a game in which there are winners and losers, and group behavior as based on competition and pursuit of self-interest.

The challenge of knowing when to make taken-for-granted beliefs explicit, assuming the teacher is able to recognize them, raises an important question about the educational background of the teacher and the pressures of the teacher's workload. Although we think some people, including teachers, are more sensitive than others to the adequacy of the "determinative memory" that characterizes this background knowledge, there is an important connection between the kind of formal education teachers receive and their ability to recognize taken-for-granted patterns. An education that emphasizes technique, factual knowledge, and a segmented and conceptually incoherent course of study is more likely to desensitize the teacher to the embedded mental processes from the past that constitute the background knowledge. The heavy workload that leaves teachers too exhausted to read or otherwise have experiences that provide a conceptual basis for obtaining a broader perspective on taken-for-granted beliefs is also a factor that undermines the teacher's ability to exercise professional judgment as we are defining it here. Whatever the cause, the inability to recognize taken-for-granted patterns of thought and behavior that contribute to current social and ecological problems is a greater contributor to being "at-risk" as a nation than problems associated with international economic competition. Economic downturns are painful for many people but are mostly survivable. The permanent loss of topsoil, contamination and depletion of water resources, and altered atmospheric conditions—because of cultural assumptions and practices that seemed progressive in the seventeenth century—may not be survivable over the long term.

Fact or Interpretation?

When primary socialization involves presenting students with factual information, there are two possibilities—with both having consequences that will affect the student's ability to think as an adult. The first is that many students will passively accept the authority of factual information and carry this expectation into their adult lives. The second possibility is that the student will view factual information as like the fuel that powers the engine (mind of the student). The expression "to turn the facts over in your mind" and the image of students as constructing their own ideas from an information base (an image popular in computer education circles) both suggest the image of the mind operating when there is an intake of factual information. Although we are having to deal with the political consequences of adults acting out both possibilities, it is important for teachers to understand the source of the problem (i.e., the myth of factual information) and the professional judgments they must make in dealing with this aspect of primary socialization.

Why it is incorrect to view the "information cells" (the words and concepts used for defining "What Is") as factual can be seen by reiterating the point made earlier about language providing the schema for understanding and interpreting. Since language is a human and thus culturally specific construct—that is, the interpretative frameworks have a cultural origin—what is represented to students as factual information is actually the result of a cultural encoding process. What is seen and interpreted from a cultural point of view becomes viewed as factual when the human-cultural authorship is lost sight of. It is easier to recognize in the spoken word the perspective (bias) and interest of the speaker; thus, in some areas of the academic community still under the control of Cartesian thought, the authority of the spoken word is not considered a valid source of knowledge. The printed word, on the other hand, appears to communicate (in conduit fashion) objective or factual information, since authorship is less visible in the text. This process of transforming human interpretations, framed by the conceptual categories embedded in the language framework of a cultural group, into objective facts is part of the process of reifying culture. When part of the culture becomes reified—that is, appears as having an existence and source of authority independent of the people who created it—then the culture (the facts, institutions, beliefs, etc.) dictates to people who feel powerless to act. Some common examples of reifications in the dominant culture include time schedules, patterns of social organization, and beliefs related to competition, winning, individualism, and the progressive nature of change. Examples of de-reification, whereby people feel empowerment to express their own voices, include movement away from sexist beliefs and practices, from hierarchical structures of social organization toward more participatory patterns, and, for many minority groups, from the values and beliefs of the dominant Anglo culture.

The process of representing someone's interpretation, which in turn is influenced by the patterns of understanding of the cultural group, as factual and objective can be seen in the following textbook explanations. The explanation of "underdeveloped economies" presented here is a typical example of how a culturally and historically specific way of thinking is transformed and presented to students as factual information:

> In many economies, such as those in Southeast Asia, little is produced except what people need to stay alive. The economy does not produce

many goods and services. Food and raw materials are the main products. At least three-fourths of the workers are farmers. If there are raw materials such as minerals, the people of the nation may have to ask foreigners to come and show them how to develop their resources. Because many people in the nations of Southeast Asia have not learned how to read, few of them know how to handle business matters or the problems that go with developing the economy. (Center for the Study of Instruction, 1977, p. 411)

And in a textbook on computers and data processing today students will encounter the following "factual" basis for primary socialization to how they should think about computers:

The computer has become a dominant force in our society. Without the computer, society as we know it would come to a standstill. Business corporations, government agencies, and other organizations depend on computers to process data and make information available for use in decision making. Because of the impact of computers on everyday life, it is essential that people gain a basic understanding of them—their capabilities, limitations, and applications. (Mandell, 1983, p. 3)

For students who are having first-time encounters with formal explanations of how to think about the significance of computers and the cultural backwardness of Southeast Asia, both examples are likely to appear as factually based. In this educational setting the ecology of ideas—which includes the printed page, the teacher who does not have the deeper understanding necessary for supplementing or critiquing the text, and students who are initially dependent on the interpretive framework encoded in the language made available to them—will convey a false impression of objectivity and finality. Instead of providing students with the conceptual basis for understanding the complex interplay among technology, cultural values and practices, and historical development, students encounter in both examples the author's Western cultural biases masked as objective fact. The only role the textbook author makes available to the students is that of passive receivers of information.

By giving "factual" explanations, teachers can also turn the information pathways that connect students to fields of study into mere conduits for the transmission of discrete and lifeless bits of information. Even the question-and-answer pattern of teaching may leave students with a false understanding. In this supposedly more open pedagogical strategy, students may either view themselves as having originated an idea or interpretation (and thus not recognize how language influences their thought process) or they may view the teacher's account as having a factual basis. If we go back to Bateson's point that relationships involve information exchanges (keeping in mind here that he does not mean information in the conventional sense in use today), we can see that students' interaction with an author, a textbook explanation, a teacher response—or whatever else represents the content of the curriculum—becomes more intellectually complex and vital as they are given the opportunity to examine the larger context (ecology) of relationships that constitute what is being studied. Instead of the information exchange that characterized the person felling a tree, it would involve processing information in a circuit that would involve students (with an understanding of their own context) with textbook writers, authors, painters, scientists, and so forth (with an understanding of their context) as well as the teacher (with an understanding of her or his context). To put it another way, the information pathways that connect students to new encounters with the collective cultural experience can be revitalized if students are encouraged to consider the relation of context to the interpretations that are given. This would include considering how their own cultural-historical context influenced the person who is giving an account of what happened in the past, as well as how the context (ecology of ideas) influenced the ideas, events, and achievements being studied.

A concern with context leads to a recognition that interpretation, shaped by the conceptual conventions of a cultural group, is the basis of knowledge. Representing knowledge as factual hides the interpretative process as well as the cultural-historical context that made one pattern of interpretation more likely than another. For the teacher managing the ecology of primary socialization, this suggests the need continually to monitor whether the communication process in the classroom is representing knowledge as facts or interpretations based on certain conventions of thinking. This does not mean the teacher is guilty of professional malpractice if some areas of the curriculum involve transmitting factual information. The sciences would be a good example of where this is likely to happen; but even in this area of primary socialization students should learn, at some point, that science involves a specific way of thinking (conventions of thought) that is historically and culturally specific and that this way of thinking, while powerful in providing explanations, predictions, and technological ways of control, is unable to deal with certain aspects of human experience.

Aside from special areas of the curriculum in which a more systematic approach may be desirable, the teacher's continual challenge is to keep the historical perspective alive as part of the primary socialization process. This may mean asking such questions as

> Where did that idea or interpretation come from?
> What were the dominant characteristics of the pattern of thinking and social activity of that time?
> What are the assumptions that we bring to our interpretations?

It may also mean using more of the resources of the community as a way of recovering a more balanced interpretation of the forces operating in the past. Regardless of the resources available, it involves exploring the historical dimension of the information pathways that connect students to the ecology of ideas and social practices.

Cross-Cultural Perspective

The teacher's gatekeeper role creates a special problem when it comes to determining the educationally significant moment when the taken-for-granted patterns of culture should be made explicit. First-time encounters with a new area of cultural experience, as we explained earlier, involve a special degree of vulnerability to being controlled by the language framework, taken-for-granted attitudes, and sense of factualness that may be communicated by the way in which the teacher orchestrates the ecology of ideas that constitute the planned curriculum. Even if the teacher makes available a complex language framework and performs the other gatekeeper functions that empower thought, it will still be difficult for students to recognize the deep cultural basis of thought and social behavior. The challenge lies in recognizing when students should be introduced to the deep assumptions that underpin the patterns of thought and social practices of other cultures and using this comparative perspective as a way of helping students recognize their own cultural patterns. As people traveling in foreign cultures have discovered, the experience of making sense of the patterns of other cultural groups often results in recognizing their own experience as based on a set of patterns and assumptions that they were previously unaware of. For students who must increasingly interact with others who are not grounded in a Western-Anglo worldview, recognizing the deep underpinnings of the dominant culture as well as the deep patterns of others seems essential to effective citizenship in a multicultural society.

To relate this point to a Batesonian perspective, knowledge of the cultural patterns of others is essential as the ecology of relationships becomes expanded through interactions with more diverse people. The information exchanges that occur between dominant and minority cultural groups will be nullified if the participants are only willing and capable of interpreting what fits their own cultural codes. Cultural differences in attitudes toward time, competition, work, individualism, and technology—not to mention the patterns of metacommunication that are critical to whether these other messages are taken seriously—constantly threaten to disrupt the communication process as members of different cultural groups interact with each other. Treating people as individuals, the rational process as culture free, and language as a conduit may, from the perspective of the dominant culture, eliminate the problem—but it is an illusion sustained by members of the dominant Anglo culture. For others, it represents further instances of cultural domination that are cloaked in the "god-words" of a modernizing ideology.

Understanding the deep assumptions of other cultures, especially those that are rooted in the narrative traditions that represent the earlier stages of consciousness of a cultural group, may be critical to the revitalization and reform of the assumptions that now appear as increasing problematic for the dominant culture. The cultural orientation generally associated with Western modernity has increased our material possibilities, but at a severe cost to the environment and our social and psychological relationships. The depletion of nonrenewable resources, growing dissatisfaction in the workplace, the increased use of drugs and prevalence of culturally caused disease, and the growing need for experts to heal an increasing range of psychological wounds all suggest that the cultural patterns borrowed from the past may not be suitable in the future. Understanding the form of intelligence that characterized the culture-nature ecology of other people may help in reconceptualizing the cultural assumptions that are increasingly being recognized as a cause of our deepening cultural and ecological problems.

As the gatekeeper in an educational setting where questions can be asked, the relationship between ideas and experience can be explored in depth, and the history of ideas and social practices can be recovered for purposes of gaining perspective on the present, the teacher has a unique opportunity and responsibility that is not available in most other areas of society. The opportunity (and responsibility) also involves helping students obtain a perspective on their own culture by viewing it through the lenses of other cultures. This may involve obtaining a perspective on the dominant cultural view of competition, success, and individualism by examining the belief system of the traditional Navajo or any other non-Western cultural group. A comparative view of technology, use of the land, and notions of progress might also be topics to focus on. The aspect of social practice and belief that can be examined cross-culturally may range from questions of gender, number system, and view of art, to myths, diet, and childrearing practices. But whether this cross-cultural perspective becomes part of the student's primary socialization depends on the kind of awareness teachers bring to the performance of their role as a gatekeeper of which aspects of the culture the student will be allowed to encounter. As we said earlier, the breadth and depth of cultural exposure are dependent on the teacher's level of understanding. If the teacher is part of an ecology of outmoded ideas, then it is likely that students will be similarly burdened—at least in those situations in which the teacher is the significant other. For in most instances of primary socialization, the culture is mediated through the teacher's patterns of understanding. To put this another way, the student's growth in communicative competence is dependent on the teacher's possessing a sensitivity, awareness, and knowledge of cultures and communicating this in a manner that empowers students to make informed interpretations of the ecology of relationships that make up everyday life and to articulate the issues in their own voices.

CHAPTER 5

Framing and Social Control

The previous chapters have been used to develop the foundations and implications of a perspective from which the classroom can be understood as an ecology of language, culture, and thought. A sociolinguistic understanding of metaphor and patterns of nonverbal communication contributes to this perspective by demonstrating several ways in which language functions not as a conduit through which teachers present information to their students, but as a guiding force in determining what information is made available and how the learning environment is organized. Primary socialization carries this theme a step further, bringing into focus forms of metacommunication that mediate cultural patterns of instruction. This metacommunication conveys implicit lessons that are critically important to how students and teachers come to view themselves as individuals and as members of a learning community.

In this chapter we shall focus on framing as still another dimension of the language-culture-thought ecology characteristic of classroom life. First, however, we want to stress how an ecological perspective differs from conventional views of classroom management as a form of social control. Foremost, it brings forward an image of control that is far more complex than one which places its primary emphasis on the teacher's unilateral decision making about classroom rules or the use of behavioral reinforcement. An image of control based on unilateral decision making assumes that individuals can be understood as autonomous and that rational processes are culture-free. These assumptions, as we have noted earlier, are challenged by Bateson's argument that if we view human intelligence in terms of the "organism plus environment," then "in no system which shows mental characteristics can any part have unilateral control over the whole" (1972, p. 317). When we apply Bateson's perspective to issues of classroom management, it highlights control and decision making as negotiated, relational processes. In this light, the teacher's efforts to establish rules, or a "work system," both control *and* are controlled by cultural patterns of interaction. Perhaps most important, this perspective offers an approach to understanding management as the process of successfully working through the give-and-take of social relationships.

We believe that this image of control as negotiated and relational will help place teaching strategies on a more sound conceptual foundation. Yet we also feel that this image is more in tune with how classroom teachers themselves intuitively understand the central concerns of their day-to-day work. Consider, for example, the comments of Peter Karlin, a high school English teacher with twenty-six years of teaching experience. When asked what *practical* advice he would offer a beginning teacher, Peter responded:

> The first thing to learn is to treat the student as a person, with the same respect you would an adult. Another thing would be to try to maintain the attitude that the students have different values than yours. Also, trust the students, and never criticize or threaten a student so that you destroy the relationship to the point where it can't be recovered. Never say anything to a student that will cause a serious break between you and him, and *you* should take the first steps toward correcting a problem with a student. That's part of treating students as people. If a student comes in upset, give him the benefit of being upset. They have bad days too. I think you should care about students. I don't think you should be their personal friend, but you should be on a friendly basis with them. You can't force students to do what you want them to do, but if they know you're working hard and care about 'em, then from there on it's gravy. . . . Definitely be aware of the students' lives outside of the classroom, and treat them as more than just an English student. I would also say not to be afraid of letting students know that you're a person and that you have a life outside the classroom. You also have to be aware that students do the same things that you did when you were in school. For instance, you loved to have the teacher forget to collect the assignment. Have the sense of humor to realize that those things are still going on. Also, use the least amount of pressure that you can. If you have to call a parent, tell the kid you're going to do it, but don't threaten them. And when you call a parent, you want to set up a situation where it's going to be a constructive rather than destructive thing at home. You don't want the parent to put the phone down and go over and hit his kid; you want him to go over and talk to his kid. (quoted in Flinders, 1987, pp. 114–115)

Several of Peter's specific recommendations will be considered later in this chapter as they relate to humor, self-disclosure, and dialogue strategies. Here we simply wish to emphasize two general points. First, taken out of context, some people might interpret Peter's advice as "mere talk," an idealized and perhaps self-serving image of teaching that has little to do with the realities of providing daily instruction. Yet the descriptive case study from which the quote is taken suggests the contrary: that Peter's comments do reflect a primary dimension of his classroom teaching. Moreover, Peter is not a unique or extraordinary teacher except, of course, in the particularities of his work situation. Like most classroom teachers, his instruction is carried out in an environment in which relationships play a prominent role in defining what it means to teach. We would be surprised, then, if other teachers did not recognize and share many of Peter's general concerns.

Second, we want to stress that Peter's practical advice is not couched in the conventional language of classroom management. He speaks, for example, of trust, respect, and mutual understanding— relational concerns that extend beyond the management of classroom rules, procedures, rewards, and penalties. Another way to put this is that the metaphor of "teacher as manager" fails to capture fully Peter's image of good teaching. The specific difficulty we face lies in the danger of neglecting forms of professional knowledge that cannot be easily explained in terms of a management perspective. In this case, the language of management relegates Peter's knowledge of how to get along with students to a marginal status, where we believe it has too often been regarded as nothing more than "tricks of the trade."

Our task in previous chapters (and one that we will continue here) can be understood as a serious attempt to reframe the current discourse on management and control in a way that helps bring into sharp focus Peter's intuitive knowledge regarding the quality of relationships that are played out through classroom instruction. These efforts have largely involved introducing a new vocabulary (e.g., *ecology of the classroom, iconic metaphor, proxemics, primary socialization*, and so forth) that makes explicit otherwise taken-for-granted cultural patterns of social interaction. In this chapter we shall develop this vocabulary further by taking a close look at the concept of framing. Our first concern will be to understand how the framing of communication influences the status of relationships and is influenced by cultural patterns. This will help clarify our image of control as a negotiated, relational process. Second, we will consider the twin concepts of power and solidarity, because they provide useful points of reference in recognizing frame and relationship connections. Power and solidarity can also be viewed as two of the primary concerns put into focus by a "teacher as negotiator" metaphor. Finally, as Peter Karlin has done, we shall identify specific aspects of student-teacher interaction (self-disclosure, humor, turn-taking, and dialogue) that help illustrate how an understanding of framing contributes to the professional knowledge of teachers.

FRAMING AS COMMUNICATION

In the classroom, as elsewhere, the forms and meaning of communication are multilayered. Deborah Tannen makes this point by observing that everything said must be said in some way (1986b). This may seem quite obvious, but it should serve to remind us that *how* something is said can be as important as *what* is said. The humor of a joke, for example, often hinges on timing, facial expressions, body gestures, and so on. After all, we enjoy the performances of comedians not only because they say funny things but also because they say things in a funny way. The "how" of speaking and writing is equally important in other situations. Asking a question, making an apology, giving advice, offering condolence, introducing oneself, ending a telephone conversation, refusing an invitation, expressing disappointment, telling a story, and greeting a friend can all be accomplished in a variety of ways, and the ways in which they are accomplished make a difference. Praise offered without any signs of enthusiasm may well be suspect, for example, while friendly advice accompanied with a great deal of enthusiasm may be interpreted as unwanted interference. As we are often quick to recognize, a phrase such as "I love you" derives its significance and even its meaning from the total context in which it is used. In short, such words and phrases do not speak for themselves.

The Metamessages of Framing

Another way in which to think about this aspect of language is to consider the "how" of speaking as a message in and of itself. This point can be illustrated if we recall, from Chapter 3, John Gumperz's (1977) example of the West Indian bus driver in London who, in asking his passengers for "exact change, please," said "please" with extra loudness, in a high pitch, and with falling intonation. Unknown to the bus driver, these prosodic cues conveyed the message that his words were to be understood as a command. Thus the passengers interpreted not one but two messages. The first, spoken—"exact change, please"; and the second (in this case mistakenly) inferred— "my words are a command." Here it is important to note that the second message provides information about the first. It is a message about a message, or what we have referred to in Chapter 3 as a meta-message. Yet to reiterate our main point, the metamessage in this example is not conveyed directly. The bus driver does not announce, "my words are a command." Instead, this information is supplied through a context of interaction that includes multiple channels of communication.

Here we also wish to emphasize that metamessages are a largely taken-for-granted aspect of day-to-day social interaction; that is, we do not self-consciously reflect on how metamessages are conveyed and interpreted unless the occasion seems to warrant special considerations (as when interviewing for a new job, making a formal presentation, or proposing marriage). In this respect, metacommunicating is analogous to many of the routine activities that comprise daily life. Walking serves as an example. As we get around from place to place each day, the action of placing one foot in front of the next, maintaining an upright position, and so forth does not ordinarily demand our focused attention. But if we find ourselves on an ice-covered sidewalk or rocky hillside, then the routine activity of walking may well become a challenging task that requires an explicit awareness of our movements and balance. Metacommunicating, much like walking, represents a tacit level of skill and understanding. Only when we find the process slippery or the territory unfamiliar (as is often the case in cross-cultural situations) do we give metamessages careful and explicit consideration.

While metamessages are communicated indirectly and at a taken-for-granted level of understanding, they are also critically important because they frame social interaction in ways that make it coherent. Like picture frames, the frames of interaction focus and structure experience within a limited context. One way they are able to accomplish this is by bracketing explicit messages. This can be illustrated visually by combining the message and metamessage of Gumperz's example into a single sentence: "My words, 'exact change, please,' are a command." Here we can see how the metamessage quite literally brackets the message on each side. In doing so, the bracket, or frame, provides a context that is necessary for making sense of the message. If we remove the frame, leaving only the message "exact change, please," then we have also removed the context, and without a context we have no way of knowing whether the message is a command, a polite request, part of a story, an example illustrating a proper use of commas, or the punch line to a joke. The point is that frames provide a footing for communication.

This function of framing is emphasized in Erving Goffman's (1974) work on frame analysis. Goffman defines frames as the organizational premises of social experience. His definition can be most clearly understood as grounded in the assumption that in everyday social interaction people are structure-seeking. In his words, "I assume that when individuals attend to any current situation, they face the question: 'What is it that's going on here?'" (p. 8). Frames such as "This is a command," "This is a joke," "This is a test," "This is urgent," "This is the beginning," "This is the end," and so on address this question, thus providing points of reference that allow us to anchor experience along the lines of some premise. Again, picture frames can be thought of as performing a similar function. In most cases, they offer a point of reference that marks off a representation of reality (e.g., a painting) from its "real" surroundings (the wall on which the painting is hung).

As we have done, Goffman also uses the metaphor of bracketing to illustrate how frames define and organize certain dimensions of social experience. He further suggests that such brackets can be seen as providing either temporal or spatial cues to expected patterns of behavior. Temporal brackets signal some point (such as the beginning, middle, or end) in the flow of episodic experience. A fairy tale, for example, is bracketed by the introductory phrase "once upon a time" and by the closing phrase "they lived happily ever after." In this example, the initial bracket "once upon a time" signals not only "this is the beginning" but also "this is the beginning of a special type of story that is imaginary, intended to entertain children, likely to be about the adventures of supernatural beings, and so on." Other examples of temporal brackets include the bang of a gavel to signal the opening (call to order) and close (adjournment) of a meeting and the use of schoolbells to bracket class sessions. In each of these cases, the brackets provide cues to occasions that are defined by cultural patterns of behavior and thought. Spatial brackets function in a similar way by offering what are primarily visual cues. The zoning laws of a city, the design of a freeway system, or the box-like architecture of a classroom serve as examples of how the use of space participates in the communication of what is expected at a given time and place. Other examples of the symbolic use of space were provided in our Chapter 3 discussion of proxemics.

We mention these examples in order to illustrate the broad scope in which framing can be understood as a primary dimension of ordinary, everyday social life. Yet we want to return for a moment to the specific issue of how framing operates within the context of spoken and written language. In face-to-face communication, pacing, pausing, intonation, body gestures, and facial expressions all help to establish the frame of a spoken message. In written language, we necessarily give up these paralinguistic and nonverbal cues, but written messages are still likely to be framed within an informationally rich context. Punctuation, for example, provides some of the information that in spoken language would be derived from pacing, pausing, and intonation, while such text divisions as chapters and paragraphs help mark off what parts of the written message are intended to stand on their own. Such cues often follow the conventions established within a given genre. Examples include the insertion of blank lines to signal a change of setting in a novel and the use of a border to frame an advertisement in a newspaper.

Even the layout, type of paper, or style of print used in publications signal metamessages that frame and are often coordinated to reinforce written messages. An example of this can be drawn from the field of teacher education by comparing two nationally recognized reports: *A Nation Prepared* (Carnegie Task Force on Teaching as a Profession, 1986) and *Tomorrow's Teachers* (Holmes Group, 1986). The first of these reports was sponsored by the Carnegie Forum on Education and the Economy. In brief, it relies heavily on economic metaphors in identifying current problems within the teaching profession. Low pay and poor working conditions, for example, are targeted as special concerns. The physical appearance of the Carnegie report features a slick, attractive cover, horizontally elongated pages, and, inside, charts and graphs provide quick visual summaries of the text. The publication looks quite similar to an annual business report; it would be quite at home in the front reception area of a large corporate office. *Tomorrow's Teachers*, by comparison, was written by a group of education deans. It gives particular attention to the academic preparation of teachers as a major concern. The physical appearance of this report features a plain cover, small, vertically elongated pages, and no graphs or charts inside. These features give the report a distinctively bookish appearance that bears a strikingly close resemblance to scholarly journals. We offer these two examples in order to illustrate that framing may involve quite subtle and often taken-for-granted aspects of language. In both cases, the reports communicate messages and provide frames (contextual information) that tell us something about the nature of those messages.

Characteristics of Framing

With these various examples in mind, we are now able to summarize a number of key points regarding the characteristics of framing.

IMPLICITNESS. Frames represent a largely taken-for-granted level of understanding. They are examples of what Mary Douglas (1975) has referred to as "implicit meanings," or what Michael Polanyi (1964) has called "tacit knowledge." In everyday social interaction, frames are understood (most of the time) without having to announce: "This is a joke," "This is a job interview," "This is a business meeting," "This is a textbook," "This is a history lesson," and so on. As Tannen observes, when all goes well, frames "do their work unnoticed and unnamed" (1986b, p. 77). Still, we do sometimes name a frame and thereby make it explicit. Yet doing so changes the frame. Consider, for example, two friends engaged in conversation. The first playfully criticizes the second, who responds to the criticism by pouting and glancing at the first friend in a way that conveys genuine distress. The first friend responds quickly to these nonverbal cues with the comment, "Hey look, I was only joking." Now the comment "I was only joking" names the frame in which the original criticism was offered, but it is not part of the frame it names. In other words, the comment is not a joke but, rather, an explanation that places the interaction on a new footing. Another way to put this is that any given frame can be explicitly recognized only from the perspective offered by a second frame.

DYNAMISM. Naming a frame is perhaps the most direct way in which to reframe discourse, but it is not the only way; and, as a communication strategy, it holds potential dangers that will be discussed later in this chapter. Here we simply want to note a second characteristic of framing—that it is a dynamic, ongoing process. Unlike picture frames, which are static, the frames that characterize social interaction change and evolve, sometimes from moment to moment. Framing is thus a fluid process negotiated and continually renegotiated by those who participate in communication. Friendly criticism, to use our earlier example, may be framed as a joke, but the response to the criticism serves either to undermine or reinforce that frame, and the response to the response continues this process. Even in written communication, authors (at least initially) imagine or expect responses, adjusting the frames of their messages accordingly. Here the point is that, in either case, unilateral control over how messages are framed cannot be maintained as interaction unfolds. One more example might help drive this point home. When we answer the telephone, we may have an initial opportunity to frame certain dimensions of the subsequent exchange, but from there on out the exchange is negotiated.

ESSENTIALITY. A third characteristic of framing is that it represents a necessary condition for language. This can be understood by noting that what framing is to language, background is to foreground. A foregrounded message, which ordinarily receives our explicit attention, always implies a backgrounded frame, regardless of whether or not the frame is recognized at a conscious level of awareness. Bateson (1972) makes a similar point in arguing that denotative messages (those with symbolic meaning) are possible only after the evolution of a "map-territory," or symbol-referent distinction. This distinction is contained in the tacit knowledge that, for example, the word cat cannot scratch or bite us. Words are thus framed as a map and are dependent on that frame. From Bateson's perspective, then, framing is foundational to language.

What this means at a practical level is that while we may be able to deliberately negotiate a particular frame, or change it, we cannot choose to avoid frames entirely. If, for example, a person consciously decided to withhold the facial expressions, body gestures, and intonation that help signal frames in face-to-face conversation, such action would in itself signal a frame. Lack of eye contact, to make our example more specific, signals a metamessage of disinterest, sorrow, or respect, depending on the cultural patterns of the particular group. Even silence is likely to be used in addressing the question of "What is it that is going on here?" For example, one reason that silence is avoided during radio programs is because the absence of sound, if maintained for any length of time, will likely signal a metamessage to the audience that technical difficulty or equipment failure is what is going on. In short, communicating without a frame is not an available option. Our motive in stressing this point is to focus attention not on whether messages are framed, but on how they are framed.

CULTURAL CONTEXT. In some of the examples above we have described framing as if it were shaped by individuals and the immediate context in which they interact. This is a simplistic (if not wrongheaded) way to understand framing, because individuals (e.g., teachers) and their immediate environment (e.g., the classroom) are embedded within a much broader cultural context. When Peter Karlin, for example, walks into his classroom, he takes with him more than his daily lesson plans and roll book. He also takes a personal history and a lifetime of experience that are based on cultural patterns of understanding. Even if Peter wanted to, he could not enter the classroom a blank slate. Another way to put this is that metaphor, nonverbal communication, paralinguistic cues, silence, and so forth do not in themselves establish frames of interaction; they only signal the presuppositions, patterns of thought, and organizational premises that anthropologists and sociolinguists define as the culture of a group. Thus a fourth characteristic of framing is that it represents a primary element of culture.

Framing as culture can be illustrated with a wide variety of examples. In Chapter 3 we cited Hall's (1969) study of proxemics, in which he identifies four zones of social distance ranging from a close, intimate zone to a far, public zone. Social distance can here be understood as a framing cue, because it helps organize and signal the footing on which interaction will proceed; that is, we associate close and far interaction with different topics and ways of speaking. Yet these expectations are not wholly consistent from one culture to another. More to the point, what defines *close* and *far* is not a yardstick or measuring tape but, rather, the cultural patterns of everyday experience. Thirty-six inches, for example, may be regarded as close by one group but not by another. This point can also be made by considering the prosodic dimensions of speech. Take, for example, the case of pacing and pausing in conversation. Tannen (1986b) notes that fast-paced questions are sometimes interpreted as a polite way of showing interest. Alternatively, they may be interpreted as a form of hostile interrogation. But here again, *fast* and *slow* are relative terms. As our own cultural stereotypes suggest, the same rate of speech as measured by a stopwatch may be perceived as fast, slow, or average, depending on the geographic region of the United States in which you happen to live.

Understanding this characteristic of framing suggests how differences in cultural experience give rise to different interpretations of the frames that guide everyday social interaction. We noted in the previous example that fast-paced questions (or, more precisely, questions perceived as fast-paced relative to what a participant's cultural experience suggests is normal) can be interpreted either as a show of interest or as a show of hostility. These two alternatives do not exhaust all possible interpretations, but how the pace of conversation is finally interpreted partly depends on the participants' membership in various cultural groups. This is why cross-cultural communication may often be particularly difficult. A participant from one culture frames messages in one way, while a participant from another culture frames messages in a different way. Because the messages are understood by each participant on a different footing, their exchange quickly leads to confusion and misunderstanding. Moreover, as long as each participant sticks to his or her original frame, more talk simply makes the situation worse. This is exactly what happens in the example described by Michaels and Collins (1984) of the white teacher who framed the task of storytelling in accordance with linear, topic-centered patterns, while her black students framed the task according to topic-associating patterns. In an important sense, the teacher and students were "speaking" different metalanguages.

Michaels and Collins's example concerns cross-cultural miscommunication between members of minority and nonminority groups. Yet, following Tannen's (1986b) lead, we would like to emphasize that membership in a cultural group can be defined at many different levels. Ethnicity, nationality, age, gender, and social class represent one end of a broad continuum; while neighborhood, family, and friendship groups represent the other end. If we recognize the full range of contexts in which cultures develop, then most communication, regardless of how alike the participants may seem, can be considered "cross-cultural" in some sense.

The misinterpretation of frames due to cross-cultural differences is particularly problematic given that framing ordinarily remains a taken-for-granted aspect of language. In other words, we may not be consciously aware of when frames are misunderstood, nor ready to attribute miscommunication to framing difficulties. Sometimes, of course, we do reexamine the footing of a message when in everyday conversation we sense that something has gone wrong. An initial reaction to confusion, for example, might well be to assume that we have somehow "misread" what a person was trying to say. Yet it is also likely that such confusion will not even be recognized; that is, we assume we understand what a person is telling us and explain away any problems by attributing them to the personality traits of the speaker. This is what happened in the example of the London bus driver's request for "exact change, please." His patron who got off the bus muttering, "Why do these people have to be so rude and threatening about it," had misinterpreted the bus driver's paralinguistic cues as an expression of rudeness. When this happens at the broad end of our continuum, such mistaken attributions reinforce dangerous stereotypes along the lines of race, class, age, gender, and nationality. When it happens at the narrow end of our continuum, it leads to the mistaken and oversimplistic labeling of individuals as rude, inconsiderate, stupid, unfeeling, and so forth. Here the important issue is not cultural or individual differences per se but, rather, the sensitivity needed in recognizing how our own cultural patterns of experience guide the ways in which we interpret and frame language.

DUAL INFLUENCE. A final characteristic of framing is its dual influence both on how messages are understood and on the social relationships that are maintained through communication. This simply restates our point that language is not used merely in order to transmit information from one person to another. In an algebra class, for example, much of the talk, as well as the way that talk is framed, has little to do with linear equations, inequalities, graphing, sets, and other strictly curricular topics. Yet it would be a mistake to label such talk as "off-task," because it does address the critical task of negotiating student-teacher involvement. Tannen (1986b), whose work has focused on how conversational styles guide relationships, notes:

> Very little of what is said is important for the information expressed in the words. But that does not mean that the talk isn't important. It's crucially important, as a way of showing that we are involved with each other, and how we feel about being involved. Our talk is saying something about our relationship. (p.15)

We do not have to look far in order to find examples of Tannen's point. In meeting an acquaintance or colleague we may ask, "How are you?", eliciting the conventional response, "Fine, and you?" Our question is not genuine in the sense that we are not seeking information about the health or well-being of our acquaintance. Nor is his or her response genuine in the sense of intending to provide such information. But, of course, this is not the point of the question and answer. Rather, we engage in such exchanges in order to signal involvement and help place interaction on a cordial footing. At issue is the relationship, not the information.

As suggested by this example, language rarely comments on relationships in a direct way. The reason for this is that being direct or indirect in and of itself signals cues about the nature of our involvement. When someone says, for example, "I am your friend," that may well be the point at which we begin to doubt their friendship. After all, if we are friends, then why is it necessary to say so directly? The statement itself does not make it true, and by keeping such knowledge unspoken it retains a special assumed status. In this example, the message and the metamessage both comment on the relationship, but they do so in conflicting ways. This can be illustrated by combining, as we have done before, both message and metamessage into a single sentence: "The message 'I am your friend' means that we are not close enough friends for it to be beyond question." Here the frame is conveyed not in the meaning of the words "I am your friend" but in the act of speaking the words.

Framing also comments on a relationship by signaling differences in the social status of those involved. Forms of address are commonly cited as an example of this. The use of titles (such as Dr., Mr., Mrs., Miss, Ms., Sir, or Madam) frames interaction as formal, while the use of first names, diminutives, and nicknames frames interaction as friendly. The differential use of these forms between communication partners also locates each participant within hierarchical patterns of social status. Consider, for example, a brief classroom exchange:

Teacher: Cindy, will you and Bob please pass out the textbooks.
Student: Which ones, Mr. Lewis?

If language were solely used to convey information, this exchange could be described simply as a request for assistance followed by a request for information with an implied response that the assistance will be forthcoming. The point of the exchange is simply to get the right textbooks distributed. But there is more to it. The teacher's use of first names and the student's use of a more formal form of address also signals the unequal status of teacher and students in the classroom. This presents something of a dilemma for classroom teachers. The teacher in our example may have adopted the practice of calling students by their first names simply with the intention of framing their interaction as friendly. Nevertheless, the frame is open to being interpreted by students as an expression of the teacher's power.

In order to illustrate how a recognition of such dilemmas contributes to a teacher's professional knowledge, we will discuss issues of power and solidarity in the following section. Before doing so, however, we want to make a more explicit connection between our discussion of framing thus far and Peter Karlin's advice that classroom teachers give particular attention to such relational concerns as trust, respect, mutual understanding, dialogue, and caring. We believe framing lends significant insight into how these aspects of the student-teacher relationship are worked out in the classroom. First, our understanding of framing suggests that relational characteristics (trust, respect, and so on) cannot be communicated directly through explicit messages—say, for example, by posting a list of rules at the front of the classroom. Indeed, the frame, or metamessage, of such an attempt may, as in the case of "I am your friend," undermine the message. Second, we have stressed that framing, as a form of control, must be negotiated and sustained through the give-and-take of social interaction. Peter's relational concerns are thus put into focus as moving well beyond images of classroom management that represent the teacher as engaged in a process of unilateral decision making. The more complex image of control suggested in our discussion of framing is similar to the one put forth by John Dewey (1938). Unlike the Cartesian view of the individual, much of Dewey's work was directed toward understanding the individual as embedded in a network of relationships (Bowers, 1987b). This emphasis on relationships (which he called communication) led him to urge those interested in understanding classroom control to consider how control operates in situations of family life, sports, and children at play. In such contexts, Dewey argued, control is exercised not by any one individual but by the set of relationships within which individuals participate. We want to substitute the term *culture* for *relationship*, because it offers a more powerful understanding of social dynamics. But here our point is simply to stress the negotiated and relational nature of control.

POWER AND SOLIDARITY

Above we have used the metaphor of "negotiation" in an effort to underscore how control involves a dual set of concerns: (1) the need to exert some degree of influence and (2) the need to maintain involvement. Tannen (1986b) uses the terms *power* and *solidarity* in order to distinguish these two basic concerns as they are played out through the framing of language. They are important concepts, because they provide points of reference for understanding how a metamessage figures into the development of relationships. Consider, for example, a high school teacher who, sitting at her desk at the end of a class period, looks up and casually says to one of her students as he is leaving the classroom, "Steve, don't forget to do your homework." How might this seemingly straightforward remark comment on their relationship? Is it a friendly reminder, a gesture by the teacher signaling that she cares about her student and wants to help facilitate his academic success? Or is the teacher telling Steve what to do, exercising her right to control his behavior? Regardless of the teacher's intentions (of *her* frame), either interpretation is possible. The former represents solidarity or involvement; the latter, the teacher's exercise of power.

How Steve interprets this message will be influenced by a wide variety of factors, including the culture of the classroom. Here we must recognize that the roles of student and teacher are in many ways unequal. Steve may very well interpret his teacher's message in terms of solidarity and respond within this frame with a reply such as, "Thanks for reminding me." Yet even so, tacit cultural expectations prevent Steve from reciprocating in kind; that is, he cannot respond, "Thanks for reminding me, and don't *you* forget to prepare your lesson plans and correct those papers for third period tomorrow!" We might also note that in this example the age of the student (as culturally defined) also makes a difference. Adolescence is often characterized within the dominant Anglo culture as a period of transition between childhood and adulthood. During this transitional period, one's status in terms of power entails a significant degree of ambiguity, and thus American adolescents are often highly sensitive to being told how to behave. Recognizing when and how such general considerations apply to a particular situation with particular students seems to be part of the professional knowledge that many teachers learn at an intuitive level.

In order to appreciate fully the complexity of such knowledge, however, we still need to take a more careful look at how power and solidarity are related. On one hand, Tannen defines power as the right to control others and the right to resist being controlled. Solidarity, on the other hand, involves the rapport established through social interaction or the feeling that the interaction is proceeding on the basis of some shared interest. Tannen also argues that all relationships involve maintaining a balance between power and solidarity regardless of whether the relationship rests on an equal or unequal footing. Where this becomes complicated is in recognizing power and solidarity as overlapping, mutually dependent concepts. Solidarity, for example, can be viewed as a form of power if we acknowledge that rapport between teacher and students clearly facilitates discipline and classroom management. This is the point Peter Karlin makes in noting, "You can't force students to do what you want them to do, but if they know you're working hard and care about 'em, then from there on it's gravy." Using solidarity as a power base works for students as well as for teachers. Robert Everhart (1983), for example, describes classroom research in which he found junior high school students who would "butter up" a teacher as strategy for gaining control that they would not otherwise have. In a similar way, power can be enlisted as a means for promoting solidarity. An example of this might be a student's praising a teacher with a comment such as, "I like her because she forces me to think."

Through these examples we can see how power and solidarity are like two sides of the same coin, distinct yet mutually dependent. Tannen describes this relationship as follows:

> It's a paradox, like the drawing of a chalice and two faces. Both images exist in the picture simultaneously, and we can see both, but we can see only one at a time. In the same way, we can see only one side of the power/solidarity dimension at a time. (1986b, pp. 94–95)

This "paradox" underpins the dilemma we noted earlier of the teacher who, by using students' first names in order to promote solidarity, also reinforces the unequal footing of the student-teacher relationship. There are no pat solutions to such dilemmas, and this makes it particularly important for teachers to develop a sensitivity to where they and their students are in terms of this interpersonal power/solidarity paradox. It may often be the case that in trying to help students (e.g., reminding them of a homework assignment), teachers find themselves confronting a defensive reaction that is due to their "help" being interpreted by students as an expression of power. In such cases, students are not being irrational or immature; they are reacting to the metamessages implied in the efforts to provide them with assistance. Recognizing this is an example of what Donald Schon has referred to as "giving the student reason" (1983, p. 68). It involves an ability to take the students' perspective and thereby legitimize their ways of thinking and feeling. But again we want to stress that this process is more a matter of receptivity than it is a matter of unilateral decision making. We will return to this issue in the next chapter, where expressions of power are explored in greater detail.

COMMUNICATION STRATEGIES

To reiterate our main points, framing signals how a message is to be understood and, at the same time, comments on the nature of relationships as they are developed and sustained through message exchanges. Framing thus provides still another perspective on understanding the classroom as an ecology of relationships. Yet, as implied above, the practical value of this perspective stems not from its offering a widely applicable set of specific teaching strategies but from its suggesting the forms of professional knowledge necessary to judging when a given strategy is appropriate or inappropriate within the context of day-to-day classroom instruction. What we are attempting here is to frame the following implications more as a set of heuristic considerations than as a set of management techniques. These considerations focus on how taken-for-granted communication "strategies" (self-disclosure, humor, turn-taking, and dialogue) can be understood in terms of framing, power, and solidarity. In dealing with them at an explicit level of understanding, we hope to make such relational strategies more open to reflection than would otherwise be possible.

Self-Disclosure

The first strategy that we will consider is self-disclosure. Peter Karlin mentions this strategy in his advice that teachers not "be afraid of letting students know that you're a person and that you have a life outside the classroom." Recall that Peter's advice focuses on student-teacher involvement, and this comment fits his focus because self-disclosure in the dominant Anglo culture generally helps frame or reframe discourse in the direction of greater solidarity. It does so as a signal of trust whereby we take others into our confidence. Yet when a teacher says to students, "I spent all yesterday afternoon preparing this lesson" or "I'm not sure whether I've made this assignment clear," such comments do more than invite sympathy and understanding; they also set an example. Talk of self and one's relationship with the curriculum signals that this is an acceptable form of discourse in the classroom; that is, part of the implicit metamessage of self-disclosure is "do as I do." In practical terms, giving information is often an effective way of getting information.

This can be an important strategy in the classroom, where the teacher's ability to teach depends on an understanding of students. However, self-disclosure can also skew the power/solidarity balance, evoking what Tannen refers to as "inappropriate equality" (1986b, p. 100). The point here is that the metamessage "do as I do" can be interpreted as an implicit command. In this case, a teacher's self-disclosure comes to be viewed by students as an imposition and threat to their privacy. Self-disclosure can thus be understood as an expression of both solidarity and power. We might also note that even when students interpret a teacher's self-disclosure in terms of solidarity, they may at a later point feel betrayed or "cheated" when the teacher's actions (e.g., assigning the student a grade) signal conflicting metamessages.

The importance in recognizing such dilemmas can again be underscored by considering self-disclosure as it relates to the cultural patterns of a particular group. In the dominant American culture, to use a simplistic example, self-disclosure is likely to be framed as an expression of solidarity. This pattern gives rise to American stereotypes of the British as impersonal and aloof, wherein a lack of self-disclosure is interpreted (or misinterpreted) as failed solidarity. On the other side of the coin, British stereotypes of Americans as pushy and aggressive can be seen in terms of self-disclosure being interpreted as an expression of power. Regardless of what these stereotypes suggest, the issue is not one of character traits (aloofness, indifference, pushiness) but rather one of cultural differences in how power and solidarity are expressed. Here the important point is for teachers to be aware of their own cultural assumptions regarding the metamessages of self-disclosure.

Humor

A second strategy that can be understood along similar lines is that of humor. Like self-disclosure, humor is often interpreted as an expression of solidarity. For example, speakers frequently begin a formal presentation with a humorous story and teachers often begin a class by telling a joke. In both situations, humor is intended to help "break the ice." When jokes work in this way, they signal a sense of shared understanding that frames interaction along the lines of involvement. But in order to recognize how it is that humor achieves this, we will need to consider exactly what is involved in the making of a joke.

Mary Douglas (1975) offers some insight into this process by analyzing jokes as a symbolic mode of expression. The central theme of her work is that jokes mime, or imitate, the social situation in which they occur, doing so in ways that resolve the inherent conflicts between community and control. Specifically, Douglas argues that jokes function to temporarily suspend dominant and conventionally accepted forms of control. In support of this thesis, she cites the two alternative perspectives on humor provided by Henri Bergson and Sigmund Freud. Bergson's perspective, on the one hand, represents humor as a way of reasserting the basic human traits of spontaneity and freedom when they become threatened by social or material mechanization. A psychoanalytic perspective, on the other hand, holds that jokes can be understood as an expression of the subconscious momentarily released from the bonds of consciousness. This temporary psychological loss of control is mimed in laughter, a temporary loss of bodily control; both produce emotional catharsis.

From both perspectives, Douglas points out, jokes are viewed as having a subversive effect on control. One way in which jokes accomplish this is by reversing subordinate-superordinate relations and thus disclosing their arbitrary nature. This can be illustrated by referring back to an example of humor that we provided at the beginning of Chapter 1. In this example the teacher, Susan Krebs, absentmindedly made a mistake in giving the class directions, and one of her students jokingly teased her with the comment, "Why, Miss Krebs, we really must be more precise in our use of language." With her serious tone of voice and intricate syntax, the student mimicked the formal "teacher talk" that Susan uses throughout the course of her work in order to frame interaction along the lines of power. In this respect, the joke replicated the social structure. However, it did so in a way that turned the tables on Susan, making her the subordinate and her student the superordinate. This achieved a momentary suspension and reversal of social control, temporarily giving control to the otherwise controlled student. In this example, the joke was accepted by Susan and her students as a joke, and its effect was to promote solidarity by emphasizing community over control.

Another way in which to understand our example, again following Douglas's analysis, is to consider the student's joke as a form of conflict resolution. The conflict inherent in the teacher-student relationship can be thought of in terms of our earlier discussion of power and solidarity as representing conflicting yet mutually dependent needs. Both teachers and students are simultaneously controlling and controlled. Humor recreates social structure in a way that brings forward the flexibility for interpreting power as solidarity and vice versa. What the joke symbolizes, in Douglas's terms, is "leveling, dissolution and recreation" (1975, p. 109).

These considerations have focused on how humor signals metamessages that promote solidarity. However, such metamessages are also open to an alternative interpretation that frames discourse along the lines of power. Humor as an expression of power will be considered further in the following chapter on the politics of language. Here we simply wish to call attention to both sides of the power/solidarity coin. In our example above, Susan responded to her student's joke with laughter. This signaled the student's frame and completed the exchange as an expression of solidarity. Yet another scenario is clearly possible: that is, Susan could have interpreted her student's joke as a form of malicious ridicule challenging her authority. Had Susan done this and signaled her interpretation back to the student (say, for example, by responding defensively), such a response would reframe their interaction along the lines of power rather than solidarity. At this point, of course, the student could defend herself by claiming, "I was only joking." In naming her original frame, the student would yet again reframe their exchange, but if such a move were interpreted as a defense, it would tacitly reinforce and perpetuate their interaction as centrally concerned with power. By the same token, a teacher who jokes with students in order to promote solidarity runs a risk that such joking may be interpreted by the students as an expression of power. In making this observation, we certainly do not mean to suggest that classroom teachers should avoid the use of humor; rather we are suggesting sensitivity to issues of power and solidarity promises to help teachers avoid perpetuating frames that undermine their ability to teach.

Turn-Taking

The third process we wish to consider is not so much a single strategy as it is a set of discourse patterns that we will refer to as "turn-taking." In day-to-day interaction—e.g., in a conversation between two friends—discourse tends to be something like a tennis game: first one person speaks, then the other, and so on. As this "game" is played out, the participants do their part in initiating topics, asking questions, responding to suggestions, acknowledging responses, evaluating information, checking for understanding, correcting mistakes, and summarizing points. How these various moves are coordinated through patterns of turn-taking also helps frame whatever messages are being exchanged. If our friend keeps interrupting us in midsentence, for example, we might well begin to interpret the metamessage of his or her interruptions as an expression of power.

Patterns of turn-taking also help frame classroom discourse. Yet in the classroom, the implicit rules that govern turn-taking often differ from those that typically guide a conversation between two friends. In part this difference can be explained as a product of the often crowded conditions of classroom life, where maintaining certain patterns of turn-taking can be seen as a way of coping with the immediate circumstances of teaching. And in part it reflects our cultural understanding of the rights and responsibilities that accompany the unequal roles of student and teacher.

How rules and status are sustained through turn-taking patterns found in the classroom is a question addressed by A.D. Edwards (1980). Edwards's central argument is that patterns of classroom turn-taking typically frame discourse for the "transmission of knowledge," a task that places the teacher in the controlling role of "sender" and the student in the passive role of "receiver." In developing this argument, Edwards cites observational research conducted by Sinclair and Coulthard (1975) indicating that teacher comments in the classroom range widely according to their function, from initiating topics, giving directions, and providing information to asking questions and evaluating responses. The range of student talk, in contrast, is often far more limited to answering questions, acknowledging information, and making bids for the right to speak. In other words, the teachers in Sinclair and Coulthard's study had more options, or "communicative rights," than did the students. Edwards views this difference as an expression of the teacher's primary "ownership" of instruction in that it represents the teacher's control over what topics are discussed, when they are discussed, who may contribute to the discussion, and who may evaluate the contributions. These various domains of control can be illustrated through an example that Edwards (1980, p. 242) provides of transcripted talk in a British classroom. A section of this transcript follows:

Teacher: Why do you think the creature (an ammonite) used to live inside a shell like that?
Pupils: (numerous bids to speak next)
Teacher: No, put your hands up please. Er, Carl?
Pupil: For protection.
Teacher: What does protection mean? Any idea, Carl?
Pupil: Sir, to stop other things from hurting it.
Teacher Right, stops other things from hurting it. Now if it came out of its shell, and waggled along the sea bed, what would happen to it? Yes?
Pupil: It might get ate.
Teacher: It might get eaten by something else, yeah.

This series of exchanges follows a common instructional pattern. The teacher initiates a topic by asking a question to which he already has a specific answer in mind ("Why do you think the creature . . .?"). Students then make bids to speak (e.g., by raising their hands); the teacher selects a speaker who responds to the question; and the teacher evaluates the response, repeating it (a signal that the response is correct) or elaborating on it (a signal that the response is partial or incorrect). Our point in making this pattern explicit is to suggest the metamessages that it conveys. These metamessages can also be understood as the presuppositions, or assumptions, that lend the discourse a sense of coherence. In this case, the presuppositions involve an understanding of teaching as concerned with the "transmission" of knowledge. The teacher's control over topics, speaking rights, and evaluation follows from this presupposed understanding. Another way to make this point is to note that the patterns of turn-taking described by Edwards have a tendency to frame messages along dimensions of power.

Recognizing the tacit metamessages of turn-taking contributes to the teacher's professional knowledge, because sound pedagogy often involves maintaining a balance between patterns of interaction that express power and patterns that express solidarity. If, for example, the turn-taking patterns represented in the exchange cited above come to monopolize classroom discourse, students are likely to learn a passive role as "receivers" of information, and such metalessons of instruction restrict a student's communicative competence as we have defined that term in the previous chapter. One of our concerns with the conventional classroom management paradigm is that it skews teaching in this direction. In Madeline Hunter's (1986) *Mastery Teaching* approach, to cite only one example, teachers are encouraged to "check for understanding" by asking questions that test the students' knowledge during the presentation of a lesson. This may well be a useful technique, but its educational use requires an awareness of the metamessages signaled by the teacher's use of questions in this particular way. Here again the important issue is not whether a teaching strategy is inherently good or bad but rather our understanding of how that strategy is likely to frame classroom interaction.

Dialogue

The transmission perspective tacitly expressed in the patterns of turn-taking noted by Edwards can also be understood as representing a Western and largely masculine cultural bias. This cultural dimension of turn-taking is brought into focus by considering that the transmission perspective characterizes a broad range of social contexts (outside the classroom) in which interaction is organized along hierarchical lines of power. Such contexts include factories, business offices, government agencies, the armed forces, courts of law, and so forth. Quite different patterns of turn-taking are suggested if we turn to contexts of interaction in which its organization is less dependent on hierarchical structuring. We can identify these patterns with dialogue as it is carried on between partners, friends, peers, or family members. Nel Noddings (1984, 1986), to cite one author who has been involved in developing a feminine approach to education, argues that dialogue is a primary dimension of a "caring ethic" in the practice of teaching. Dialogue may often involve an exchange of information, but as Noddings (1986) puts it, "true dialogue is open; that is, conclusions are not held by one or more of the parties at the outset. The search for enlightenment, or responsible choice, or perspective, or means to problem solution is mutual and marked by appropriate signs of reciprocity" (p. 223). Thus we are likely to find dialogue playing a central role in relationships wherein negotiation predominates.

At this point we will outline some of the characteristics of dialogue in order to identify the semantic options that teachers might use in fostering their students' communicative competence. In ordinary dialogue, say between two friends, turn-taking is negotiated in the context of interaction. Initiation or change of topics is open to either participant, and next speakers are self-selected rather than "called on" after they have made a bid to speak. Questions are used to check one's own understanding and signal involvement, and less often to test the understanding of the other participant. Even in well-coordinated dialogue, much of the talk is overlapping, with interruptions, digressions, and backtracking tolerated insofar as they signal interest and desire to participate. Of course, dialogue is not a free-for-all; there are "rules." Pronouncement, for example, as well as passivity are likely to be considered bad form. Dialogue is, nevertheless, a "locally managed" approach to interaction.

In the classroom, two factors would seem to mitigate against dialogue: (1) large class size and (2) presuppositions of student ignorance. However, many of the classroom teachers we have observed are able to overcome these barriers by organizing instructional time and activities in particular ways. A number of these practical strategies are aimed at promoting dialogue between students. For example, a third-grade teacher we observed, Kathy Robinson, conducted most of her science lessons in the form of small-group activities. During these lessons students worked in groups of four on a cooperative task (one that could not be accomplished solely by an individual). Once the students began, Kathy would step back, allowing her students to assume primary ownership of their activity. When students asked Kathy questions, a pattern that persisted in spite of the small-group format, her preferred response was, "Ask someone in your group." During social studies lessons, this same teacher often divided her class in half, asking each half to silently read different sections of a chapter from their textbook. Afterward, students from each half of the class had the opportunity to ask other students questions about the chapter sections they had not read. This procedure put students in the position of being asked questions not in order to be tested (as if they were contestants on a television quiz show), but in order to share information with their peers. Finally, in all types of lessons, Kathy often asked individuals, or sometimes pairs of students, to leave their desks, come to the front of the classroom, and explain to the class some procedure, example, or concept relevant to their lesson. During these brief explanations, Kathy sat off to the side of the room, allowing the student or students temporarily to assume her role as teacher. This often did not engage the students in genuine dialogue, because even these seven- and eight-year olds were quick to establish turn-taking patterns that signaled their control over the interaction. Yet it did get students listening to other students and the teacher listening to them.

Kathy's strategies are aimed at fostering student-student dialogue, but we have also observed teaching strategies aimed at promoting student-teacher dialogue. Here we might note that the teaching schedules of most elementary and secondary teachers do not include any periods of time officially designated for teachers and students to interact on a one-to-one basis. Even so, such interaction does take place, and teachers often structure their lessons to include pockets of time for this purpose. For example, a middle school algebra teacher whom we observed routinely held open the last ten minutes of class in order to provide students with individual help. Another teacher, George Katz, routinely set aside one day each week in each of his classes for what he called "miniconferences." During this time the students worked independently on assignments while George moved down each row of desks briefly talking with individual students. When questioned, George was quite explicit about the use of this routine. As he explained, "It's nice to talk one-to-one, and it helps break the mannequin-like image of me standing up in front of the room. It really pays tremendous dividends—allows them to ask questions, and I find out a lot. Some students won't say anything in class, but sitting eye-to-eye, we can talk" (Flinders, 1987, p. 179).

Even during whole-group instruction, as in the case of lecture-type presentations, we observed that some teachers were able to maintain a sense of shared ownership in the lesson by framing their comments and questions in ways that signaled a balance between power and solidarity. These teachers did so by asking questions that did not call for prefigured answers or information that had already been presented. Instead, their questions were often intended to elicit new information, examples, and interpretations. When these teachers did ask students to summarize or paraphrase information that had already been covered, they would often accept the students' responses with subtle forms of acknowledgment (a slight nod of the head, for example) and refrain from further elaboration, thus minimizing their evaluative role. In a literature class, a high school teacher we observed, Paul Arkwright, was explaining a particular reference to segregation in the novel *To Kill a Mockingbird* when one of his students interrupted to ask, "Isn't this story really about education?" The student's question was not directly relevant to the teacher's point, and he responded only with a thoughtful expression and a softly muttered "humm . . ." After several seconds of silence, a second student responded to the question. A brief exchange between the two students followed, their comments focusing on how the term *education* might refer to life experiences outside the classroom. Paul did not interrupt or directly participate in their exchange, nor did he attempt to evaluate or relate their discussion to his original topic. Had he done so in this particular instance, Paul might well have co-opted the students' engagement, making their exchange a part of his own agenda and thus tacitly delegitimizing the students' active role in the classroom.

The examples we have provided cast teachers into a receptive role wherein their sensitivity to relationships is expressed in what they do not do as well as in what they do. Their professional knowledge is thus, in some ways, analogous to what auto mechanics refer to as "stopping-sense." This is the tacit knowledge that tells the mechanic when to stop tightening a bolt so that it will hold but not break or when to stop applying pressure to a gasket so that it will seal but not crack. In each task, success is a matter of balance. Our analogy may be inappropriate to the extent that it puts out of focus the cultural dimensions of teaching. Carburetors and brake drums are not influenced by cultural patterns in quite the same way that teachers and students are. Nevertheless, providing occasions for dialogue in the classroom does seem to require a certain amount of "stopping-sense"—professional knowledge (grounded on cultural awareness) that tells teachers when to temporarily stop asking questions, providing answers, evaluating responses, enforcing rules, rewarding compliance, and so on.

RENEGOTIATING INSTRUCTIONAL FRAMES

We have focused on dialogue in order to suggest some of the practical implications that follow from understanding how patterns of turn-taking tacitly frame classroom interaction. In this context it is quite easy to recognize that framing is more a matter of negotiation than of unilateral control; that is, dialogue cannot be forced. Frame analysis, however, does hold broader implications for teaching. Even, for example, when patterns of turn-taking represent a "transmission of knowledge" frame, that frame is tacitly negotiated. We are most likely to recognize this only when negotiation fails and we find our lessons being reframed by students along unanticipated lines. Consider an example offered by Tannen (1986b). She describes a personal experience that she encountered while giving a lecture to a large audience. During this lecture, two people in the front row began asking questions and making comments that directly challenged Tannen's statements. At first she tried to minimize any disruption by keeping her responses to their questions brief and forging ahead with the development of her lecture. Yet her two inquisitors persisted, and Tannen began to debate, quite successfully, each of their points at length. She recalls that, "At the end of the lecture I felt like a victor following a battle: exhausted and emotionally spent, but relieved that I had prevailed" (p. 85).

The important issue in this example is not how well Tannen was able to respond to the challenging questions of her "students." Rather, the issue is how the questions reframed their interaction from lecture to confrontation. Tannen herself notes that by providing lengthy responses to the questions she was unwittingly drawn into a confrontational frame. We might note here that even in confrontation, power *and* solidarity are both at play; that is, the challenging questions by the two members of the audience can signal interest and involvement as well as a bid for control. Still, in this instance, Tannen felt manipulated by being caught up in a frame that undermined her original intentions.

The practical question now is how Tannen might have renegotiated the footing of her exchange with the two vocal members of her audience. One option would have been to make the questioners' frame explicit by naming it. In other words, she might have stated flatly, "I find your questions disruptive and confrontational." The problem with being so blunt, however, is that it often reinforces the very frame that is being named, thus signaling a metamessage of failed solidarity. Another option would be to make explicit not the confrontational frame itself but the perceived limitations of that frame within the immediate context of instruction. For example, as the questions became increasingly disruptive, Tannen might have avoided responding to them directly by making a comment such as, "We don't have very much time, and I would like to make a number of other points. When I finish with those, we can come back to your questions and other questions that anyone else may have." This option, of course, offers a compromise—let me control the frame now, and you can control it later. Compromise, a basic negotiation strategy, here signifies not an act of appeasement, but (as the Latin root of the word suggests) a process of arriving at mutual agreement.

Tannen's example illustrates a case of framing in which the central concern is power. Yet frames that evoke solidarity may be equally problematic from an educational point of view and thus in need of renegotiation. In order to demonstrate this, consider a brief student-teacher exchange that we observed at a middle-class, suburban high school. Two students approach Jane Owen, an English teacher, as she walks back to her classroom after lunch. Both students had been in Jane's freshman literature class the previous year. In the corridor they now greet Jane with broad smiles and enthusiastic hellos. Reciprocating these friendly overtures, Jane asks how they are, and one of the students (still smiling good-naturedly) launches into a series of complaints about his current English teacher. He begins with some thinly veiled flattery of Jane, saying, "Gee, I sure wish *you* were teaching our class. Mrs. Hudson is too strict. She won't even let us talk about what we've read." The other student supports his peer, noting in a relaxed tone of voice, "She sees something in a story, and that's what you're supposed to get out of it; nothing else." Jane nods her head and offers a sympathetic smile, but responds, "Well, you know, that's sometimes the way they teach artists and painters. For years and years the only thing they're allowed to do is copy the masters. Then after a time, they get to do their own work."

The two students in this example took the initiative to frame their interaction with Jane in terms of complaining. Yet the context of their exchange (including the students' nonverbal and paralinguistic cues) signaled that their complaints served a particular function; that is, to promote solidarity. Here the metamessage could be understood as something along the lines of, "Jane, we can complain to you because you are not just a former teacher, but also a friend." Complaining about teachers is a ritual that often characterizes student culture, but this is simply a specific case of a more general "complaining-for-solidarity" cultural pattern. Indeed, Jane had engaged in a similar form of metacommunicating during lunch with her fellow teachers (they had complained at length over a largely insignificant change in school policy) only moments before she encountered her two former students. Another way to put this is that neither Jane's complaints in the faculty lunchroom, nor the students' complaints about Mrs. Hudson make sense solely as literal messages. Imagine, for instance, what would have happened had Jane taken her former students' complaints strictly at face value. She might have responded, "This is terrible! Something must be done! You should talk to Mrs. Hudson, or maybe the principal." In eliciting such a response, the two students would no doubt have become equally concerned, not with the quality of Mrs. Hudson's teaching but with Jane's failure to recognize the frame of their interaction.

The real problem Jane faced, of course, was not that she had misread the students' frame but rather that "complaining-for-solidarity" signals a peer relationship in which she as a teacher cannot fully participate. In other words, Jane would have evoked inappropriate (dishonest) solidarity had she sought to maintain the students' frame by responding to their complaints in kind (e.g., "Yes, Mrs. Hudson is an old bat, isn't she?"). At the other extreme, Jane would have undermined their rapport had she responded solely as a superior (with a chastisement, for example, such as, "How dare you students criticize a teacher!"). Jane's solution was to offer the students a compromise by indirectly reframing the interaction in a way that upheld both their right to "complain" and her own right not to.

As the example suggests, reframing strategies depend on quite subtle forms of interpersonal skill. Moreover, they are not easily disentangled from the total social context of a particular discourse. Still, we can use our example in order to summarize several key points. First, the whole process that we have been describing was carried on at a tacit level of understanding. Jane's former students did not announce their frame, nor did Jane announce her attempt to change frames. It would have been difficult, if not impossible, for them to make all the presuppositions of their talk explicit. Yet, more to the point, their implicit understanding was in itself a metamessage of rapport.

Second, the words exchanged between Jane and the students did not "speak for themselves." They required Jane (if we assume her perspective for a moment) to make an inference regarding "what it is that is going on here." Why were these students complaining about Mrs. Hudson? Were the students malcontents? Were they spreading malicious gossip? Were they expressing legitimate concerns about Mrs.

Hudson's teaching abilities? Or were they expressing solidarity and their desire to maintain our relationship on the basis of mutual trust? The information that must be brought to bear in addressing such questions was not contained solely in the students' spoken words. Rather, Jane's interpretation called on a broad understanding that encompassed the total context of their interaction, cultural patterns of nonverbal communication, Jane's knowledge of student culture, her previous experience working with these two particular students, and so on.

Finally, our example illustrates how framing shapes and is shaped by the social status of relationships. As noted earlier, Jane's efforts to reframe the interaction away from "complaints" and toward discussion reflected her implicit assessment of where their relationship was in terms of power and solidarity. To accept the students' frame would have been to deny the cultural status differences between student and teacher roles. But to reject their frame out of hand would have been to deny the relational and negotiated nature of their interaction. In this respect, Jane's response served to recalibrate her relationship with the students. Thus the question of "what it is that is going on here" turned out to be concerned with power and solidarity as much as with understanding.

Although our example focused on an instance of interpersonal communication, we would like to bring the discussion back to the types of interaction that distinguish formal instruction. In doing so it is important to emphasize that all teaching and management strategies signal tacit metamessages about the ecology of relationships that constitute classroom life. For example, when a teacher posts a list of class rules at the front of the room, we may say that the students thereby receive information regarding what behaviors that teacher considers acceptable and unacceptable within that context. But students will seek meaning in the teacher's actions as well as in the posted messages. What is it that is going on here? Is our teacher trying to help us by making expectations clear? Or is the teacher exercising power by telling us how to behave? A teacher reading passages from a text, to take another example, does more than simply convey curricular information. His or her actions also comment on the textbook as a source of authority. This is the same point that we have made in relation to self-disclosure, the use of humor, and patterns of turn-taking.

A critical awareness of how interpersonal, instructional, and management strategies frame classroom interaction provides a basis for evaluating such strategies, and it is in this context that we view framing as most relevant to the professional knowledge of teachers. At issue is not only what constitutes sound pedagogical judgment but also the teacher's ability to model for students a culturally responsive approach to communication. Still, framing is only a part of this much broader theme. We can also gain insight into culturally responsive teaching by considering the politics of language. This is our primary focus in the next chapter.

CHAPTER 6

The Classroom as an Ecology of Power

Our task here is to explore further how power can be understood as a primary dimension of social relationships in the classroom; but unlike the discussion in Chapter 5, where the teacher's exercise of power was viewed as in a state of tension with achieving solidarity with students, we want to place the discussion within a larger and more political context. In doing so we will bring into focus a basic characteristic of classroom life that the professional education of teachers often ignores, namely, that educational processes are inherently political. Our concern for understanding the political processes operating in the classroom highlights yet another difference that separates an ecological perspective from the conventional technicist approach to teaching and classroom management. The former perspective recognizes that the teacher's gatekeeper role in primary socialization and in responding to the multiple levels of student communication legitimates certain cultural beliefs, values, and practices while delegitimating others. Yet the latter approach, with its Cartesian view of the rational process as providing objective knowledge, neglects these issues by representing the teacher as simply engaged in processes of behavior management and politically neutral decision making.

Although the technicist orientation to the classroom as a process of management involves a hierarchical pattern of social relationship, with power supposedly exercised by the teacher, who occupies the apex of this mini-social system, there is total silence in the supporting educational literature on the political nature of the teacher's role. Walter Doyle's (1986) authoritative summary of the massive research efforts used to legitimate the management role of the teacher, covering nearly 300 articles and books, does not mention that the exercise of power that characterizes the teacher's role is political—and thus may involve fundamental issues that teachers must be prepared to consider as part of their professional decision making. Several quotations from this summary clearly point to the taken-for-granted attitude that prevails toward the teacher's exercise of power:

Both policy-directed and descriptive studies indicate that life in classrooms begins with the creation of a *work system,* and the setting of rules
and procedures to hold the system in place, and that a considerable
amount of energy is devoted to this process. . . . The fact that knowledge of classroom rules and procedures cannot be taken for granted
suggests that *rule setting* has important socialization functions as an acknowledgment of the importance of order and a symbol of the level of
vigilance and accountability that will prevail in a particular classroom.
(p. 413; emphasis added)

In summary, the need to restore order in the classroom is a sign that the
mechanisms that establish and sustain order are not working. The *repair*
process itself is complex and risky as are the decisions concerning how
and when to intervene. Successful *managers* appear to be able to decide
early whether an act will disrupt order and to intervene in an inconspicuous way to cut off the path to disorder. In attending to misbehavior
and interventions, however, the emphasis remains on the *primary vector
of action* as the fundamental means of holding order in place in classrooms. (p. 422; emphasis added)

These statements about the teacher's role, while using metaphors
taken from a highly mechanistic view of the workplace, are really
about the exercise of power. And as the exercise of power always involves legitimating certain patterns of thought and value over others,
it is inherently political. Aside from a discussion of teacher modeling,
where Madeline Hunter warns that "in selecting a model, it is wise to
avoid controversial issues where the emotions aroused can divert
learners' attention from what is being taught" (1986, p. 46), this fundamental point has been ignored. It was even missed in a discussion
that recognized that "any class is to some extent heterogeneous: No
two students are alike." According to Emmer, Evertson, Sanford,
Clements, and Worsham, the primary implication of diversity in the
classroom for the teachers is that

attempting to cope with heterogeneity by using different assignments,
providing an individualized, self-paced program, or using small group
instruction extensively in secondary classrooms increases the complexity of classroom management, requires a great deal of planning and
preparation, and may require instructional materials that are not readily
available. (1989, pp. 141–142)

The heterogeneity, to recall a central theme of earlier chapters, can
also be understood as expressing differences in group affiliation that
may range across a wide spectrum—from age and gender differences

to social class and the even deeper cognitive and behavioral patterns rooted in the student's primary culture.

These differences, which should be recognized as part of the ecology of the classroom, are expressed in the metaphorical frameworks that provide the conceptual scaffolding for new understandings as well as in the patterns of nonverbal communication, framing, turn-taking, and other social-cultural processes used by the teacher and students to find their respective sense of balance between the exercise of power and solidarity. As we wish to examine more fully how the exercise of power in the classroom raises political issues that teachers have a responsibility to consider, we shall introduce several insights of Michel Foucault's that seem particularly useful for illuminating the interconnection between knowledge (which teachers use, along with the notions of role and function, as the basis of their authority) and power.

THE NATURE OF POWER

Power is one of those metaphors that is used in a variety of common-sense contexts. At times it is used to describe social and economic differences between people, with one group seen as possessing an excess of power and the other (dominated) group as lacking in power. The connection of technology with power is perhaps one of the most widely shared notions; the image of a power-enhancing tool, which may range from a screwdriver to a computer, rests on a cultural orientation that values predictability, efficiency, and the reduction of manual labor. Educators often equate more schooling with obtaining the means of power, while other experts uphold a variety of nostrums and techniques as the source of power. Although power is associated with a wide range of meanings and forms of expression, in popular thought it is perceived as a quality, force, or process that can be obtained, lost, or absent. Academics tend to equate the generation of knowledge with truth and progress; by leaving it to the more commercially oriented segments of society to make the connection that equates knowledge with power, academics can maintain the myth that inquiry is objective and nonpolitical.

Foucault's Analysis

Michel Foucault, the late French social theorist, provides a more coherent way of understanding power. In recognizing that power is expressed through all the relations that constitute and sustain the patterns of social life, his view of power complements the ecological perspective of Bateson. Where Bateson stresses the information exchanges that sustain a system (such as a classroom), Foucault focuses on relations as the expression of power. In a statement that has a definite Batesonian ring to it, Foucault states:

> The individual is not to be conceived as a sort of elementary nucleus, a primitive atom, a multiple and inert material on which power comes to fasten or against which it happens to strike, and in so doing subdues or crushes individuals. In fact, it is already one of the prime effects of power that certain bodies, certain gestures, certain discourses, certain desires, come to be identified and constituted as individuals. (1980, p. 98)

But individuals are not just "normalized" in patterns of thought, speech, and behavior by the exercise of power; they also become the agents for the expression of those forms of power that constituted them.

Foucault explains the exercise of power, in its most basic and general sense, as "a way in which certain actions modify others." As he puts it, "What defines a relationship of power is that it is a mode of action which does not act directly and immediately upon others. Instead it acts upon their actions: an action upon an action, on existing actions or on those which may arise in the present or future" (1983, p. 220). In separating his view of power from the stereotypical images of violence directed toward the powerless and subjugated (though his position does not exclude this as one possibility) and the romantic notion of power as accumulated and stored as a personal possession (also a possibility), Foucault provides a way of understanding that the use of the spoken word, the fixing of another person in one's gaze, the long, silent pause following the other person's comment, and so forth are actions that modify the actions (thought process and behavior) of others. At the interpersonal level, communication about relationships (the subject of Chapter 3) can be understood in Foucault's terms as involving the exercise of power. In fact, relations ("information exchanges" in Bateson's framework) cannot exist without the exercise of power, since power "consists in guiding the possibilities of conduct and putting in order the possible outcome" (1983, p. 221). Stated differently, the form that the exercise of power takes is really the expression of government, where "to govern," in Foucault's sense, means "to structure the possible field of action of others"

(1983, p. 221). For example, the teacher's actions when the students' episodic narrative style did not fit her natural attitude toward a topic-centered and linear style of development not only involved interruptions and discomfort on the students' part as they were made to feel the objects of a negative judgment; it also imposed a new pattern that they were to follow (or else remain silent).

This interpersonal level of relationship, where personal intentions are most visible, is not, however, the main focus of Foucault's analysis of power. It also tends to contribute to the basic misconception that the exercise of power is the result of the individual's conscious intent. As the earlier statement suggests, Foucault views the individual as largely constituted (in terms of self-concept and way of thinking and acting) by networks of relations that make up the culture (the multiple dimensions of a sense of reality). These networks encode the traditions and norms that regulate the language patterns, status systems, social customs, patterns of expression, and so forth. In discussing how the exercise of power is to be studied, Foucault does not start with the conscious intent of the autonomous individual. Rather he focuses on the programs, strategies, and techniques that are expressions of a particular set of social orientations. The discourse of one group in society—a language that constitutes what will be accepted as real and having authority, what strategies and status system will be used for relating to others, and how to identify and resolve the problematic—determines how power is exercised within the network of relations that encompass and constitute a particular form of individualism. To quote Foucault, "There is no power relation without the correlative constitution of a field of knowledge, nor any knowledge that does not presuppose and constitute at the same time power relations" (1979, p. 27).

The Power/Knowledge Connection in the Classroom

Although there is a need to understand more fully the historical connection between the emergence of the discourse (field of knowledge centered on the importance of surveillance) that guided the establishment of the modern prison, and more recently the industrial model of production, and the current discourse that dominates the approach to teacher education in the United States, we shall use the language of classroom management as an example that will further clarify and ground Foucault's way of thinking about power as acting on (and helping to constitute) the actions of others.

The key words used in classroom management literature for defining "What Is," and thus "structuring the possible field of action," for both teacher and students include the following: *classroom management, rules and procedures, workplace, behavior, rewards and penalties, accountability procedures, monitoring student behavior, classroom order, ontask behavior, seatwork,* and so on. The strategies of power encoded in this vocabulary, what Foucault terms "normalizing practices," include a hierarchical set of social relationships, a transmission model of the learning process, use of constant surveillance to detect and punish inappropriate behavior and reward appropriate behavior, and systematic preplanning of all classroom activities. If teachers accept this view of the classroom, the language/power connection acts on their own self-understanding and thus on the kinds of relationships they will have with students; the metaphor of "self as a manager of student behavior" also establishes the norms to be used in separating the good student from the "problem" student.

The "field of possibilities" for thought and behavior excluded by the view of reality constituted by this language must be noted in order to recognize that the knowledge of "What Is" is based not on an objective understanding of the classroom and the purpose of education but on a set of beliefs and social practices taken for granted by a particular segment of society. References to the student as a "product," as well as the many ways of identifying the work-like characteristics of the classroom ("seatwork," "on task," "workplace," not to mention "homework" or, as it is now called, "output"), suggest the linkage between the discourse of the classroom management paradigm and the way of thinking that underpins our cultural approach to technology and the organization of the workplace—both of which are now being seriously questioned because compliant workers in our society are now recognized as one cause of shoddy and unwanted goods, while the forms of technology being used are increasingly recognized as a major cause of ecological damage. Student-teacher relations, learning activities, and curricular materials excluded from the "field of possibilities" by the classroom management paradigm include those which reflect a view of the educational process as combining a concern with consciousness-raising (which involves becoming aware of taken-for-granted cultural patterns and practices) and an attempt to develop a sense of responsibility for and connectedness with the processes of civic renewal. That the development of understanding (learning) is a negotiation process involving teachers and students who bring to the educational moment different backgrounds of knowledge, experience, and expectations is also ignored. Nor are teachers whose self-image is that of a manager likely to be sensitive to the metaphorical nature of language, their gatekeeper role in this process of primary socialization, or the cultural patterns encoded in the student behavior used to communicate about interpersonal relations. Although these "information pathways," to use Bateson's term, will be ignored as having any real educational significance, they will be not immune from the exercise of power. For example, not recognizing that a student's body language is signaling a sense of doubt or disagreement, or disregarding a student's use of a different metaphorical framework or cultural pattern for communicating, also involves an "action upon an action." But in an ecology of power where only the teacher's definitions of behavior are rewarded, the teacher's nonresponse may, in many instances, be interpreted as a rejection and invalidation of the student's thoughts and values. The interaction of the teacher's self-understanding with the student's self-understanding, given the formative and vulnerable stage of development that the latter is undergoing, is perhaps one of the most significant aspects of the power/knowledge relationship under the teacher's control.

Another example of how the exercise of power is influenced by an interacting set of roles, status distinctions, and way of thinking can be seen in Raymond McDermott's (1976) study of the differential treatment given to top and bottom reading groups. With the top group of readers, the power/knowledge connection involved the teacher's use of a sequential pattern of turn-taking, with the teacher counting the number of pages to be read aloud by the group and then sequentially assigning the amount each student is to read aloud. The students, as McDermott reports, "act[ed] out the order rather perfectly" (p. 36); but the important issue in terms of how the procedure caused the students to adapt their experience to the expected norms is that the knowledge of when their turn would come in the sequence resulted in a relative degree of freedom for each member. With the low reading group, the power/knowledge connection (the way of thinking that guides how the actions of the teachers impinge on and influence the actions of the students) was played out in a different way. Because of the greater difficulty members of this group had with the basic decoding skills, as well as forty interruptions of this group's activity by other activities in the classroom (compared with two interruptions of the top group in the same thirty-minute period), the students seldom had a sense of the story line that would have made reading a meaningful experience. Moreover—and here we see how the exercise of power (and its effects on the student) can express the teacher's way of understanding—the teacher used a different strategy for allocating turns. Instead of calling on students in terms of a fixed (and thus known) sequence, the teacher negotiated the right to read with each child. The student who wanted to read was expected to call out, and the teacher would then allocate turns. The system, as a technology for exercising power over the students, had the effect of "giving no one, either teacher or children, any time out from monitoring each other for some idea on what to do next" (p. 39).

In Foucault's view, power is always an aspect of a relationship. Thus our concern in thinking about an ecological approach to teaching is not to eliminate the exercise of power, as though this would be a necessary condition for establishing education on a just and equitable basis, but to recognize the characteristics of the belief system that guides and legitimates the exercise of certain forms of power in the classroom. The multiple levels of communication in the classroom (nonverbal communication, the mingling of metaphorical frameworks, and the mental patterns encoded in the artifacts and spatial arrangements of the classroom) all involve limits on the "field of possibility" of student thought and behavior. We want to go beyond this microlevel of political action by identifying two primary areas in which the teacher's failure to reflect on the guiding pattern of thought can lead to the exercise of power that has an alienating and subjugating effect on students—the privileging of the literate over the oral tradition and of masculine over the feminine patterns of thought. For the sake of brevity, we shall refer to these areas of concern as "literacy" and "gender." In each of these areas, structural characteristics of society having to do with the form of economy and technology, as well as supporting traditions of belief, status, and privilege, have influenced the process of schooling—including the criteria that guide the selection and education of teachers and the entire range of materials and objects that make up the curriculum. Teachers cannot directly change the structural characteristics that influence the form that the exercise of power takes at the interpersonal level of classroom action, but they can become aware of the linkages that connect limiting educational practices with assumptions and values that sustain the current structural characteristics of society. This awareness, in turn, can lead to changes at the level of micropolitics that has been the focus of previous chapters. Through the use of metaphor, nonverbal communication, framing, and so forth, the teacher brings into play strategies of power that act on the student's self-awareness, thought processes, and behavior. With regard to the issues relating to literacy and gender, we would like to suggest some alternatives to the normalizing practices that occur when teachers reproduce in their relations with students the patterns of power that they have taken for granted as a condition of their own existence.

LITERACY AND ORALITY

The patterns that constitute the school act on the student's patterns of social, psychological, and (later) economic life. These patterns include, among others, the layout of space (arrangement of desks, classrooms and hallways), the schedules that designate when shifts can occur between being under direct teacher control and being able to move freely about the halls and classroom, the content of the textbook that provides the vocabularies and schemata for organizing knowledge, the system of collecting data on student performance, and the evaluation process. The "actions upon an action" that make up the ecology of the classroom, to recall Foucault's phrase, are guided by the thought processes of the school architect, the planners of time schedules, and writers of textbooks, as well as the teacher, who must orchestrate all these established patterns in a way that guides the students' actions and thoughts toward goals that are supposed to be educationally significant. Although the strategies of power often involve treating students as subjects to be acted upon, the students themselves are not entirely passive, since they continually—through accommodating smiles, question-asking strategies that draw attention to themselves or disrupt the teacher's line of thought, and bodily rhythms that subvert the teacher's sense of timing—act in ways that "structure the possible field of action for others" (i.e., the teacher, administrators, and other students). Of the many avenues through which power is exercised in the classroom, some involve the use of specific strategies guided by powerful ideological orientations. Classroom practices influenced by deeply held beliefs about the power and authority of measurement constitute one of these avenues. Other disciplinary practices (in the sense of shaping the students to a set of norms) are rooted in long-held assumptions that privilege the written over the spoken word. In fact, many of the learning activities and evaluation processes in schools are directed toward making students literate.

The disciplinary practices designed to foster the transformation from membership in the oral culture of the home and primary social relations to the more autonomous status of the literate citizen and worker are justified by a widely accepted set of claims about the efficacy of reading. At the beginning of a textbook designed to introduce future teachers to strategies of reading instruction, the author reproduces the following quotation from a California manual on reading:

> Individuals who can read with understanding hold the key to all of the stored knowledge of civilization. They are able to enter a limitless arena

of thought, imagination, exploration, and enjoyment; to stop and reflect on what is read, leading to more intensive critical thinking about a given subject; to organize ideas from many sources; and to fulfill personal needs and interests. (Lemlech, 1984, p. 122)

The promises of providing universal access to all stored knowledge, strengthening the basis of rational and autonomous thought, and fostering a more critical way of understanding are likely to be viewed by most teachers as part of the justification for staying in the field of education. The belief in the emancipatory characteristics of literacy go even further back, to the earliest days of the public school movements on both sides of the Atlantic. These claims, as well as others that have connected literacy with social development, the advancement of democracy, and enlightenment itself, have caused most classroom teachers to ignore giving serious consideration to how literacy might differ from the oral tradition. Nor are they likely to have considered either the various forms that literacy can take or the possibility that schooled literacy produces a new form of truth that, at the same time, leads to the subjugation of those forms of knowledge associated with oral communication.

The privileged status of literacy within schools has been further strengthened by both media advertisements and the advocates of educational computing, with the latter attempting to make the use of the computer in the classroom the new symbol of educational progress and modernity. As a language-processing technology, the computer is part of the print tradition of communication. Thus its use in the classroom is not only dependent on the ability to read; it also contributes to shaping the students' sense of reality in the same way as other forms of print communication (Bowers, 1988). Like the printed word, the computer has largely been viewed as a neutral technology (in both cultural and political terms) even though, like the tradition of print, it is also associated with progress and modernization. What is being replaced (subjugated, in Foucault's terms) by these modernizing print technologies has not been given serious consideration by educational profession—which reflects a bias shared by the other sectors of society that control the processes of knowledge production and legitimation.

Differences Between the Spoken and Written Word

Teachers, in our view, should have a deeper understanding of the forms of communication they utilize in the classroom than now characterizes the general public. More specifically, they should understand the cultural and political consequences that result when they continue the traditional practice of privileging literacy as the primary avenue to knowledge and individual empowerment. In clarifying how the written word differs from the spoken word—that is, how the two involve differences in ways of thinking and relating to others—we want to stress that the issues should not be interpreted in terms of either/or categories. We are not urging that books and computers be barred from schools; rather, the issue is one of knowing how print, as a technology, influences the more constitutive aspects of student experience and knowing when its use is inappropriate.

The earliest assessments of how the printed differs from the spoken word involved viewing the two forms of communication in dichotomous terms. As Walter Ong stated it, "The mind does not enter into the alphabet or the printed book or the computer so much as the alphabet or print or the computer enters the mind, producing new states of awareness there" (1977, p. 47). The spoken word, as an "action upon an action," was viewed as natural, involving all the supplementary channels of communication associated with the senses and thus leading to participatory relations with others. While the printed word was seen as encoding a static form of knowledge, the spoken word was viewed as tied to the rhythms of community life. "Oral utterance," Ong wrote, "thus encourages a sense of continuity with life, a sense of participation, because it is itself participatory" (1977, p. 21). Additional influences attributed to print included the rise of individualism (writing and reading are solitary experiences) and the acceptance of the decontextualizing characteristics of abstract and analytic thought (Havelock, 1986), a sender-receiver model of communication whereby the writer communicates to an anonymous public rather than to a known person, the treating of knowledge as a commodity that can be stored and allocated in terms of special social interests, and the fixing of norms in print (as laws) that allows individuals to define their rights and interests as distinct from those of the community (Goody, 1986).

The Scollons summarized how the privileging of print, as the basis of new strategies of power that act on thought and social relationships, led to basic changes: "The word comes to take precedence over the situation, analysis takes precedence over participation, isolated thought takes precedence over the community" (1985, p. 10). Along with Deborah Tannen, they have also helped us understand that the basic differences between reading the printed word (literacy) and speaking to others (orality) has to do with how the two modes of communication differ in utilizing context and thus in affecting the social relationships that are part of context. Rather than understanding literacy and orality as contributing to radically distinct cognitive and social differences, they suggest that differences be understood on a continuum, where print (directed to a friend) may take on some of the characteristics of the spoken word, and where the spoken word (the lecture) may manifest characteristics associated with literacy.

Tannen's contributions to understanding how the strategies of power associated with speaking differ from those associated with writing seem especially useful for clarifying how the classroom teacher's decisions involve reinforcing a particular cultural orientation over other possibilities. The critical distinction between spoken and written discourse, as she sees it, turns on the "relative focus of personal involvement and relative focus on content or information conveyed" (1986a, p. 127). Although a variety of variables enter into both modes of communication, a key dimension that separates the two is "whether it is one-way or two-way communication" (1986a, p. 130). Writing (or print, as it appears to the reader) involves an emphasis on the message, or content, that is being conveyed; speaking, on the other hand, involves a greater focus on interpersonal relationships. As Tannen observes, "In speaking, everything that is said must be said in some way: at some pitch, in some tone of voice, at some speed, with some expression or lack of expression in the voice and on the face of the speaker" (1986a, p. 130). These metamessages, along with body rhythm, gestures, and use of space, communicate both the speaker's and, in turn, the listener's attitude toward the message. By way of contrast, the inability to take account of the attitudes communicated through immediate interpersonal relationships means that the writer must make certain assumptions about the intended audience and then provide the lexical and other cues that will guide the reader's comprehension of the message.

In contrast to the Scribner and Cole (1981) study of the interconnection of literacy and forms of consciousness among the Vai people of northwestern Liberia, which purported to show that schooling rather than literacy contributed to an abstract and decontextualized way of thinking, Tannen's focus on the degree of involvement versus emphasis on message seems particularly important to taking seriously (though perhaps more cautiously) the early formulation of the orality-literacy distinction. The emphasis on message, the stabilizing of texts that allows for analysis, and the linear and abstract form of thinking that is required to organize thoughts into sentences that will eventually constitute a coherent conceptual statement all suggest patterns of interaction that reinforce the view that authority is to be located in the judgment of the individual. That print allows the individual to attain a degree of autonomy from group norms by reaching audiences beyond the immediate social and temporal context must also be recognized in any discussion of whether print, in spite of influential cultural variables, contributes to a further integration of community or to the emergence of individualism and the sense of an abstract public. In writing for other audiences, for example, only individuals can have the sense of removing "themselves in mind from their social place" (Leed, 1980, p. 56).

As both oral and literacy traditions involve myriad forms of social expression and use (Graff, 1987; Heath, 1983), it is essential that we focus on the implications of the differences that separate the two modes of communication within the context of schooling. Thus we wish to focus on some of the implications of "schooled literacy," as Jenny Cook-Gumperz refers to this special variant that combines decoding skills, the decontextualized content of textbooks, and the use of tests to assess performance (1986). However, before we begin identifying the critical judgments facing teachers, we wish to bring out another dimension of the classroom that relates directly to the question of whether literacy (in the context of the cultural variables usually present in an American classroom) acts on the action of students (their patterns of thought, values, and social relationships) in a way that further reinforces a decontextualized, message-centered, and individualistic pattern of thought.

Although there is a wide variation among teachers and grade levels, not to mention regional differences, there is still a shared ideology that, to varying degrees, guides the intellectual process in the classroom. In some classrooms, its presence may be limited to a faint echo in textbooks, while in other classrooms, it serves as the guiding pattern for thinking and discussing issues. This ideology, what Alvin Gouldner terms the "culture of critical discourse" (1979), provides the justification for a particular set of rules that are to guide all serious thought. Essentially, the rules include the following:

1. Speakers must be prepared to justify their assertions (i.e., provide supporting arguments and further evidence).
2. The justification of knowledge claims cannot be based on the authority of tradition or special status of other persons.
3. Although listeners must be free to make up their own minds about the knowledge claims, they are expected to be persuaded by the authority of the evidence or argument.

4. This mode of inquiry can be directed toward any aspect of cultural life (i.e., nothing is immune from being questioned and decided anew on the basis of the critical thought of individuals).

Although many teachers invoke other forms of authority, and some may even view these rules of thinking as the expression of secular humanism, we nevertheless think that this ideology, though highly diluted in many classrooms, is a taken-for-granted ideal of many teachers. The point we want to make is that when the ideology of critical discourse exists as part of the intellectual life of the classroom, it strengthens both the analytical (decontextualized) pattern of thought and sense of individualism (authority as located in the rational process of the individual) associated with literacy. Since knowledge claims in literate traditions are based on a process of justification, which requires an elaborate language code for presenting arguments and the "objective" evidence of other experts, they also strengthen the stratification process that is an integral aspect of schooled literacy. Oral traditions, on the other hand, accept a wider variety of knowledge claims and sources of authority: formulaic sayings, living traditions, persons who have special standing in the community, sacred texts and stories, and so forth. Unlike the literacy/critical discourse tradition fostered in universities and, to a lesser extent, in public schools, the oral tradition does not view truth and progress as emerging from an arena (an intellectual market place for the free exchange of ideas) in which individuals engage in an ongoing competition to establish a new basis of understanding.

Classroom Context

The issues we wish to take up here are not entirely separate from the heated debates that have occurred over whether minority children should be allowed to use the colloquial speech of their primary culture group or required to learn to speak and write in so-called standard English. Although we do not wish to enter that debate in a direct way, we are going to identify how an understanding of some of the basic differences in the spoken and written word can lead to professional judgments that are more sensitive to the problems of cultural (and thus political) domination in the classroom. But it is important to reiterate Courtney Cazden's observation that "all human behavior is culturally based" (1988, p. 67) in order to remind ourselves that we are not suggesting that all strategies and patterns that involve the exercise of power can be eliminated from the classroom, even if teachers commit themselves to some form of cultural democracy. Our primary concern here is with those strategies and patterns that are not recognized by teachers because of their taken-for-granted nature; when these strategies and patterns, even in the hands of well-intentioned teachers, conflict with the norms of the student's primary culture, power is then exercised on students in ways that force certain aspects of their experience to be repressed. In these situations the double-bind caused by conflicting norms and expectations can lead a student to experience a divided self that is being pulled in different, and often irreconcilable, directions.

It would not be incorrect to view all first-time students, regardless of ethnic background, as entering a cultural environment that has distinctly foreign elements to it—even though most of the norms that regulate classroom activities have their origins in white middle America. For example, most preschool children have lived their lives in an essentially oral culture. When faced with the task of learning to read, they may experience problems of making a transition in patterns of thought and communication that are not dissimilar from other bilingual experiences. The transition (or "normalizing" process, to use Foucault's term) that must be undergone can be seen in a comparison of colloquial vocabulary (e.g., "guys," "stuff," "yeah") and sentences (e.g., "I'm doing *this* big thing with Bill" and "Tell yo' momma where we went today"; Chafe, 1985, p. 115; Heath, 1983, p. 158) with the lexical and grammatical norms of written discourse. The extreme divide that separates the two modes of discourse can be seen in a writing guide that states that the emphatic words of a sentence should be placed at the end of a sentence and urges the writer to remember that the use of the "active voice carries with it a tone of greater assurance and decisiveness than the passive voice" (quoted in Beardsley, 1966, p. 97). These and many other rules that separate the lexical and grammatical characteristics of speaking from those of writing must be internalized by students and substituted for the patterns that are a natural part of speaking. Wallace Chafe's (1985) discussion of how "idea units" are handled differently in spoken and written discourse seems especially important to recognizing the changes students must undergo in order to succeed in the literacy culture of most public schools. An idea unit, as Chafe uses the phrase, refers to the amount of information a speaker can comfortably retain in short-term memory and verbalize. As short-term memory appears to change approximately every two seconds, the idea units of speakers are usually verbalized in seven words of English. Analysis of how these idea units are constituted has yielded insight into other characteristics of speaking. According to Chafe, a typical idea unit possesses the following:

> (1) It is spoken with a single coherent intonation contour, ending in what is perceived as a clause-final intonation; (2) it is preceded and followed by some kind of hesitation, ranging from a momentary break in timing to a filled or unfilled pause lasting several seconds; (3) it is a clause—that is, it contains one verb phrase along with whatever noun phrases, prepositional phrases, adverbs, and so on are appropriate; and (4) it is about seven words long and takes about two seconds to produce. (1985, p. 106)

In addition, speaking involves the use of distinct elements that control the flow of information—"like sluice gates in the stream of speech," to use Chafe's metaphorical image (1985, p. 112). Because speaking can become rapid and quickly overwhelm the listener with more information that can easily be handled, words and phrases such as *anyway, by the way, for one thing, let's say now, Oh, OK, well, right on,* and so forth, serve to slow down the momentum of information flow. What Chafe terms "disfluencies"—the "false starts, afterthoughts, repetitions, corrections and fumblings" (1985, p. 112)—also serve to limit the rate of information exchange. As an example of a disfluency, Chafe cites a typical utterance containing pauses and false starts: "Cause . . . um . . . there were . . . four fam . . . four? Yeah, four families" (1985, p. 113).

In addition to lexical differences (e.g., the use of slang we mentioned earlier as not being appropriate to most written discourse—and certainly not accepted in most English classes), learning to read and write involves acquiring the ability to adapt the thought and communication processes to idea units that have fundamentally different characteristics from those associated with speaking. Time plays a different role in writing in that information does not have to be chunked into the short and rapid bursts that characterize most speaking (academics and other intellectuals who have adapted their thought and speaking process to the format of writing represent, of course, an exception to the norm). Second, the act of writing itself slows down the whole process, allowing the writer to craft long and complicated idea units by using a variety of grammatical devices to introduce subordinate ideas, midsentence disclaimers, and connections with previous idea units. Unlike speaking, the writer can edit and rewrite, and only after long reflection and polishing do the idea units appear in print—that is, as a text that acts on the reader's thought process. The solitude and relative freedom of the writing process, according to Chafe, leads to the average use of eleven words per idea unit, with some sentences reaching such lengths that the central organizing ideas may become lost in a morass of words.

Textbook writers often use shorter sentences and limited vocabularies in order to replicate the conceptual patterns associated with patterns of oral discourse. But there are fundamental differences that mark the student's transition from a predominantly oral culture to the more rule-bound discourse patterns associated with the literacy orientation of the classroom. Differences in cultural background, where the grammatical patterns and metaphors of the student's native language help to constitute a different awareness of reality than that experienced by the English-speaking teacher, must also be taken into account. As the students making this transition from the oral culture of childhood to the culture of schooled literacy face long-term risks of being stigmatized and shunted into tracks for lower achievers, it is imperative that teachers have a clear understanding of how their judgments can make this transition both easier and more equitable. Unfortunately, the teacher's own background of ethnic and social-class embeddedness, as well as educational experiences, often creates a taken-for-granted attitude toward using the conceptual attributes associated with schooled literacy as the norm for assessing a student's level of intelligence, attitude, and thus social potential. It is here that the teacher needs to begin the process of reducing the political inequities that characterizes many classrooms.

Although there is a growing awareness among teachers that there are different forms of intelligence and learning styles, we want to urge that consideration also be given to the interconnections between the student's primary culture and the distinctions that separate the spoken from the written word. The emphasis on involvement with relationships (speaking) versus the emphasis on communicating information or messages (writing) involves more than different ways of thinking (the person who uses a mode of communication inappropriate to context is likely to be seen as not knowing what is going on— i.e., as unintelligent); it also involves reinforcing cultural orientations that relate to the larger political questions of whether we are primarily a technologically oriented society, where efficient and impersonal information exchange is seen as the norm of communication, or a society that values the forms of relationships essential to bonding people to a sense of community. The question of student aptitude, as measured against the cognitive and cultural requirements of literacy, is thus inseparable from the political orientations that are reinforced by the teacher's decisions. The points we would like to have teachers consider, as they orchestrate the dynamics of the classroom, are described below.

AWARENESS OF RELATED COGNITIVE ABILITIES.   The learning activities involving the cognitive abilities associated with literacy are not of a higher order than those associated with the effective use of the spoken language. To make this point in a slightly different way, the inability to master the decoding skills and decontextualized pattern of thinking associated with reading should not lead to judging the student as a slower learner—a judgment that, in too many instances, leads to inferior educational opportunities and, thus, life chances. As shown by Raymond McDermott's (1976) study of the consequences of ability grouping in the teaching of reading, the top group gets instruction and the bottom group gets discipline—often for reasons having to do with the teacher's willingness to let the latter group be caught up in an ongoing process of interruptions because they are not expected to achieve. In the higher grades, a student who fails to succeed with a curriculum based on possessing literacy skills is often assigned to a lower (and slower) educational track, where the cycle of failure is accelerated by lowered and, too often, indifferent expectations.

UNDERSTANDING DISTINCTIONS.   Teachers should become sensitive of the need to help students obtain a clearer understanding of the difference between the spoken and written word. This would help students better understand themselves and their relationships with an educational process (indeed, society) that privileges forms of knowledge associated with literacy over those associated with spoken discourse. There is some evidence that a better understanding of the patterns that distinguish speaking/listening from writing/reading might help students acquire more easily the special skills associated with reading. Understanding the expectations associated with communication that is more "situation dependent" (involving multiple channels of communication) and communication that is more "text dependent" (involving primarily the lexical-semantic-syntactic channel) might enable students to recognize which channels they should pay attention to when reading. Herbert D. Simons and Sandra Murphy (1986) note that a student's ability to recognize and treat language abstractly is related to reading acquisition. "Subjects who exhibit phonological awareness have a strong tendency to be better readers than subjects who lack such awareness. Awareness of the segmental nature of spoken language appears to be an important factor in learning to read" (1986, p. 201). They also found that "the prediction that children who used situation-dependent language would exhibit poor reading skills was also confirmed" (1986, p. 201).

Clarifying the differences between spoken and written language may also help students understand the difference between speaking, which is facilitated by the use of contextual cues, and writing a paper as part of a class assignment. Tannen identifies several important distinctions that students should keep in mind as they gear themselves up to engage in a highly decontextualized form of communication. In contrast to speaking,

> a writer and reader are generally separated in time and place, so immediate context is lost. Second, the reader cannot ask for clarification when confused, so the writer must anticipate all likely confusion and preclude it by filling in needed background information and as many as possible of the steps of a logical argument. Third, because the writer and reader are likely to share minimal social context, the writer can make fewer assumptions about shared attitudes and beliefs. (1986a, p. 128)

Other important distinctions include Chafe's point about listeners (and readers) being comfortable with idea units of a certain length and the difficulty and even irritation readers accustomed to the short and accessible idea units of spoken language feel with regard to the more complex idea units of written discourse.

Failure to explain these differences to students results in the school environment's reinforcing the stratification patterns that advantage students from a cultural background that more heavily relies on print as the means of information exchange. Conversely, students who are more accustomed to the communication patterns associated with the spoken word are operating at a disadvantage when it comes to demonstrating those skills usually associated with academic ability—as though the phrase were culturally neutral. As we have attempted to show, the spoken and written word involve different patterns that act on the actions of students. But these relationships, where the exercise of power is "guiding the possibility of [thought and] conduct and putting in order the possible outcome" (Foucault, 1983, p. 221), are not politically or culturally neutral. To put it another way, tying the reward system of the classroom to one mode of communication (literacy) makes the teacher's role a highly political one. We are simply suggesting here that students should be informed about some of the rules (the hidden distinctions between spoken and written discourse) by which the game is being played.

ALLOCATION OF FINANCIAL RESOURCES. The current imbalance between the amount of a school budget allocated to the purchase of computer software programs and the amount given to enrich the curriculum with the spoken word—with specialists in storytelling and members of the community who are the bearers of the oral traditions—suggests another area of professional judgment that needs more critical attention. We chose computer software, rather than books in general, as the basis of comparison because the software program is the current high-status representative of the literate tradition, which has, in recent years, become associated with the view that knowledge is essentially data and that data is the basis of problem solving and thus has economic value.

Although narration, which Jean-Francois Lyotard calls the "quintessential form of customary knowledge" (1984, p. 19), is a characteristic of good literature, we want to stress here the importance of incorporating into the classroom curriculum learning through the spoken word. In an important essay exploring the cognitive differences between the scientific and narrative approaches to knowledge, Jerome Bruner (1985) makes the point that the narrative acts on the student in a different way from the scientific mode of knowledge, which is concerned with how to verify knowledge claims. The narrative, he writes, "leads to good stories, gripping drama, believable historical accounts . . . [its domain] is the landscape of consciousness: What those involved in the action know, think or feel. . . . [It] is concerned with the explication of human intentions in the context of action" (pp. 98–100). In short, learning from the spoken narrative not only provides students a model of "knowing-how," "knowing how to speak," and "knowing how to listen" (Lyotard, 1984, p. 21), which are essential to the bonding process of community life; it also provides students the analogues of human (cultural) experience essential for the clarification of their own values and sense of identity. The narrative form of knowledge is based on a continuity of events and experiences; thus, unlike the factual knowledge that appears to be free of context and time itself, it provides a basis of understanding how the present life of intentions, meanings, and perplexities have continuities with the past. Spoken narratives also encode the moral analogues of the community. These analogues or models represent in human terms the personal and social consequences of lessons not learned—such as the consequences of pride and selfishness. Narratives also provide the models of what constitutes inner strength of character, honesty, generosity, and fairness. In short, narrative provides the symbolic web of meaning that guides human action and thought at the same time that it renews the patterns of the cultural group.

All classrooms involve the spoken word as a natural part of the classroom ecology. Teachers need to give verbal instructions and engage in discussions that range over a variety of issues. Talk is also a natural aspect of student interaction. But the inevitable presence of talk does not overcome the privileged status literacy has been given as the primary avenue to knowledge. In most instances talk is essential for sustaining the authority of literacy in the learning process. We do not want to be misunderstood here as advocating the abandonment of literacy; instead, we are urging teachers to recognize the importance of bringing a better sense of balance to the curriculum. This balance, which will vary from community to community, can be better attained by utilizing people who are the storytellers and thus bearers of the oral traditions of community life. Many students whose primary culture gives importance to narrative knowledge experience, as they sit immersed in the decontextualizing thought processes of print culture, what Richard Rodriquez (1981) terms "radical self-reformation" (p. 67). The sense of self-alienation that Rodriquez experienced ("my need to think so much and so abstractly about my parents and our relationship was in itself an indication of my long education"; p. 72) can be lessened as the teacher expands the meaning of curriculum to include the narrative traditions of the different ethnic groups that constitute our pluralistic society.

To ignore in the transmission process of the classroom the forms of knowledge encoded in the various oral traditions is to engage in a subtle yet powerful form of discrimination. Although there is a tendency to associate the oral tradition with special groups—Native Americans, Irish, Jews, and so forth—the dominant Anglo culture also has its storytellers and folk knowledge—stories of epic events and characters, both anonymous and highly publicized, who serve as analogues for how to live. As students have the opportunity to encounter both their own narrative traditions and those of other students, they will not only learn how different groups give meaning to experience; they will also have legitimated, within the context of the classroom, the essentials of community membership—learning "what one must say in order to be heard, what one must listen to in order to speak, and what role one must play . . . to be the object of a narrative" (Lyotard, 1984, p. 21). This is the positive dimension of the political process that results from an "action upon an action."

THE POLITICS OF GENDER

The classroom continues to be an arena where the politics of gender are often played out according to cultural and linguistic patterns of which neither teacher nor students are fully aware. But this lack of awareness in reenacting these cultural patterns does not make the impact on students who are in such a formative stage any less significant. Cultural patterns that regulate nonverbal communication and organize experience—as well as determine who possesses higher status, who has the right to perform certain tasks, and who may express certain thoughts—serve as the templates that guide the exercise of power in the classroom. These patterns also encode the gender differences that are to guide thought and action across a whole spectrum of activity. In thinking about the professional judgments that teachers must make with regard to gender distinctions in the classroom, it is important to recall our earlier discussions of how students may be members of different primary cultures and how much of the literature dealing with overcoming the subjugated status of women is based on a set of Western (Anglo-European) cultural assumptions. These assumptions about the nature of the individual, freedom, and equality—while fundamental to bringing social attitudes and practices in line with the political rights guaranteed by the Constitution to all members of society—are not always interpreted and given the same importance by members of cultural groups that do not share what Highwater (1981) terms the "cultural package" of the dominant white, Anglo society. Among some Native American and Hispanic groups, for example, the women may view oppression not in terms of lacking a wider choice of careers outside the home and the freedom from the family and group responsibilities, but rather in terms of having their cultural values as a cohesive group subverted by the materialism, anomic individualism, and technologically driven change of the dominant culture. For some Native American groups the primary concern is surviving as a viable cultural group, which means not only recovering and maintaining traditional customs and ceremonies but also insuring that enough children are born and nurtured to avoid tribal extinction. As the introduction of a cross-cultural perspective into any discussion of gender politics is likely to be viewed by some with great suspicion that the argument is simply a thinly disguised excuse for maintaining the patterns of male dominance, we think it necessary to quote a few extended passages from *The Primal Mind* (Highwater, 1981) that explain the basic differences that separate the dominant cultural view of individualism from that of many Native Americans who are rooted in their traditions:

> From the Native American perspective the most fearsome dogma of
> Western reality is probably the fact that personal identity is both abso-

lute and final at the same time that it is unavoidably public. It is inconceivable to the traditional Indian that *the self* is not allowed to exist in the West unless it is willing to be on perpetual public display. Indians find it incredible that a person must retain one identity, one name, one persona for his or her entire existence, no matter what immense changes may take place in that person's life. These contrasting attitudes about personal realities and the place of *the self* in the group make it clear that there are great differences between the way Indians and people of the West regard identity. . . .

The ego orientation and social narcissism of the West, along with the popular elaborations of a show-stopping entity called the *psyche*, are almost inconceivable to the primal populations of the world, which invest very little importance in every machination, twist, and turn of the private person. . . .

It is through relationships that Native Americans comprehend themselves. Such relationships are richly orchestrated, as we have already seen, by elaborations of languages and ritual activities. Underlying the identity of the tribe and the experience of personality in the individual is the sacred sense of place that provides the whole group with its centeredness. . . .

The relatedness of the individual and the tribe extends outward beyond the family, band, or clan to include all things of the world. Thus nothing exists in isolation. Individualism does not presuppose autonomy, alienation, or isolation. (pp. 168–172)

To Chicana feminists, addressing the problems of both survival and liberation as a cultural group means overturning the racist and economic domination practiced by Anglo men and women alike. From their perspective, the feminist movement has not addressed the problem of racism, and thus its agenda of social progress for women is viewed as continuing the forms of cultural and economic domination that have given rise to the cult of *machismo*. The interconnection of sexism and racism thus leads to challenging the most basic cultural values (among others) that may cause the Chicana student to find in the teacher a person who "does not conform to her expectations of female behavior"; the Anglo teacher is seen as "aloof, assertive and independent" and as fostering the values of individuality and achievement—values quite different from those of *la familia*, which are based on respect and cooperation (Enriquez & Mirande, 1978, p. 13).

Although this discussion of cultural difference may appear to be a digression from the problems of gender inequities in the classroom, it is, in fact, directly related to several critical points that must be kept in mind in translating feminist concerns into classroom practice. The first is that the main body of literature that has served to raise consciousness about the wide range of inequities that left women in an inferior status has largely failed to address the issue of using the values and assumptions of one cultural group to dominate other cultural groups, especially when the latter are perceived as backward in terms of middle-class, Anglo culture. Thus the second issue becomes especially important to our discussion of the classroom. Since there are different ways of understanding the gender issue, wherein notions of rights, dignity, and responsibility are understood in terms of different root metaphors that constitute the reality of the cultural group, it is dangerous for teachers to apply a set formula when they may simultaneously face students from the dominant culture, students whose parents are assimilating to the values and assumptions of the dominant culture, and students of parents who are attempting to keep their traditional culture alive and who may view the dominant culture as a source of racism and economic oppression. As members of non-Anglo cultural groups continue to articulate alternative ways for understanding the issue of gender equality, the teacher's responsibility may become clearer in terms of steps that can be taken to reconcile a notion of cultural democracy in the classroom with equitable treatment of students.

In the meantime, we want to identify alternative classroom practices to the sex-role socialization that has become so problematic for people within the dominant culture. However, many of the practices that have served to limit the student's "possible field of action" to gender-specific roles are simply not appropriate, regardless of the student's primary culture.

The effects of power, Foucault reminds us, "circulate through progressively finer channels, gaining access to individuals themselves, to their bodies, their gestures and all their daily actions" (1980, p. 96). The network of disciplinary practices that contribute to normalizing students to the dominant cultural patterns that encode gender distinctions for living superior and inferior social lives is part of the ecology of the classroom. The disciplinary practices are integral to both primary socialization and the ongoing process of communication (both verbal and nonverbal) that reinforces attitudes and patterns first learned outside the classroom. As Sandra Lee Bartky (1988) observes, to be feminine involves internalizing the dominant attitudes about the female mind and body: body size and patterns of movement through space, appearance of the face, deportment that does not communicate either aggressiveness or intimidating intelligence, and so forth. The woman who is obsessed with body weight as an adult, with whether she is too assertive, and with the effects of the weather on hairdo or makeup is engaged in a "relentless self-surveillance" in ways that men are not (p. 81). The norms that are the basis of this self-policing are reinforced throughout the network of disciplinary practices that make up society. Of specific concern to us, however, are the disciplinary practices in the classroom that reinforce the sense of inferiority and thus the need to judge the self in terms of masculine expectations. The three areas of concern include language and curricular content, humor, and differential attention.

Language and Curricular Content

Although considerable attention has been given to how language—more specifically, use of the pronouns *she* and *he*—contributes to attaching gender stereotypes to social roles, many teachers have not fully worked out how to teach students to write in a more gender-neutral manner. Students (and some authors) who are attempting to avoid reinforcing patriarchy through the use of the masculine pronoun often use *she/he* or just *she*. Both are awkward, with the latter merely substituting a new bias for an old one. Yet students can be taught to write in the plural form that allows for the use of the gender neutral *they.*

Some parts of the curriculum, including educational software programs, still contain stereotypical thinking about the masculine nature of social roles. The software program *The Oregon Trail* (mentioned in Chapter 4) is a good example of how the technology of the new "information age" encodes centuries-old, masculine biases about competence, decision making, and competition. This simulation of decision making involves adopting male roles: a banker from Boston, a carpenter from Ohio, a farmer from Illinois. Women are represented in supporting roles, not as the makers of decisions related to the progress and survival of the group. As Bateson's ecological perspective helps us to recognize, books, software programs, and film encode the mental world of the people who produce them, and these people are influenced unconsciously by a mental ecology that extends even further back in time. We want to reiterate the importance of being constantly alert to the gender stereotyping that may be internalized by the student as the norm for human action. But as we think this problem has already been widely documented, we want to turn to other aspects of language and curricular content that have not received such widespread attention and thus remain a problematic aspect of the classroom ecology.

The first has to do with the metaphorical language, including the analogues, used to demonstrate a point an author wishes to make. As students learn something for the first time (primary socialization) they often need examples, models, and analogues that relate to their own experience. In presenting a new idea or procedure by constructing a bridge to understanding that is grounded in some aspect of familiar experience, authors often select experiences with which males can easily identify. The metaphorical language of computers we identified earlier is a good example: "bomb," "checkpoint," "logic bomb," "purge," "command," "execution," and so forth. And in science texts the students might read such statements as, "The brain is an awesome computational instrument" (taken from the literature in the new field of cognitive science) and descriptive accounts that represent the inquiry process as objective, factual, and carried out essentially by male scientists. The generative metaphors that help constitute understanding ("survival of the fittest," "competition," "mechanisms," etc.) generally reflect the types of experiences that characterize the gender of the scientist; and with the field of science largely populated by males, it is not surprising that cultural biases infiltrate science by way of the metaphorical language that is, in part, grounded in personal experience.

Although the following quotation is not from a public school textbook, it clearly shows the masculine gender orientation in scientific explanation:

> Two concepts of genetic mechanisms have persisted side by side throughout the growth of modern genetics, but the emphasis has been very strongly in favor of one of these. . . . The first of these we will designate as the "Master Molecule" concept. . . . This is in essence the Theory of the Gene, interpreted to suggest a totalitarian government. . . . The second concept we will designate as the "Steady State" concept. By this term . . . we envision a dynamic self-perpetuating organization of a variety of molecular species which owes its specific properties not to the characteristic of any one kind of molecule, but to the functional interrelationships of these molecular species. (quoted in Keller, 1987, p. 244)

The metaphors in this statement—"mechanisms," "Master Molecule," "totalitarian government"—frame understanding in terms of what has become recognized as the Cartesian/masculine way of thinking that is now widely associated with a modern form of consciousness. The masculine categories of understanding include power, a detached attitude toward observation, a procedural way of thinking that is based on understanding relationship in terms of linear causality, acceptance of hierarchical relationships, and the acceptance of a culture-free form of rationalism as the only source of authority. The root metaphor that provides the most basic template of understanding is that of the machine.

The Cartesian/masculine pattern of thinking is particularly evident in the above quotation, but it is also present in textbook descriptions of how things function, procedural approaches to problem solving, techniques that increase our power to control nature, and our sense of autonomous individuality. In a mathematics textbook, for example, problems are framed in a manner that requires this detached procedural thinking: "There are nine players on a baseball team. In how many ways can the coach choose players for the first four batting positions from the nine players" (Vannatta & Stoeckinger, 1980, p. T53). A newer mathematics textbook intersperses names and pronouns that suggest a sense of gender balance, but the problem-solving process retains the detached and procedural pattern of Cartesian/masculine thinking: "As she enters the preserve, the club director sees a sign that suggests that each visitor contribute $1.85. How much should she put in the contribution box if she pays the suggested amount for each of the 21 members?" (Fennell, Reys, Reys, and Webb, 1988, p. 85). Throughout the text the problem-solving process is framed in terms of sporting events, work situations, and the uses of technology.

When the metaphors and style of thinking in the curriculum reflects an essentially masculine orientation, only part of the culture is being validated in the students' minds. This bias, in turn, acts on both male and female consciousness in ways that help to solidify future misunderstandings and miscommunication. For the former, it reinforces a taken-for-granted attitude toward a Cartesian view of the world (Chodorow, 1978); for the latter, it involves invalidation and self-ambivalence. A number of feminist writers—Mary Field Belenky (1986), Susan Bordo (1987), Nancy Chodorow (1978), Carol Gilligan (1982), and Sandra Harding (1986), to cite just a few who are contributing to a powerful critique of gender orientations in consciousness—have identified aspects of feminine consciousness. The consensus of this literature is that women's "ways of knowing" are more contextual, involve a sense of connectedness, are framed by a concern with nurturing relationships, depend on multiple channels of communication (including voice and intuition), and are more constituted through an ongoing process than discovered through detached observation. The metaphors that suggest mental images and provide the templates of understanding will be very different when they are derived from these more connected, as opposed to detached and power-oriented, ways of knowing.

In suggesting that teachers be alert to the metaphorical language and conceptual-mapping characteristics of the curriculum, particularly with regard to the gender orientation that is being reinforced, we are really returning to an earlier theme; namely, that a crucial aspects of the teacher's professional responsibility involves judgments about the mental ecology of the classroom. More specifically, teachers should recognize what Bateson terms "pathologies," or an "ecology of bad ideas" (1972, p. 484). The gender bias in the curriculum not only involves a field of power relations and disciplinary practices that shapes the mental processes of both female and male students to accept the superiority of patriarchy (in ways of knowing, social institutions, and forms of technology); it also perpetuates the Cartesian presumption that rational and detached individuals can exercise technological control over the whole environment. As the following observation by Bateson suggests, the awareness of gender bias in curricular content is not simply an issue of equity and fairness: "When you separate mind from the structure in which it is immanent, such as human relationship, the human society, or the ecosystem, you thereby embark, I believe, on fundamental error, which in the end will surely hurt you" (1972, p. 485). For, as he notes, "the unit of evolutionary survival turns out to be identical with the unit of mind," and the unit of survival is *"organism* plus *environment"* (1972, p. 483).

Classroom Use of Humor

As was pointed out earlier, humor is an important and necessary aspect of the classroom ecology. The continual process of meeting expectations and performance standards—assignments, classroom participation, behavioral norms, demonstrations of what has been learned—requires that teachers often operate more at the power end of the power/solidarity continuum, even when their exercise of power is obscured by the use of more participatory processes. Humor provides the opportunity to suspend momentarily the givenness of the social order, with all its heavy expectations and consequences for deviant or poor performance, thus allowing students and teachers to share a moment of spontaneous laughter and the sense of solidarity that is associated with a shared (and perhaps unorthodox) perception. When the teacher, for example, breaks the routine of a high school class by commenting on the static noise coming from the intercom speaker fastened to the wall (e.g., "Big Brother is listening again so we all better think right thoughts and be on task"), the humor serves to bring teacher and students together in a highly ritualized (and safe) response to the faceless nature of bureaucratic intrusion and control. But classroom humor does not always bring students and teacher together in a moment of solidarity; it can also be used to divide students from each other by playing on deep-seated (even unconscious) cultural stereotypes. The telling of ethnic jokes is a prime example, as are jokes directed against the athlete or the student who is perceived as too intellectual or too serious for the norms of the other students. Gender bias can also be communicated through this more invasive type of humor.

We want to identify three categories of classroom humor based on treating females as a special group and as essentially inferior. The first type involves dismissing females with humor. In the elementary grades, it may take the form of an "isn't that cute" comment by the teacher, followed by a quiet and friendly chuckle as the conversation is directed back to a boy's remarks about what was really happening in the game. In high school it may take the form of a teacher comment such as "not bad for a girl" or "that's a good try" as a female student responds to a domain of cultural experience usually perceived as masculine. The laughter that accompanies these off-the-cuff comments helps to hide the gender stereotyping by framing it as a humorous response. In this form of humor, where solidarity is attained along gender lines, the potential subverting of the social order—women demonstrating competence and asserting rights in previously masculine domains—is challenged and trivialized through humor. If the female student reacts, thus challenging the controlling frame that demeans her contribution by turning it into a joke, she then may encounter a remark like "can't you (women) ever take a joke?"—followed by another round of laughter.

A second category of gender-based humor involves situations in which the teacher (upper grade) selects out certain female students in order to engage in a teasing type of humor. This type of humor, whereby the teacher attempts to achieve a sense of solidarity with special students (sometimes the more attractive and physically developed), can involve humorously intended remarks that are thinly disguised forms of sexual innuendo. In using humor based on the student's looks, body, or dating experiences, the teacher may be pushing the student to the edge of the comfort zone in order to see the expression of embarrassment. A response that communicates embarrassment also signals to others the student's subordinate position.

A third category of gender bias is communicated through jokes that are treated as gender-specific. In some instances, the teacher may preface the joke with an apology or other remark that frames the joke as one that only the "boys" will understand and appreciate. In other instances the joke may be of the locker room genre, and the female students may simply be treated as invisible—with no preface such as "you girls probably won't like this one." This type of humor may also be used among teachers to maintain a sense of solidarity within faculty groups. In a study of teacher collegiality, Charles Bruckerhoff (1985) describes the practical jokes and games played by a clique of male high school teachers. He quotes a teacher who explained one of these games involving female students:

> A teacher would select the most outstanding girl in class for the day based upon revealing dress, beautiful breasts, general good looks, etc. and give her a book to deliver to one of the others in the clique as a little present. To give the game a new twist, a teacher sent the fattest and ugliest girl he had on the same kind of errand to another as a "little present." (p. 16)

This, we suspect, is an extreme example, but it does illustrate problematic dimensions of cultural patterning reproduced in the school.

As with Mary Douglas's observation about the characteristics of the social system being encoded in the patterns of nonverbal communication, classroom humor encodes the gender distinctions worked out in the larger social system. The status system in schools allows teachers more latitude than students in reframing the perceptions of the social world through humor; it also allows the teacher to use humor to reassert control in the classroom when a student attempts to subvert the classroom sense of order. In terms of student-initiated humor, there is less margin for error in terms of timing, spontaneity, and the momentary subverting of the established order and power relationships—all of which are required for the joke to work. The social system also authorizes certain groups to use humor in a manner that empowers themselves; in effect, the uses of humor are expressions of the structures of power that make up society. As a colleague pointed out, recalling a line from a recent movie, the privileged status of the masculine view of reality makes it nearly impossible for a female to respond to a male's comment that "that suit goes so nicely with your eyes" with "thanks, your nose goes so well with your tie." Similarly, female students cannot easily or safely challenge sexist humor in the classroom, as the teacher's authority still has the backing of a social system that privileges the masculine over the feminine.

In identifying the categories of sexist humor we want to emphasize the types of humor that teachers should avoid; we are not trying to suggest that all teachers are guilty of being sexist. We also want to point out that the use of humor in the classroom, as elsewhere, can be utilized to express attitudes that mask a whole series of psychological states that cannot be communicated in a more open and direct manner. The sense of anger, rancor, spitefulness, and desire to detract from another person's sense of well-being—all characteristics of the ressentient personality that Friedrich Nietzsche (1888/1967) identified—can be triggered in a classroom situation where the student's performance threatens the teacher's own sense of competency. When the teacher makes a self-comparison with the student's ability and feels impotent to challenge the source of threat in a direct manner, or when the teacher lacks the maturity to acknowledge that the student may have a quicker mind or a greater sensitivity and deeper understanding of the issues being discussed, the use of humor can serve as a powerful yet safe way of putting down the student. One of the characteristics of ressentiment is that it is expressed by the person (teacher and student) who cannot confront the source of threat or discomfort in a more open manner—which could lead to a clarification of differences and perhaps a different basis of understanding. The teacher whose own athletic performance has always been a source of discomfort can use humor to put down the athletic student (the jock), just as the teacher who has a more procedural way of thinking can put down the student who is able to recognize the answer without plodding through all the steps, again through a joke that masks a sense of rancor and a desire to detract. We think that sexist humor may be, in part, rooted in ressentient attitudes, wherein a sense of powerlessness and inferiority (there are multiple bases of personal comparison in a school setting) lead to the use of humor as a way of putting students and others "in their place."

Where humor is based in ressentient attitudes we can see how it expresses a form of power that cannot easily be dealt with. The following dialogue, as recalled by a female (university) student, captures the way in which humor and the demeaning put-down get mixed together in such a way that a response would appear to disrupt the sense of good fun and humor:

"*Ms.*? You don't use Mrs.? Maybe you can explain to me this new thing of names with women today—why you aren't proud

of your husband?" (general laughter in the room). "So *Ms.*
Jones, what do you do for a living?" He knew I was a student, so
he left me with a choice of identifying myself as a low-status student or identifying with my husband. When I replied that I was
a student, mother, and wife, he asked: "In that order?" (to
smiles and chuckles around the room). When I flushed with anger, he responded: "Oh, isn't that cute? *Ms.* Jones is blushing.
Well, I certainly hope it is not because of the answer to the question."

The disguised aggression, framed in the form of a humorous exchange that supposedly strengthens group solidarity, cannot be
openly challenged in situations in which the student is in a subordinate position—unless she is prepared to face severe reprisals from
the teacher and censure from some students for being "too sensitive"
to take a well meaning joke. The ambiguity that surrounds the situation, as well as the sense of powerlessness in achieving clarification
(and validation) about one's own existential situation, contributes to
the development within the student of the same sense of powerlessness that may eventually spill out in rancorous, spiteful, and demeaning statements to others. In effect, ressentiment in teachers contributes to its spread among the students (Nordstrom, Friedenberg, &
Gold, 1967). Although, we want to reiterate, it is not limited to the
domain of gender, it is likely to be more widespread there, as consciousness-raising around issues of gender threatens male dominance. The oft-heard jokes among men that they will need a sex
change if they want a job in a field where employment decisions are
responsive to the need for gender balance in the workplace is a typical
example of how a sense of powerlessness gets transformed into rancor. As there are many bases for interpersonal comparison, and many
institutional characteristics of schools that can contribute to the teacher's sense of powerlessness, ressentient humor can be directed toward both male and female students. Thus we want to end this discussion by emphasizing again that this is not a gender-specific
phenomenon.

The Classroom Problem of Differential Attention

Differential treatment of students that reflects gender distinctions
varies with grade level. For example, elementary teachers might say,
"Boys, be quiet," "The girls may line up first," and "You'll have to go
sit with the girls if you don't behave." Although this type of gender

categorization is not likely to be heard in a high school classroom, many forms of differential treatment appear to cut across all grade levels. The differential treatment that students encounter, depending on their gender, reflects how the taken-for-granted patterns and attitudes of teachers encode the mental ecology that was the basis of their own socialization. We want to emphasize that these classroom practices reproduce the taken-for-granted attitudes of the larger society in order to avoid a possible misinterpretation that teachers are more prone to gender stereotyping than other members of society.

In reviewing nearly thirty years of classroom research on differential treatment in classrooms, Craig Flood (1988) makes the following summary:

1. Girls tend to be called on if they sit in the front rows, while boys tend to be called on regardless of where they are seated.
2. Teachers have a tendency to help boys get started with an assignment and then let them go ahead on their own. Girls are given more continuous guidance.
3. On the whole, boys experience more positive and negative teacher contacts combined than girls. While girls experience a higher proportion of positive contacts, boys encounter an average of two and a half times more disapproving comments from teachers.
4. Girls receive more teacher attention in reading classes and less in math classes.

Differential treatment also exists in the allocation of turn-taking rights. Teachers tend to grant more rights to speak (to ask a question or to make a comment) to boys and to follow up the boys' comments with an acknowledging response.

These patterns of differential treatment are based on gender stereotyping about boys being more competent in certain cognitive and skill areas, as well as more independent and assertive. When these assumptions guide the teacher's response, a cycle of self-fulfilling prophecy is set in motion. The higher level of activity (and assertiveness) on the part of boys requires teachers to respond to them more (in terms of both discipline and reinforcement), but this (according to the stereotype) is what is expected of boys. Girls are expected to be docile, and the teacher often evaluates and responds to them accordingly. Persistence in pressing a point in a discussion and the assertion of claims for equal treatment in terms of turn-taking will be seen by teachers who have a stereotyped image as deviating from the norm, and thus this behavior may be labeled as insubordinate and aggressive. The same behavior on the part of boys will be seen as normal; and while it adds an additional element of stress to the classroom management process, it is unlikely to result in a negative label or grade.

In getting back to Foucault's point that all actions—the spoken word, smiles, body gestures (plus the maneuvers that cause the student to avoid recognition)—influence the subsequent actions of the other and thus shape the possibilities of being, we want to make a few suggestions for reducing the patterns of actions that are embedded in, and continue to reinforce, gender stereotypes. We think these suggestions will, at the same time, reflect a sensitivity to cultural differences among students.

The first step in consciousness-raising, where the taken-for-granted patterns can be made explicit, is to develop the language framework for naming what is happening in the classroom, including the casual relationships. This is, in part, what we are laying the foundation for here in our discussion of differential treatment. A second step is to have a colleague observe your classroom and, in the process, document the patterns of interaction with students. Were male students given more opportunities to speak? Was the eliciting of responses evenly distributed between male and female students? What assumptions were communicated about competence being related to gender? As so many of the cultural patterns are invisible to the person who lives them as part of everyday life, the third-party documentation will allow the teacher to escape a form of cultural blindness. After the teacher has worked to reduce the patterns of differential treatment, the colleague should be invited back to document whatever changes have been made. We will further explore such observation strategies in the following chapter.

Another aspect of the solution is to recognize that changing the pattern of interaction will not, by itself, resolve the problem of meaningful communication in the classroom. To put this another way, calling on female students as often as males is a positive step, but if the teacher is unable to engage in a dialogue with the student little of real substance will have been achieved. The elements of a dialogue, as opposed to the monologue that characterizes the sender-receiver model of education, were first identified by Martin Buber (1965). Paulo Freire (1974) and, more recently, feminists have emphasized that dialogue is essential to a non-Cartesian form of education (Belenky et al., 1986; Noddings, 1986). Although Buber's own language is highly gender-specific, he nevertheless illuminated the characteristics of a dialogue that have relevance to communicating in a classroom, where the problems of differential treatment have been largely resolved. After the acknowledgment of the student as a speaker, it is essential, according to Buber, that the student be confirmed (recognized) in terms of his or her distinctness as a person. Thus the teacher's part in the unfolding of a dialogue involves speaking with the student in such a way that the content (and the answer) of the discussion is not entirely determined in advance. Confirmation of the student as a person, the careful listening to what the student says (both verbally and nonverbally), responses that take account of the legitimacy of the student's comments, and the continual respect of the student as a bearer of convictions and knowledge—even when these become the focus of the educational moment—are all essential to the openness and mutuality that characterizes dialogue. If these elements are not present in the interchange between teacher and students, simply allocating reinforcement on equal terms or granting equal rights to speak will not meet the students' need to be confirmed as persons and in their relationships with others as they encounter the often perilous world of adult knowledge.

Although the ability to engage in dialogue may have a psychological basis, as well as a relationship to the teacher's own self-confidence in relation to a body of knowledge, growth can be engendered by becoming sensitive to how the nonverbal dimensions of communication signal the teacher's attitude toward the student. It is also possible to attend to whether the student's response is being dismissed because it did not conform to the answer the teacher was looking for and to whether the communication is characterized by mutual involvement that extends the understanding of both student and teacher.

Dialogue is not an exception to Foucault's observation about the disciplinary nature of actions that act upon the actions of others. But it involves the exercise of power that is not rooted in social networks and cultural beliefs that restrict the possible field of thought and action to what has previously existed. Dialogue is different in that it confirms the participant's sense of self-worth, validates the mutuality of meaningful social relationships, and empowers in the sense of deepening and broadening understanding. In fact, it moves the politics of the classroom to an entirely different level—one that we will address more fully in the discussion of the educational needs of the twenty-first century.

CHAPTER 7

Culturally Responsive Supervision

Metaphor, nonverbal communication, the teacher's gatekeeper role, framing, gender-specific uses of humor, and the privileging of written over spoken language are topics that have helped us bring forward some of the hidden cultural patterns of classroom teaching. We would like to emphasize that such patterns are hidden not because they are obscure or peripheral to the daily lives of teachers and students, but for the opposite reasons. That is, they are so very obvious and so integral a part of ordinary experience that we take them for granted, too familiar and too "true" to warrant explicit attention. By naming them and suggesting the ways in which they shape understanding, our aim is to provide perspectives from which teachers may recognize relationships that would otherwise remain hidden and thus beyond any form of reflective consideration. We view this effort as critically important not only to promoting the teacher's professional knowledge as a basis for informed judgment but also to legitimizing the wide range of teaching skills (including those associated with caring and imagination) that have been put out of focus by technicist approaches to classroom instruction.

One implication of our work, from an ecological perspective, concerns the truism in education that teaching—like swimming, driving a car, or playing the violin—is learned not from reading books or from completing the coursework required for teacher certification. Rather, it is learned "on the job" from the demands of providing day-to-day instruction in real classrooms with real students. It is this more role-contextualized experience that the folk wisdom of the teaching profession holds as most meaningful to both novice and veteran teachers alike. On the one hand, we believe that preservice coursework can play an important role in the education of teachers and that college instructors can, at times, serve as powerful models for both good as well as poor teaching. On the other hand, an ecological understanding of how teachers learn and develop professional skills highlights the broad social, cultural, and institutional contexts of their work. What this means, in practical terms, is that teachers who have developed a high level of sensitivity to the deep cultural patterns of language and understanding are likely to feel constrained or alienated if they find themselves in schools with an institutional culture that values prescriptive techniques over responsive judgment.

In this chapter, then, we want to expand our considerations of teaching and classroom management to encompass the process of supervision as another aspect of the teacher's professional culture. We could have selected a variety of other support activities as the focus for this expansion, including inservice staff development, curriculum design, program evaluation, and administrative leadership. Such activities are indeed closely related to and often intertwined with the supervision of teachers. Nevertheless, supervision offers some clear parameters for focusing our discussion on the practice of teaching and its institutional rewards. At the same time, supervision is carried on both during preservice (with student or intern teachers) and, increasingly, throughout the teacher's career. Finally, a growing body of research and an increasingly large community of scholars, as well as new approaches, academic journals, and professional organizations, focus on teacher supervision as a distinctive field of activity.

Our main task is neither to account for recent developments nor to sort out the relationships between supervision and other support activities. Instead, it is to pin down the conceptual and practical implications that an ecological perspective holds for how we understand and evaluate supervision models. We will refer to these implications collectively as culturally responsive supervision. In combining these terms, we hope to underscore the receptive role and sensitivity demanded by supervision as a form of inquiry, while at the same time playing down the implied hierarchical relationships that the "supervision" metaphor brings with it from other fields (e.g., business and industry). Moreover, it should also be clear that we will strive to develop an image of responsive supervision more as a framework for understanding supervisory activities than as a prescriptive model.

In order to develop this framework, our first concern will be to identify the major presuppositions that guide the diversity of supervision techniques now being proposed. This will help clarify how, when, and where an ecological understanding of the classroom can contribute to the professional knowledge that supervisors bring to their work. Second, we will suggest a number of points at which responsive supervision is informed by qualitative forms of social inquiry. This task of bringing an ecological perspective together with qualitative methods is important in maintaining a close match between the content and procedures of supervision. We will also consider issues related to the supervisor's subjectivity. Here our concern will be not with eliminating the subjectivity, but with ways of fostering greater awareness on the supervisor's part of how it directs supervision with various degrees of subtlety.

SUPERVISION AS TECHNOLOGY

For the purposes of our task here, we intend to provide neither a review of the literature on supervision nor a comprehensive treatment of its historical development. We want only to suggest some connections between dominant models of supervision and a broadly based set of assumptions that Donald Schon (1983) has referred to as "technical rationality." We view these connections as deeply rooted in a long intellectual history that has been dominated by Cartesian and largely masculine patterns of thought. To illustrate these patterns, however, we need only go back some fifty or sixty years to when teacher supervision emerged as a field with the distinctiveness by which it is recognized today.

Frances Bolin (1987) argues that early efforts in the United States to articulate teacher supervision as a field of professional activity were shaped by some of the same social forces that guided developments in the curriculum field. In particular, she notes the influence of scientific management principles, what Raymond Callahan (1962) called "the cult of efficiency," that emerged broadly as an approach to certain forms of industrial production. This approach, based on the metaphor of social engineering, was soon wedded to a growing body of research in psychology by those working in the newly emerging fields of supervision and curriculum. In supervision, this merging of approaches led to Arvil S. Barr and William H. Burton's 1926 book, *The Supervision of Instruction*, a work that, according to Bolin (1987), "linked Burton's interest in the principles of supervision, based on an understanding of human growth and development, and Barr's interest in teacher efficiency" (p. 373). Beginning in 1927, Burton and Barr helped edit an NEA Yearbook, *The Superintendent Surveys Supervision*, that was published in 1930. The foreword of this yearbook offers the following definition: *"Supervision has for its object the development of a group of professional workers who attack their problems scientifically, free from the control of tradition and actuated by the spirit of inquiry"* (quoted in Bolin, p. 376; emphasis original).

This 1930 definition may seem to us today as exceedingly bold in its focus on scientific inquiry. Yet the assumptions upon which it is grounded have not changed, for they continue to guide systematic approaches to defining the supervisor's role. They include an implicit belief that supervision is based on forms of rationality divorced from tradition and culture. This primary assumption is played out, at the expense of understanding the cultural embeddedness of the participants (students, teacher, supervisor), by defining this field of professional activity as concerned foremost with the discovery of techniques for achieving prespecified ends—in this case, those identified with the teacher's professional development. Supervision, from this perspective, is only a tool or method for engineering social change, and the supervisor can be thought of as a technician who applies a learned set of techniques to repair or improve the teacher's performance in a wide variety of areas. The supervisor's own professionalism, in turn, is established by possession of whatever technical skills and knowledge are required by this task.

This orientation, which could be labeled "supervision as technology," has had a broad influence on various approaches ranging from clinical supervision to peer coaching. We will consider more closely a model of clinical supervision in order to clarify the connections between a technicist orientation and supervisory practices. While clinical supervision has been defined in many ways (see, for example, Smyth, 1986), a recent emphasis on teacher effectiveness skills is not atypical of the types of thinking that have dominated the field. In this respect the model we will consider offers some important lessons for understanding the limitations as well as the practical implications of technical approaches to supervision.

In the second edition of *Techniques in the Clinical Supervision of Teachers* (1987), Keith A. Acheson and Meredith D. Gall defined supervision as "the process of helping the teacher reduce the discrepancy between *actual* teaching behavior and *ideal* teaching behavior" (p. 27). Here again we find the implicit assumption of rationality as concerned with problem solving, in this case translated in instrumental terms. The supervisor's task is specifically threefold: first, identify goals (ideal teaching behaviors); second, identify "actual" teaching behaviors; and third, identify procedures that will close the gap by changing behavior toward the ideal. Of particular significance is that techniques that are used throughout this entire process, a characteristic that places this approach in the same tradition as Ralph Tyler's

(1949) rationale for curriculum development. Acheson and Gall (1987) describe a total of thirty-two techniques, the first four of which (pp. 61, 64, 66, 69) address the process of identifying goals. They include:

> Identify the Teacher's Concerns about Instruction (Technique 1)
> Translate the Teacher's Concerns into Observable Behaviors (Technique 2)
> Identify Procedures for Improving the Teacher's Instruction (Technique 3)
> Assist the Teacher in Setting Self-Improvement Goals (Technique 4)

In applying these techniques, the supervisor looks primarily to the teacher in defining ideal teaching behaviors. Nevertheless, Acheson and Gall also provide a review of teacher effectiveness research findings to be used, we assume, in further guiding this process. Supervisors thus come to their work twice armed with a set of techniques and a body of knowledge based on empirical research, both of which are based on the assumption that goals are like rocks, bacteria, or solar particles—they can be discovered through objective observation as "out there" in the real world.

One of our concerns is that this assumption, necessary to a technicist approach, puts out of focus the cultural patterns and values that are encoded in the techniques themselves. Consider, for example, the technique of translating the teacher's concerns into observable behaviors. Most teachers and supervisors would quite reasonably find it impossible to state all of their professional aspirations in behavioral terms. Teachers might hope, in particular, to be warm, imaginative, confident, respectful, caring, clear in expressing ideas, and sensitive to how their students relate to the world. Such metaphors are, to use Michael Polanyi's (1964) term, "logically unspecifiable." They cannot be captured by any list of behaviors. If a translation is forced, teachers have only one of two choices: either to trivialize certain goals (warmth defined by smiles per minute) or to let them fall by the wayside. In this way, the technique itself prefigures what goals will even be considered (a point on which Acheson and Gall remain silent). The issue is not whether such techniques should be ruled out in every case, but rather what constitutes informed judgment on the part of supervisors and their awareness of how techniques "use" them at the same time as they use techniques.

While goal identification is recognized as critically important, clinical supervision's strong suit is found in addressing another task:

the specification of actual teaching behaviors. Acheson and Gall describe seventeen techniques related to this task. These techniques focus on classroom observation and include, for example, procedures for recording selected teacher questions, feedback, and directions verbatim; making records of selected behaviors, verbal flow, and movement patterns based on seating charts; collecting anecdotal information; administering checklists; and using timeline coding schedules. The supervisor's role in applying these techniques is made quite explicit. As Acheson and Gall note, "Clinical supervision, in its most basic form holds up a mirror so that teachers can see what they are actually doing while they are teaching" (p. 15). This metaphor of the supervisor as instrument ("mirror") again underscores the primary assumptions that represent technical rationality as culturally neutral. The supervisor's role is to reflect back reality "in the raw," to provide a true image ("data") undistorted by cultural bias. As with goals, actual teaching behavior is assumed to exist independent of the supervisor, out there waiting to be discovered. This is achieved through techniques of counting and recording those observable behaviors that correspond to a set of "low-inference" categories, such as teacher question/student response, on-task/off-task behavior, praise/criticism, direct/indirect style, and so forth.

Clinical observation techniques are thus designed to lend supervision a semblance of objectivity that Acheson and Gall see as highly valuable when it comes to the process of giving information back to teachers. In describing Technique 22 (Providing the Teacher with Feedback Using Objective Observational Data), they claim that "many conferences are difficult because the data are 'soft' (i.e., subjective, inaccurate, irrelevant). . . . 'Hard' data alleviate this problem" (p. 156). They go on to suggest that a characteristic of "important information" is that it is "objective (unbiased)" (p. 157) and that "persuasive data contain no value judgments. Inferences and generalizations the *observer* may have formed about the activity are not included in the data presented in a conference with the teacher" (p. 161).

We have serious doubts that data (persuasive or otherwise) "contain no value judgments." Even video and audio recordings, which Acheson and Gall describe as "probably the most objective observational techniques" (p. 123), are selective, limited, and thus biased in what they are able to pick up and re-present. The camera lens, for example, quite literally frames observation, and "human factors," as any filmmaker can testify, are very much present in camera placement, direction, editing, and so on. Yet our primary concern is not with whether such claims to objectivity can be justified but with how they hide the sociocultural and political nature of professionalism by limiting the supervisor's role to that of a technician. This is a far more problematic issue, for if we accept an image of supervisors that denies their cultural embeddedness, then observation techniques operate foremost as a set of blinders; that is, they restrict rather than enhance perception.

Consider, as an example, a supervisor and teacher interested in increasing student participation in classroom activities. In order to collect data relevant to their interest, the supervisor considers various clinical observation techniques and decides to use a checklist of teaching behaviors that are assumed to increase student participation. Such behaviors identified in a sample checklist offered by Acheson and Gall include

1. Calls on nonvolunteers
2. Redirects questions
3. Praises student responses
4. Invites student-initiated questions (p. 135)

As an observer, the supervisor's task is to identify and record each time the teacher engages in one of these behaviors. This will provide data relevant to the teacher's "actual" behavior during classroom instruction.

In practice, the supervisor will initially find this simple task of recognition more difficult than suggested by how we and its authors represent it. When a teacher is in a small room with twenty-eight young people, troublesome questions quickly arise: Should a smile or nod of the teacher's head be counted as praise? Should the teacher's verbal response, "good answer," be counted as praise even when it seems automatic and detached from the flow of interaction? When the teacher steps out from behind the front desk and sits down close to a student, does that count as an invitation? Or when the teacher asks abruptly for questions twenty seconds before the end of class, is that an invitation? The supervisor soon learns that these and many other "judgment calls" can be avoided by attending to only one or two dimensions of classroom interaction–say, the literal meaning of the teacher's verbal comments or specific behaviors that can easily be disconnected from their social context. This restricted focus, the supervisor assumes, is necessary to assure "objective (unbiased) observational data." At the same time, however, it teaches the supervisor to selectively ignore whatever does not conveniently fit into the behavioral categories of the checklist.

In this example our primary concern is not with the limited number of categories used in any given checklist. Focused attention is necessary, not for the sake of objectivity but for the sake of coherence and understanding. Nor do we want, at this point, to become entangled in a debate over what specific categories should be included and excluded in the development of checklists. Instead, we believe the central issue is one of recognizing how a claim to objectivity itself introduces cultural biases by restricting what counts as data to the observable behavior of others. To put this another way, observation techniques prefigure what is observed. Returning to our example, the checklist technique itself puts out of focus a broad range of sociocultural patterns, and many of these (such as the teacher's use of nonsexist language in praising student contributions, or the ability to encourage patterns of turn-taking that build solidarity) may well be the most crucial factors in sustaining student participation. Such patterns cannot be captured by a behavioral checklist because whatever meaning and logic participation holds for those in the classroom is a matter of experience, not behavior. Further we want to reiterate an earlier point: Behavior is a language used to communicate about relationships and thus expresses the most deeply held (and unconscious) assumptions of the students' primary culture. Checklists and other supposedly objective techniques are equally effective in putting out of focus the cultural patterns of understanding that guide the supervisor's thought and actions.

A similar line of argument has been advanced in the field of supervision by Thomas Sergiovanni (1987). He suggests, for example, that "when caught up in the language of the teacher-effectiveness research, we view teaching and supervision in a certain way. An evaluation system based on such research is a subjective artifact of this thinking" (p. 226). This is a significant point, given the current propensity for making unquestioned claims that one's particular training program is research based. Sergiovanni's main argument, nevertheless, is that while the field of supervision has been dominated by a "rationalistic tradition," its evolution now depends on rethinking the nature of professional activities in ways that are securely anchored in the concept of culture. He summarizes this argument by stating:

> Teaching and supervision are fields within the domain of the cultural sciences. Models of knowledge generation and use in practice within the cultural sciences are both mind dominant and mind dependent. They emerge from a series of subjective decisions, but once established these models become dominating mindscapes that program our thinking and create our reality. (p. 231)

To this image of supervision as "mind dominant and mind dependent," we would like to add Bateson's (1972) notion that "the individual mind is immanent, but not only in the body. It is immanent also
in the pathways and messages outside the body" (p. 461). It is this
way of viewing students and teacher as part of a larger mental ecology that opens the door to understanding supervision as culturally
grounded.

Having identified the cultural biases encoded in the technical
form of rationality that guides models of clinical supervision, we must
reemphasize that such a critical awareness is not meant to imply a
blanket condemnation of this approach. On the contrary, clinical supervision can be understood as motivated by a desire to move away
from past images that portrayed the supervisor as an "inspector"
whose job was to maintain unilateral control over the transmission of
a particular sociopolitical belief system. Moreover, the techniques of
clinical supervision, if coupled with an ecological sensitivity, can be
useful in highlighting certain behavioral manifestations of the deep
cultural patterns that guide classroom interaction. Acheson and Gall
(1987), for example, provide two illustrations of how observation
techniques included in their model have been used by researchers to
recognize and document differential patterns of verbal interaction
corresponding to student gender and ethnic differences. Our point is
only to suggest the limitations of thinking about this process
(whether it be research or supervision) as merely a technical activity
of mirroring objective reality. This perspective simply provides no basis for recognizing how techniques use us as we use them and thus
become the "dominating mindscapes that program our thinking and
create our reality" (Sergiovanni, 1987, p. 231).

Acheson and Gall (1987) are not insensitive to this issue, for they
advise supervisors that "you will need to use judgment in incorporating them [techniques] into your supervisory behavior and in applying
them to a particular supervisory situation" (p. 72). What concerns us
is that this advice alone only leaves us with the unanswered question
of what types of understanding might inform this judgment. Addressing this question is one of the central points at which we view
culturally responsive supervision as making a contribution to the
field. Our aim, then, is to develop an ecological understanding as it
applies to recognizing the tacit presuppositions that guide supervisors throughout the various phases of their work. This understanding
fosters such recognition by shifting attention from technical rationality to cultural awareness; from the autonomous individual to processes of information exchange; and from a conduit view of language

to the historically grounded patterns of thought embedded in metaphor, nonverbal communication, humor, framing, turn-taking, and so on. Our first step in outlining the primary dimensions of culturally responsive supervision is to reconceptualize supervision as a form of qualitative inquiry.

SUPERVISION AS INQUIRY

In the past two decades, educational researchers have become increasingly interested in qualitative studies, the methods they employ, the presuppositions that guide their focus, and the particular forms of insight they are able to provide into the nature of classroom life. This trend has included foremost a basic concern for defining what qualitative inquiry is. At the outset we want to suggest that there are no clear lines of demarcation between the many different forms of qualitative inquiry and conventional—often referred to as quantitative—research. The labels "qualitative" and "quantitative" are themselves somewhat misleading, because the rough distinctions that can be made have little to do with qualities and quantities. Rather, they primarily concern the epistemological assumptions that underpin each of these two orientations. On the one hand, quantitative inquiry takes its lead from the physical sciences, assuming a Cartesian view of knowledge that endeavors to maintain a separation between researchers and the focus of their study. Qualitative inquiry, on the other hand, assumes a relational view of knowledge that highlights the interdependence between researchers and what they study. These assumptions are played out at the practical level of doing educational research not only in terms of methods and procedures but also in terms of focus. Frederick Erickson (1986), for example, labels qualitative inquiry as *interpretive*, not because the qualitative researcher develops an interpretation (all researchers do this) but because the focus of qualitative inquiry tends to be on learning how people and groups interpret and thereby gain meaning from their experience. These assumptions and this focus are what align qualitative inquiry with culturally responsive supervision.

In locating the avenues through which this orientation might inform supervision, we will rely on the work that Elliot Eisner (1982, 1985) has done in his efforts to clarify the scope and purpose of qualitative inquiry. Eisner views qualitative inquiry as having two primary components. The first centers on what researchers bring to their work, including cultural patterns of understanding, contextual knowledge, and skills of perception. We will consider this first component in two sections: one focusing on the implicit curriculum of the classroom and the other concerning context. In both cases our intent is to suggest perspectives that facilitate the supervisor's ability to see and hear dimensions of classroom learning that would otherwise remain taken for granted.

The second component of qualitative inquiry Eisner defines as the process of disclosure. It concerns making public what is seen and heard. In the case of supervision, this involves the educational efforts of sharing with teachers whatever insights might have been gained through observations of their teaching. It is achieved through a three-fold process of critical description, interpretation, and evaluation. Critical description seeks in language an expressive equivalence of experience (what the supervisor has learned); interpretation provides for its meaning; and evaluation addresses the question of its significance. While these dimensions of disclosure are clearly interdependent, a consideration of each, later in the chapter in a section titled "Doing Responsive Supervision," will allow us to develop a coherent image of what this approach might look like in practice.

The Search for the Implicit Curriculum

The field of supervision has, by and large, focused not on subject- or discipline-specific methods but rather on approaches and procedures (e.g., clinical supervision) that can be applied across a variety of subject areas. Although we see implications of an ecological and qualitative perspective that are subject-specific, our concerns with curriculum will also cut across subject areas. This is in keeping with the scope of previous chapters.

It is, in any case, the explicit, or advertised, curriculum that most typically defines subject-matter learning. This curriculum includes those intentions that are made explicit through such documents as course descriptions, curriculum guides, and lists of instructional objectives (all of which, of course, are subject-specific). While such intentions are very much relevant to supervision, students in a classroom learn much more than what is in the curriculum guide. This point was made by John Dewey (1938):

> Perhaps the greatest of all pedagogical fallacies is the notion that a person learns only the particular thing he is studying at the time. Collateral learning in the way of formation of enduring attitudes, of likes and dislikes, may be and often is much more important than the spelling lesson

> or lesson in geography or history this is learned. For these attitudes are
> fundamentally what count in the future. (p. 48)

Such "collateral learning" is now often referred to as the implicit curriculum. It is taught not only by teachers and textbooks but also by
the way schools are organized. Its lessons are generally taken for
granted; they include all of the tacit patterns of understanding that
allow teachers and students to make intelligible ordinary, day-to-day
experience.

In this regard, the implicit curriculum encompasses much of
what we have already discussed in relation to the classroom as an
ecology of ideas. The previous chapters on metaphor, nonverbal communication, primary socialization, framing, and the politics of language are each aimed at making explicit some of the cultural patterns
that make up this mental ecology. Rather than repeat those efforts
here, we will instead focus on dimensions of this cultural patterning
that are of special relevance to supervision as a form of inquiry. These
include specifically the multidimensionality of language and the
teacher's gatekeeper role in the classroom.

Understanding how language functions at multiple levels and
through multiple channels contributes to responsive supervision by
bringing into sharp focus the metamessages of classroom interaction.
It is from these metamessages that students learn about the nature of
a specific subject and its relative status. In learning to read and write,
for example, students also learn a tacit way of thinking about what it
means to read and write. If certain metaphors and ways of describing
these activities are used during instruction, students may also be left
with the implicit understanding of language as a conduit; that is, their
task as reader and writer is one of encoding (*putting their* meanings
into words) and decoding (*getting out* the meaning of others). A more
ecologically sensitive curriculum might convey (again through metaphor and ways of speaking) that meaning is not in the text, nor in the
individual, but rather is the *shared* and culturally *interdependent* aspects of their *relationship*. In a similar way, metaphor, nonverbal communication, and framing signal metamessages regarding the relative
status of subjects, as when reading and math are taught only in the
mornings, while storytelling, art and play are tacitly relegated to the
afternoons.

From the metamessages of the classroom, students also learn
what it means to learn, the norms of school life, what forms of knowledge are regarded as legitimate, differences between home and
school, who and what has authority, the nature of thinking and feel-

ing, the value of competition, what it means to be an individual, and so on. Such implicit lessons represent various strands in an intricate web of meaning, each held in place not by messages transmitted from sender (teacher) to receiver (students) but through the ecology of language that characterizes the classroom. The implicit curriculum is thus found in the multiple levels of exchange at which, for example, analogic, generative, and iconic metaphors reproduce cultural patterns of understanding. The high school student who complains that "I've been struggling with this quadratic equation for forty-five minutes!" and the teacher who responds by recommending a different "plan of attack" are talking as much about the background assumptions that frame how to think about algebra as they are about algebra as a rule-governed symbol system. This multidimensionality of language is also seen in the use of nonverbal cues (including proxemics, kinesics, and prosody) that frame messages, in patterns of turn-taking that guide classroom discussions, and in the use of humor as a symbolic mode of expression. These dimensions of language thus serve as primary landmarks for supervisors learning to recognize the implicit lessons of classroom life.

Another approach to this aspect of the supervisor's professional knowledge can be achieved by reconceptualizing the role of classroom teachers. As we think of the classroom as an ecology of relations and patterns, teaching comes to be understood as directed toward "managing" not students but rather the level and quality of intelligence embedded within the classroom as an ecology of ideas. This is the teacher's gatekeeper role in primary socialization.

An understanding of the teacher's gatekeeper role brings forward an array of questions relevant to the supervisor's awareness of implicit classroom learning:

> At the most basic level, how do teachers and texts define what is?
>
> What vocabulary, concepts, and perspectives are made available to students?
>
> How, for example, does this science teacher define science?
>
> How does this definition (encoded in the vocabulary the teacher makes available) serve to establish the boundaries of what will and will not be considered?
>
> Does the teacher supplement the perspectives represented by the text?
>
> Is the teacher able to connect elements of the explicit curriculum to the students' lives inside and outside of school?

Are attempts made to bring forward particular areas of implicit knowledge and cultural presuppositions that would otherwise be taken for granted?

Are students encouraged to assess the ways of thinking encoded in language?

Are they helped to recognize that "the map is not the territory," or are they learning to regard information as simply factual?

Are attempts made to locate information in its historical, political, or social context?

Are written and spoken discourse given equal authority?

Are cross-cultural perspectives introduced?

This list of questions could be extended. Yet its length and diversity already suggests that the teacher's gatekeeper role alone covers an overwhelming number of concerns. The purposes of supervision thus include a need for focus. We view this as largely a matter of what cultural patterns are salient within a given classroom at a particular time. The salience of these patterns, nevertheless, depends not only on what happens in classrooms but also on its significance in terms of student learning. In clarifying questions of significance, the concept of "communicative competence" offers culturally responsive supervisors some guidance. As we have used this term in previous chapters, it calls attention to how classroom experience shapes the students' ability to participate in community life. Informed and active participation involves the abilities to recognize taken-for-granted patterns of understanding as well as the language frameworks that enable students to reconceptualize problematic beliefs and cultural practices in a manner that takes into account new contextual elements. This is the issue of learning to learn, and not all interpretive frameworks are equally powerful as contributors to this process. As Bateson (1972) wrote, "There is an ecology of bad ideas . . . and it is characteristic of the system that basic error propagates itself" (p. 484). Views of the self as the basic unit of survival, of learning as the acquisition of facts, of language as a conduit, of rationality as culture-free, of students as objects of behavior management, and of supervision as technology are, we believe, examples of such basic error.

The Search for Context

A second major dimension of professional knowledge is reflected in the supervisor's ability to contextualize interpretations of classroom interaction. We want to be particularly explicit in how we are using the term *context*, because this term is used in a quite different way by authors who have approached supervision from a technicist orientation. Acheson and Gall (1987), for example, advise the clinical supervisor that:

> You should be alert also to the *context* of the teacher's lesson; for example:
> "The room is warm; wall thermometer reads 78 degrees."
> "Teacher shows map to class. Map is faded. Names of countries are difficult to read."
> "Lesson is interrupted by announcement over intercom."
> "One of the fluorescent lights starts to hum loudly."(p. 121)

As their examples suggest, Acheson and Gall use the term *context* in keeping with their focus on behavior. To put this another way, the contexts of behavior can be understood in terms of how we measure time, space, temperature, and so forth. Yet the contexts of experience are not bounded by such factors. Instead, they are intimately connected with relationships and situations that may be physically far removed from behavior. It is in connection with experience that we will use the term *context*. By doing so we want to bring forward an image of the classroom as an ecology of relationships. The word *ecology*, after all, is commonly used in reference to the study of relationships.

Classroom relationships can be viewed as embedded in a number of contexts. We will briefly consider three: sociocultural, political, and historical. The first is brought into focus by recognizing the classroom as a pluralistic culture in which diverse patterns of understanding and communication are represented along such lines as gender, age, social class, and ethnicity. Perhaps the central issue here, for the purposes of supervision, is that insensitivity to the identity of such groups and the differences in experience they bring to the classroom will only reinforce ethnocentric views whereby those cultural patterns not shared by the teacher or textbook writer come to be disregarded. When such taken-for-granted views are the sole basis for interaction, cultural stereotyping is sustained and relationships proceed on that basis. An example of this can be found in metaphorical language (e.g., the "hard" sciences) that tacitly reinforces stereotypes of gender-specific abilities.

The political context of classroom learning highlights a somewhat different set of concerns, those which focus on power and empowerment. At issue in this context is how the implicit lessons of instruction "structure the field of possibilities" for individuals and cultural groups. This is simply another way of saying that stereotyped thinking holds significant consequences for how students are treated in the classroom and the opportunities they receive for gaining access to the explicit curriculum. Raymond McDermott's (1976) study, cited in Chapter 6, illustrates this point in describing the differential treatment of high- and low-ability reading groups. The political context of instruction also surfaces in how print is given greater authority than the spoken word, thus tacitly reinforcing a content-focused, individualized, and decontextualized approach to learning. The use of humor (e.g., locker-room jokes) that builds solidarity with some students by excluding others is still another dimension of the classroom as an ecology of power. Sensitivity to this political context of language and instruction offers supervisors a perspective from which to conceptualize discourse in ways that redirect it toward empowering both teachers and students as partners in an ongoing dialogue.

The context of classroom relationships may also be expanded to include a historical perspective. All classroom interaction has a history, but in saying so we do not mean what might have occurred yesterday, or last week, or last term in a particular class. As important as this personal history is to teaching, we instead want to focus on the broader implications of what Bateson refers to as the "determinative memory" of any system (e.g., language) that shows mental characteristics. Specifically, we have in mind the question of how elements of classroom discourse (such as the iconic metaphors of "individual," "work," "progress," "learning," "knowledge," and so on) generate patterns of thinking worked out in the past. In similar ways, determinative memory is also represented by patterns of nonverbal communication, the hierarchical organization of schools, and other cues that help frame the explicit curriculum. A key issue for supervisors is whether these historical dimensions of language and subject matter are, at appropriate times, made explicit or whether they remain at an implicit or taken-for-granted level of understanding.

Once again this brings us back to the question of significance in terms of how instructional contexts shape the communicative competence of students and their ability to recognize the sociocultural, political, and historical frameworks that guide relationships. Yet context is also important if teachers and supervisors are to avoid forms of miscommunication that may arise when the cultural diversity of the classroom is ignored. Recall, for example, Michaels and Collins' (1984) description of the teacher who, in failing to recognize the different language styles of her students, pursued strategies that quickly

led to a breakdown in their communication. Finally, context is further
tied to what Basil Bernstein (1971) describes as the development of
"uncommonsense" educational knowledge (p. 58). This concerns the
boundaries between in- and out-of-school ways of knowing. When
the contextual dimensions of the curriculum are neglected (as can be
seen in highly abstract treatments of math, science, art, and so on),
then these boundaries are strengthened, separating classroom learning from the lives of students.

DOING RESPONSIVE SUPERVISION

At this point we turn from the supervisor's professional knowledge to
the process of supervision itself. This process is typically thought of
as a recurrent cycle that includes three phases: preconference, observation, and postconference. In order to align this sequence with the
ecological view we have developed, our task is to reconceptualize it as
a form of qualitative fieldwork. In doing so we will be less concerned
with the exact order of events than with dimensions of inquiry that
inform the total process. Specifically, we will focus on description, interpretation, and evaluation.

Before addressing these specific dimensions of inquiry, we shall
first return to the issue of focus. Our discussion of what supervisors
bring to their work—their ability to recognize the multiple dimensions of language and context—should reinforce the notion that no
one comes to inquiry as a blank slate, regardless of the approach
taken. Yet, at the same time, the sheer number of ways in which cultural patterns are played out in instruction represents far more than
could occupy anyone's conscious awareness from moment to moment. While aspects of culture can be made explicit, we cannot, nor
would we want to, simultaneously focus on all of the implicit knowledge that shapes classroom instruction. Doing so, if it were possible,
would only create total confusion. It is in this regard that cultural renewal is analogous to repairing a ship at sea. If we intend to stay
afloat, we cannot take the ship apart and rebuild it from scratch;
rather we must limit our repairs to only one or two sections at any one
time.

This leaves us with the question of knowing which aspects of culture are, for the supervisor, most worth the efforts required to make
them explicit. In qualitative research, this basic question of focus is a
matter of debate. Some researchers emphasize that the focus of fieldwork should be allowed to emerge inductively from direct observa-

tions. Ethnographers sometimes operate from this premise (see, for example, Agar, 1980). Others stress that perception is by definition selective and that focus is always guided by the interpretive frameworks brought to an observation.

Our perspective suggests that the critical issue involves developing interpretive frameworks that enhance the supervisor's awareness of how cultural patterns are played out in the classroom. In cases where supervisors have not had prolonged experience in recognizing these patterns, a written list of concepts and terms, perhaps arranged thematically, could be useful for reminding them of certain key perspectives during their classroom observations. Three examples are provided in Figures 7.1–7.3. Each is intended to serve as a memory aid. Figure 7.1 illustrates how some of the concerns raised by an ecological perspective might be integrated within the context of a conventional lesson structure. Figures 7.2 and 7.3 provide for a more detailed analysis of instruction. One (Figure 7.2) is focused on primary socialization; the other (Figure 7.3) is focused on metaphor. Additional lists could be developed for nonverbal communication, power and solidarity, culturally specific values, and implicit knowledge.

Again, such lists (which could take a wide variety of forms), include far more "topics" than it would be possible for a supervisor to address unless observations were extended over a considerable period of time. The focus of any particular supervision episode, then, is open to being informed by the salience of patterns observed in a given classroom and their significance in terms of student learning. In observing a civics lesson, for example, the supervisor might note how a generative metaphor such as "the branches of government" guides class discussion and introduces students to a framework for understanding the interdependence of public systems.[1] The role that a generative metaphor plays in providing an initial schema for understanding could then serve as a point of focus for describing the lesson and discussing it with the teacher. Other concepts (such as framing, metacommunication, power and solidarity, and so forth) might also be drawn into this discussion, but the supervisor should not feel compelled to "cover" every cultural dimension of any given classroom interaction.

The reason we emphasize this point is because in supervision, as in teaching, less can be more. A focused discussion of metaphor, humor, turn-taking, kinesics, or reframing that fosters a deep cultural

---

1. We are indebted to Petra Munro for this example.

Figure 7.1 Structure of the Lesson

Teaching often follows an identifiable structure. Although different approaches to learning will influence the structural characteristics (or pattern) of the lesson, certain key elements are generally present. How students are to be involved often depends on how the teacher frames the opening and closing of the lesson, communicates expectations for students, and adjusts teaching style to the flow of classroom events.

A. Introducing the lesson: Framing
1. Clear opening frame that establishes the purpose or context of the lesson
2. Acknowledgment of how the main issues of previous lessons relate to current lesson
3. Overview statements
4. Clarification of how students are expected to participate in the learning experience

B. Teaching the lesson: Matching purpose with appropriate teaching style
1. Use of appropriate examples for clarifying concepts or for modeling student performance
2. Exploration of students' ways of understanding new concepts (use of dialogue)
3. Attendance to different dimensions of primary socialization process (language, tacit knowledge, historical, and cross-cultural perspective)
4. Display of sensitivity to cultural and gender differences among students
5. Orchestration of student participation in a manner that makes all students feel involved

C. Closing the lesson: Reviewing and providing for continuity with next lessons
1. Clear summary of concepts that have been clarified, questions raised, and consensus achieved during lesson
2. Brief overview of how concepts and performances relate to next lessons

understanding of these elements is far more likely to be constructive for teachers and supervisors than a discussion that sacrifices coherence for the sake of coverage. Again, the breadth of taken-for-granted knowledge that guides both teaching and supervision is simply too vast to be made fully explicit within the constraints of any given episode of teacher-supervisor interaction.

We also recognize teachers themselves as a potential source of focus. Another way to put this is that supervisors have much to learn from teachers about what they view as the central concerns of their

Figure 7.2   Primary Socialization

Primary socialization involves a number of professional judgments that are part of introducing students to new concepts or providing a basis (language, schema, etc.) for understanding some aspect of the culture they have learned from previous experience. Culturally responsive supervision involves helping the teacher understand how their decisions in this dynamic process influence student understanding.

A. Controlling language (sharing a conceptual scheme): Vocabulary
   1. Adequacy for representing conceptual complexity of issue or aspect of experience
   2. Clarification of vocabulary being used
   3. Appropriateness to maturity and cultural background of students
   4. Establishment of connections between vocabulary and students' experience
   5. Appropriateness of metaphors in terms of gender and cultural differences

B. Making explicit taken-for-granted (TFG) beliefs
   1. Recognition of TFG beliefs and attitudes in curriculum material
   2. Recognition of TFG beliefs in class discussion
   3. Recognition of teacher's own TFG beliefs that are unconsciously shared
   4. Recognition of TFG beliefs that communicate gender, age, and ethnic biases

C. Putting "facts" in historical perspective
   1. Identification of subjective, cultural dimensions of knowledge
   2. Introduction of historical perspective (social origin of knowledge, facts, etc.)
   3. Introduction of cross-cultural perspective (i.e., how other cultural groups would interpret issues, events, "facts," etc.)

work. Regardless of the prevailing technicist approaches to teacher education and professional development, we view these concerns of practice as closely aligned with an ecological understanding of the classroom. This is suggested, for example, by Peter Karlin's comments in Chapter 5 that focus on the relational dimensions of his day-to-day teaching. They reflect an intuitive understanding of the concerns put into focus by a culturally responsive approach to supervision. In this regard, the supervisor's role is to help teachers develop a vocabulary and frames of reference that acknowledge the ecological dimensions of their professional/practical culture. Qualitative studies of teaching offer a contribution to this effect. Yet the primary lesson we have learned from such research is that the professional culture of

Figure 7.3 Metaphorical Basis of Thought

Robert Frost observed that understanding the nature of metaphorical think-ing, including when it provides a basis for new understanding and when the metaphor breaks down, is an essential part of the teacher's knowledge. Understanding a new concept or experience is dependent on relating it to the familiar—which is the essence of metaphorical thinking. In addition to this process of analogic thinking, there are two categories of metaphor—root and iconic—that play important roles in providing a basis (schema) of under-standing.

A. Using metaphor to introduce new concepts: *Analogic thinking* (under-standing the new in terms of the familiar)
   1. Appropriateness of generative metaphor
   2. Explanation of the dissimilarities between what is being compared
   3. Recognition of the "as if" dimension of metaphorical thinking
   4. Relevance of generative metaphor (reference point for understand-ing new concept) to student experience
   5. Avoidance of a cultural or gender bias in generative metaphor

B. Recognizing the role of *iconic metaphor* in reproducing past ways of understanding
   1. Avoidance of a pattern, or schema, for thinking that is now out-moded
   2. Placement of iconic metaphor in historical context
   3. Recognition of how iconic metaphor encodes a culture- or gender-specific way of thinking

C. Making explicit *root metaphors* as cultural worldview or paradigm
   1. Explanation of how patterns of thinking, including taken-for-granted assumptions, are grounded in root metaphors
   2. Introduction of a cross-cultural comparison into discussion in order to make root metaphor explicit
   3. Appropriateness of root metaphors used for understanding current problems

teaching is anything but monolithic (Feiman-Nemser & Floden, 1986). This is an important point because it suggests that supervision must rely on receptive modes of inquiry, such as "ethnographic monitor-ing," if its aim is to alert supervisors both to their own cultural presup-positions and to the often subtle ways in which teachers communicate their professional cultures. The first issue is a matter of guarding against stereotyped images of teaching that supervisors bring to their work. The second is a matter of developing a sensitivity to the teach-er's world that will guide the supervisor in knowing when and what questions to ask.

In summary, culturally responsive supervisors do not approach their work empty headed. They begin, rather, with professional knowledge and skills that are grounded in an understanding of the classroom as an ecology of language, culture, and thought. Still, they do not know at the outset exactly what they will learn from observing and interacting with a particular teacher. In practical terms, this is how we view the purpose of supervision as a form of fieldwork. It is foremost a process of learning.

If we continue this line of reasoning, the active nature of this role brings us back to the task of reconceptualizing supervision as a form of qualitative inquiry. At this point, we can further clarify the dimensions of qualitative inquiry by focusing on description, interpretation, and evaluation. Throughout the process of supervision, these processes are interdependent. In considering them, therefore, we will give particular attention to how each one informs and is informed by the other two.

Description

Descriptive accounts in qualitative inquiry are drawn from a number of sources. They include the observer's fieldnotes, audio recordings, interview notes, sample text materials, lesson plans, video tapes, and so forth. These in themselves are descriptive accounts in that they represent perspectives on instruction. They can be shared outside of the immediate context in which they were made, or they can be fashioned by the observer into some form of report. In qualitative inquiry, specific forms of report range widely from ethnographies and case studies (which are perhaps most common) to what Sara Lawrence Lightfoot (1983) terms "school portraiture" and a form that Elliot Eisner (1985) calls "educational criticism." These various genres are distinctive in their focus and methods, but the central concern of each is to render observations in the form of a story, narrative, or vignette. Examples of short vignettes include the description of Susan Krebs that introduces Chapter 1 or the account of Richard Dodds' lesson on "work" that begins Chapter 2. Such brief vignettes may be particularly appropriate to supervision given the limited resources (particularly time) with which supervisors often work. Reports may also take the form of verbal descriptions that supervisors provide teachers, typically at some point after a period of classroom observation.

We have already considered how interpretive frameworks serve to focus the supervisor's perceptions of classroom life. These same considerations apply to processes of description with equal force. Frederick Erickson (1986), for example, writes:

Even the most richly detailed vignette is a reduced account, clearer than
life. Some features are selected in from the tremendous complexity of
the original event (which as we have already seen contains more information bits than any observer could attend to and note down in the first
place, let alone report later) and other features are selected out of the
narrative report. (p. 150)

The metaphorical nature of language is particularly useful in understanding this process of selection and focus. Metaphors such as
"classroom management," "diagnostic testing," "homework," "individualized instruction," "engaged academic learning time," "off-
task," "behavioral reinforcement," and "teacher productivity" not
only mirror reality but also generate broadly based patterns for
understanding what it means to teach. The point we wish to emphasize, however, is that such interpretive frameworks not only inform
what gets into a description and what gets left out; they also inform
how teaching and learning are described. The metaphorical way of
thinking about language as a conduit, for example, will direct the supervisor toward the purpose of transmitting explicit messages
through discursive, propositional statements such as: "Nine students, or one-third of the class, remained on task throughout the
work period," "The teacher's lesson lasted a total of twenty-eight minutes," "The teacher provided verbal praise to sixteen different students at the overall rate of twenty per hour," "The focus of the lesson
was on identifying topic sentences," "The teacher called on individual
students by name seven times during the 50-minute observation period," or "The teacher checked for student understanding three times
during the first fifteen minutes of instruction."

Such propositional language tells us something about the behavior of teachers and students. It is also interpretive and evaluative, regardless of whether the supervisor recognizes it, because in addition
to telling us about behavior, its propositional form communicates metamessages about the purposes of supervision, the teacher's status,
and what dimensions of teaching are worth consideration. Such metamessages, in practice, arise from the very dimensions of language
put into focus by the cultural understanding that we have advocated
as central to the supervisor's professional knowledge. This understanding informs description in two ways. First, it shifts the focus of
description from behavior to the cultural frameworks through which
experience is constituted. It does so by bringing forward the cultural
patterns of thought that give behavior (e.g., praise, time on task, the
use of questions) some meaning for teachers and students. Second, a

cultural understanding of language moves description into a tradition in which discursive propositions become only one of many elements that play into the telling of a story. This underscores the power of metaphor, tone, voice, diction, connotative meaning, imagery, alliteration, and other cues that contribute to the framing of written and spoken messages.

Such expressive forms used in qualitative description are, like propositional language, both interpretive and evaluative. They highlight certain dimensions of classroom experience and signal the metamessage that these dimensions are in some way significant. Nevertheless, from the perspective of responsive supervision, our main point concerns the ability of supervisors to develop frameworks that foster their recognition and explication of these metamessages. This raises issues that are centrally involved with the interpretive dimensions of inquiry.

Interpretation

Interpretation is a matter of how observations come to be made intelligible. This is done not so much by individual observers as it is by the cultural patterns of understanding brought to an observation. We have already (in the previous two sections) discussed interpretive frameworks that provide supervisors with a perspective from which they may recognize these cultural patterns and, at times, make them explicit. At this point, therefore, we will simply illustrate this perspective within the context of supervision. Consider, for example, the experience of a supervisor, Karen Adler, in the process of observing a high school English teacher, Glen Watson. Glen's class includes thirty sophomores, two of whom are international exchange students from Japan. The supervisor notes that Glen begins his class by approaching the two exchange students, who are sitting together in the front, right-hand side corner of the classroom. He asks these students to work on an essay during the class period. Glen then takes roll, turns to the class as a whole, and begins a discussion on a novel that the students have just finished reading. Throughout this discussion, which at times becomes quite animated, the Japanese students work independently on their own assignment.

This description briefly summarizes what Karen has recorded in her fieldnotes. She now faces the question of what significance, if any, this descriptive accounts holds for coming to a better understanding of Glen's teaching. It is at this point that the supervisor's interpretive frameworks are most clearly at work. If, for example, Karen assumes a sociocultural understanding of language, as opposed to the conduit view, this perspective will bring forward the tacit cultural patterns and taken-for-granted presupposition on which classroom interaction is based. This would allow Karen to consider at an explicit level the teacher's strategy of giving the exchange students separate assignments as a communicative act in and of itself. Another way to put this is that a cultural understanding of language raises the question of what metamessages are signaled by Glen's actions in this particular case.

Such metamessages, as we have discussed in previous chapters, are open to different interpretations by those involved in the interaction. The teacher in our example might well interpret his own actions as an expression of regard for his students. That is, Glen may wish to assure that his two exchange students receive individualized assistance, and having them work apart from the rest of the class facilitates this. Moreover, Glen may be unsure of the students' spoken English abilities (they do, after all, seem very quiet), and he thus does not want to risk their participation in class discussions for fear that it will, for them, lead to embarrassing situations. With further observations, the supervisor notes that Glen attempts tacitly to signal this metamessage of support not simply by making special assignments but also by nonverbal cues, such as standing close to the two students when giving directions, smiling, and maintaining direct eye contact. The two students, however, might well interpret quite different metamessages from Glen's actions and nonverbal cues. Being singled out for special treatment might be understood within their cultural patterns of experience as a form of rebuke, signaling a metamessage that the teacher lacks confidence in their abilities to contribute to group activities. Cultural patterns also influence whether Glen's nonverbal cues of smiling and maintaining eye contact are understood in terms of rapport or reprimand. In considering these possibilities, Karen's mind is brought back to a proverb she once learned from a Japanese friend: The nail that sticks up is the one that's hit.

In this particular example, the teacher may or may not be aware of the cultural patterns of thought that shape how his actions and nonverbal cues will be understood and the potential for miscommunication that differences in these patterns introduce. Nurturing such an awareness is, as we see it, a central aim of supervision. Karen might do so in a number of ways: by introducing a cross-cultural perspective; by calling Glen's attention to particular aspects of nonverbal communication; or by discussing how metamessages, unlike written and spoken messages, comment on classroom relationships. Here,

Karen's foremost consideration is to make explicit her own interpretive frameworks—specifically, those relevant to a sociocultural understanding of language—for this process allows supervisors to offer teachers not only insight into otherwise hidden dimensions of classroom experience but also new ways of seeing and hearing. This simply restates the educational function of culturally responsive supervision.

Our example further helps us recognize how interpretive frameworks are informed, on one side, by direct observations of teachers, including the salient patterns of interaction that characterize what goes on in a particular classroom. Yet, on the other side, it may be less clear how interpretation is informed by the evaluative (and political) dimensions of inquiry. In making these dimensions a bit more explicit, we want to point out that all forms of inquiry are evaluative in at least two distinct ways. First, the methods of inquiry are in themselves actions and, as such, they signal metamessages regarding the nature and value of whatever is being researched. For example, methods that rely exclusively on counting the frequency of prespecified teacher behaviors reduce teaching to a sequence of discrete, isolated tasks and thereby tacitly signal the value and relative status of teaching as a profession. Second, methods prefigure the focus of an inquiry and thus "structure a field of possibilities." This also signals metamessages regarding what is valued and what is not. The time-on-task research, to take one example, tells teachers less about classroom learning than it does about what researchers believe to be important.

Evaluation

Supervision is evaluative in similar ways. The approach and methods a supervisor adopts in observing and conferring with teachers serve to frame what concerns are to be regarded as legitimate. Another way to put this is that supervisors, regardless of their approach, do not seek understanding simply for the sake of understanding. Instead, their work aspires in some way to improve teaching.

Some of the specific evaluative questions addressed in supervision include: What is the significance of educational experience in this classroom? What is being learned? And what are the consequences of this learning? As we have argued earlier, much of what is learned in the classroom, in the way of cultural patterns, is learned at a taken-for-granted level of awareness. In our previous example, the evaluative issues thus concern what Glen's two exchange students learned from working independently. This includes not only an explicit curriculum—how to write an essay—but also an implicit curriculum that holds lessons about learning as individually centered, about school expectations, and about "being different." These implicit lessons may or may not be problematic, depending on how consistently these students are treated as special and their interpretations of Glen's nonverbal cues. It is in this sense, we might note, that evaluation is informed by description and interpretation. Our main point, however, concerns the supervisor's sensitivity—first in identifying these implicit lessons of instruction and second in recognizing their consequences for how students and teachers understand the ecology of learning in which they participate.

This is important because not all of the learning that takes place in classrooms is educational in the sense of promoting communicative competence or the ability to recognize the deep cultural patterns of experience and the interconnections between language and thought. Bateson (1972) provides an example of such miseducational learning:

> When you narrow down your epistemology and act on the premise: "What interests me is me, or my organization, or my species," you chop off consideration of other loops of the loop structure. You decide that you want to get rid of the by-products of human life and that Lake Erie will be a good place to put them. You forget that the eco-mental system called Lake Erie is a part of *your* wider eco-mental system—and that if Lake Erie is driven insane, its insanity is incorporated in the larger system of *your* thought and experience. (p. 484)

Both explicit and implicit classroom learning can contribute to the type of thinking and actions that Bateson describes. As examples, we could cite the use of such metaphors as "wilderness," "genetic engineering," and "homework," or the biology student who is ridiculed by classmates for being squeamish at the prospect of dissecting a live specimen. Once again this takes us back to the supervisor's cultural understanding of metaphor, the teacher's role in primary socialization, patterns of turn-taking, the use of humor, and so forth.

As an additional consideration, we wish to emphasize that the consequences of instruction follow not only from what is learned explicitly and implicitly but also from what is not learned. Elliot Eisner (1985) makes this point in reference to the "null" curriculum—that which schools fail to teach. He writes:

> It is my thesis that what schools do not teach may be as important as what they do teach. I argue this position because ignorance is not simply a neutral void; it has important effects on the kinds of options

one is able to consider, the alternatives that one can examine, and the perspectives from which one can view a situation or problem. (p. 97)

This way of thinking should serve to alert teachers and supervisors to perspectives, concepts, images, and vocabulary that both are and are not made available through instruction. For example, students who are taught history as a collection of facts, science as value-neutral, and language as a conduit are not likely to learn the frameworks and vocabulary that would allow them to reconceptualize these politically and historically grounded patterns of understanding. The consequences of such a null curriculum are played out in terms of stereotyped thinking, miscommunication, sexist attitudes, and passive acceptance of an environmentally damaging lifestyle.

Awareness of Cultural Patterns

In considering above the interdependence of description, interpretation, and evaluation, we have placed our main emphasis on the supervisor's ability to recognize the tacit cultural patterns that guide day-to-day classroom interaction. Once again, it is in this context that metaphor, nonverbal communication, framing, primary socialization, and the politics of language offer powerful frameworks for learning. The supervisor's role, nevertheless, is one of both learner and teacher. In the context of the latter, educational functions of supervision, what becomes critical is the ability of supervisors to make explicit the interpretive frameworks (metaphor, etc.) that shape their own patterns of understanding. Like the cultural patterns of classroom life, those that guide supervision typically remain below the level of explicit awareness.

This issue has drawn close attention in qualitative inquiry, where the assumed interdependence between observer and observed makes the interpretive frameworks of the observer one of the focal points of inquiry. In describing ethnographic methods, for example, Michael H. Agar (1980) writes:

The problem is not whether the ethnographer is biased; the problem is what kinds of biases exist—how do they enter into ethnographic work and how can their operation be documented. By bringing as many of them to consciousness as possible, an ethnographer can try to deal with them as part of methodology and can acknowledge them when drawing conclusions during analysis. In this sense, ethnography truly is a personal discipline as well as a professional one. (pp. 41–42)

We would argue that ethnography is a cultural as well as personal and professional discipline, but the level of awareness that Agar calls for is the main point, not only for ethnography but for any genre of social inquiry. It can be thought of as another aspect of "ethnographic monitoring," in this case directed toward the observer's cultural and professional background.

Alan Peshkin (1988) addresses how this form of ethnographic monitoring applies to his own fieldwork in a multiethnic high school. He argues, persuasively, that simply acknowledging the subjective nature of inquiry is of little benefit unless researchers are willing systematically to seek out their own cultural perspectives throughout the entire inquiry process. Peshkin's own strategy for doing so involved monitoring his affective reactions to whatever he observed in the field. As he puts this, "I looked for the warm and cool spots, the emergence of positive and negative feelings, the experiences I wanted more of or wanted to avoid, and when I felt moved to act in roles beyond those necessary to fulfill my research needs" (p. 18). In such cases, Peshkin recorded his reactions on notecards, and this record then became a source of information about the cultural values and presuppositions that guide his work. It is interesting to note that even the brief examples that Peshkin offers suggest the diverse complexity of the cultural perspectives from which he views education. This should caution fieldworkers, for the danger of applying stereotypes to one's own cultural patterns of understanding is equal to that of applying stereotypes to the cultural patterns of others.

Such monitoring strategies, although highly useful, must be coupled with a cultural understanding of language and the professional ecology of researchers (or supervisors). It is this linkage that fosters their communicative competence. This is doubly important in supervision, where the ability to recognize the deep cultural patterns of learning is both the process and product of inquiry.

GETTING THINGS RIGHT

Any form of inquiry includes a concern for avoiding mistakes and misinterpretations, assuring that one's inferences are well grounded, or simply "getting things right." In supervision, such concern may be augmented when the goal of this process is to inform hiring and promotion decisions. In part this might explain why, as Sergiovanni (1987) puts it, "Dominant models of supervision and teaching emphasize uniform answers to problems, value-free strategies, separation of process from context, objectivity, and a uniform-technical language system" (p. 224). What we are suggesting is Raymond Callahan's (1962) vulnerability thesis. Specifically, claims to objectivity protect supervisors by obscuring the political and evaluative dimensions of their work. In doing so, the difficulties of recognizing cultural bias are addressed by denying its influence.

Such models (e.g., clinical supervision) have taken their lead from conventional quantitative research, where "getting things right" is foremost a matter of *validity*, as that term is defined in a technical sense to mean objective or free of bias. This perspective could be termed procedural validity, for it relies primarily on methods that are intended to maintain a strict separation between observer and observed. But our intent is to reconceptualize supervision as a form of interpretive inquiry, and validity in this paradigm means something quite different from what is suggested by conventional approaches to research. It is neither procedural nor dependent on the observer's self-extrication, but rather more outcome oriented in its focus on the development of insight. Here we might paraphrase Agar's comments, cited earlier, in arguing that validity is not concerned with whether observers (e.g., responsive supervisors) are biased, but with their ability to recognize and make explicit whatever cultural biases are most relevant to the contexts of their work. It is this that serves the development of insight by highlighting the interconnections between language and thought, the cultural diversity of the classroom, and the tacit metamessages of nonverbal communication.

Another approach to understanding this notion of validity is to consider supervision from the teacher's perspective. Given this approach, valid supervision is that which teachers find telling or informative. It broadens or deepens their understanding of what they are about as professionals, or it provides them with a vocabulary for articulating knowledge that would have otherwise gone unrecognized. Sometimes this comes as a flash of insight that allows teachers to make sense of what was previously regarded as a loose collection of disparate experiences. At other times it is a slow, arduous process of learning to recognize bits and pieces of habituated response patterns. Yet when either process is nurtured by supervision, teachers are likely to feel that the supervisor is "getting things right."

Rather than risk confusion between this conception of validity and its technical meaning in statistical and experimental research, some qualitative researchers argue that the term *validity* should simply not be used in the various genres of interpretive inquiry. Harry Wolcott (in press) makes this argument, suggesting that the term *understanding* might serve as a suitable replacement. By *understanding*, he refers specifically to "the power to make experience intelligible by applying concepts and categories" (p. 25). Procedural techniques alone cannot lead directly to such power. Still, Wolcott does describe nine heuristic considerations that he, as an ethnographer, has found useful in doing fieldwork. We have summarized these below as we understand them, recognizing that some more than others are applicable to responsive supervision:

1. Do more listening than talking in the field.
2. Record fieldnotes during observations or as soon as possible thereafter.
3. Take your time.
4. In recording descriptive accounts, let those you observe "speak for themselves" as much as possible.
5. Remember that you cannot and do not understand everything.
6. Do not hesitate to put yourself (your voice) squarely into descriptive accounts.
7. Share descriptive accounts with others who are knowledgeable.
8. Use subsequent observations to check the balance, fairness, completeness, and sensitivity of descriptive accounts.
9. Give close attention to details in revising descriptive accounts.

These considerations are useful in capturing some of the practical dimensions of observing, describing, and conferring with classroom teachers about their work. It is, nevertheless, the issue of understanding that is most central to our task of reconceptualizing supervision as a form of qualitative inquiry.

If we return for a moment to Wolcott's definition of *understanding* as the power to make experience intelligible, this perspective allows us to recast the supervisor's role in terms of the same issues that we previously considered in connection with primary socialization. While our earlier considerations of primary socialization focused on the teacher's gatekeeper role, we now turn to the supervisor's gatekeeper role in mediating a curriculum for professional development. Doing so will serve as a way to summarize some of our main points.

First, the supervisor's approach and methods participate in defining "What Is," for they are guided by presuppositions that constitute the boundaries for what will be considered and communicated throughout the process of supervision. Recognizing and negotiating these boundaries involves foremost a cultural understanding of supervision that sensitizes supervisors to the metamessages communicated by nonverbal cues (e.g., supervision methods as well as the supervisor's gestures, facial expressions, tone of voice, dress) and to patterns of thought generated by metaphor. The supervisor, for example, who describes students as "on-task" or a lesson as well "delivered" is speaking metaphorically, and these metaphors themselves guide both patterns of thought and teacher-supervisor relationships. A cultural understanding of supervision should also alert supervisors to possible differences between the supervisor's world (professional culture) and that of the teacher. This is one area in which qualitative classroom research can inform supervision by breaking down stereotyped images of teachers and teaching. Such images are highly problematic in supervision, because they create the potential for misinterpretation and miscommunication on both sides. In practical terms, avoiding this requires that the supervisor adopt a language that is meaningful to teachers and relevant to their professional lives.

Second, the supervisor's gatekeeper role involves recognizing moments when it is appropriate to bring forward particular elements of implicit classroom knowledge by introducing cross-cultural comparisons, historical perspectives, examples of metacommunication, and so forth. This basic issue of focus highlights the supervisor's judgment in assessing the quality of intelligence encoded in the classroom as a mental ecology. In this context, the supervisor's professional training might offer significant contributions toward fostering informed assessments on the part of supervisors and their ability to recognize the connections between the mental ecology of the classroom and the communicative competence of students. Yet such contributions are possible only if the supervisor's professional training is grounded in a cultural rather than merely technical understanding of supervision.

Finally, the supervisor's gatekeeper role in primary socialization brings into sharp focus the interpretive frameworks that guide classroom observations and teacher-supervisor interactions. When such frameworks are ignored or put out of focus by claims to objectivity, conferring with teachers is likely to assume a transmission model in which the supervisor is viewed as a "mirror of *actual* teaching" and the teacher is viewed as a passive receiver of factual information. Casting the teacher and supervisor in these roles signals important metamessages regarding their relationship and relative status. In contrast, if we rethink supervision as a form of interpretive inquiry, the supervisor's frameworks and cultural patterns of understanding become a part of the inquiry process. Understood as interpretation, the supervisor's contribution is in many ways less concerned with getting *things* right than it is concerned with getting *relationships* right. Among other issues, this suggests that teacher-supervisor interactions are more culturally interdependent and less inherently unequal than suggested by the "transmission" metaphor. The practical implications of this view stress the importance of supervisors' making clear the interpretive nature of their work. In doing so at the outset of supervision, they would avoid many of the Cartesian presuppositions that have long guided the conventional models of their work and at the same time reaffirm the teacher's role as an educator.

CHAPTER 8

Afterword:
Educating Teachers for the
Twenty-first Century

In their summary of research findings on "Teacher Behavior and Student Achievement" (1986), Jere E. Brophy and Thomas L. Good reached an important conclusion about the simplistic thinking that links, in deterministic fashion, teacher behavior to student achievement.

> The data reviewed here should make it clear that . . . what constitutes effective instruction (even if attention is restricted to achievement as the sole outcome of interest) varies with context. What appears to be just the right amount of demandingness (or structuring of content, or praise, etc.) for one class might be too much for a second class but not enough for a third class. Even within the same class, what constitutes effective instruction will vary according to subject matter, group size, and the specific instructional objectives being pursued. (p. 370)

What they recommend for the education of teachers—to provide a conceptual basis for interpreting the multiple levels of message exchanges that characterize the context of the classroom and to learn to adapt their style of teaching accordingly—is part of what we have attempted to address in the previous chapters.

The importance of taking into account the context of the classroom as an essential aspect of professional decision making is one of the main reasons we have been critical of classroom management techniques and teaching strategies that are often represented in teacher education textbooks as having universal applicability. As we have attempted to show, each classroom ecology involves patterns of thought and communication (behavior being just one channel of communication) that are influenced by the primary culture of both students and the teacher as well as other cultural factors relating to age, gender, social class, and so forth. Personal idiosyncrasies relating to mood, style of humor, and ways of thinking and responding to the myriad events that characterize interpersonal life in school and the larger society are also part of classroom ecology. It is important to recognize that this aspect of the classroom ecology cannot be explained entirely in terms of cultural patterns. Our emphasis on developing a broad conceptual foundation for recognizing how thought and behavior in the classroom are, in part, expressions of shared cultural patterns suggests our concern that the context of the classroom not be viewed as too fluid and relative to warrant teachers' having any professional knowledge base other than a knowledge of their subject area and management techniques.

Concern about basing the education of teachers on a way of thinking that separates the learning of behavioral management and teaching techniques from contextual considerations is not, however, the only reason for our attempt to sketch out a more culturally sensitive approach to understanding the classroom. We think that in the immediate years ahead there will be an increasing awareness that the twenty-first century will not present the same challenges that have been the major preoccupations in the West over the last several hundred years. The main concerns will not be how to expand personal freedom or the challenge of developing technologies that will extend even further a material sense of progress. Nor are they likely to be connected with the need to store and process the mountains of data that are supposed to characterize the new "information age" society. Yes, there will be a need to develop new technologies, including the use of computers. But we suspect that the overriding concern will be with repairing the damage to the ecosystems caused by the Western mindset and with responding to the resulting disruptions in the fabric of cultural life. We should say here that we will be fortunate as a society if these become our major preoccupations in the early years of the next century, as it is entirely possible that we will continue to be driven by the Enlightenment patterns of thought and behavior that were based on the assumption that rationally (technologically) based progress offers an ever-expanding horizon of material and personal opportunities. Misunderstanding the basic problem, which has to do with a culture that disrupts the natural systems in a manner that diminishes the prospects of the next generation, might lead to more conflict between social groups within society and between societies. This would be the worst scenario.

Before explaining why we think the Cartesian/management approach to the education of teachers will not help foster a form of education appropriate for the next century, and why an approach based on a Batesonian way of thinking may be part of the solution, we want to lay out more carefully some dimensions of the growing ecological crisis. The "evidence" of disruption and failure of natural systems should not be viewed as grounded in a complete understanding, as many of the variables are now only partly understood. We have no reliable analogues for understanding the full consequences of disrupting natural systems that are integrated on a global scale. Nor can there be any totally adequate estimations of future ecological damage caused by current and past cultural practices, partly because the taken-for-granted attitude toward our cultural practices has desensitized us until now from considering their impact on the environment. The use of chlorofluorocarbons serves as a good example of not being able to recognize the ecological consequences of cultural practices that seem at the time to serve useful purposes. The use of this family of chemicals seemed useful as a propellant for aerosol spray cans and efficient refrigerants; no one at the time foresaw the damaging effects these compounds would have on the ozone layer. Since a nearly endless list of similar examples could be cited, it is important to view the following discussion of the ecological crisis as only a preliminary understanding of the challenges we will have to meet in the next century.

THE ECOLOGICAL CRISIS

In a recent report of the Worldwatch Institute, Lester Brown and Sandra Postel (1987) summarize the known evidence that points to an accelerating rate of change in atmospheric chemistry, soil composition and fertility, global temperature patterns, and the abundance of living species. The changes suggest that critical thresholds in the life-sustaining characteristics of natural systems may have already been crossed. In other instances the data are less conclusive, but the consequences that would result if the current rates of change continue are too enormous to be ignored by policy makers, educators, and others concerned with achieving a sustainable relationship between the world's cultures and the ecosystem.

Recent exploitation of fisheries, forest lands, and aquifers can be fairly precisely calculated in terms of when a critical threshold has been crossed that leads to a downward spiral in the system's ability to regenerate itself. Other natural systems are more difficult to understand, partly because of their complex interdependence with other natural systems and because of their global scale. But a pattern is clearly visible. The rising atmospheric levels of carbon dioxide, which are related both to the use of certain technologies and to the rapid depletion of plant life, suggest a global warming trend that could raise ocean levels, change weather patterns, and radically alter food production. A study of warming trends in recent history (1860–1984) found that the three warmest years were 1981, 1982, and 1983. Analysis of air trapped in glaciers indicates that the level of carbon dioxide in the atmosphere has also significantly increased, with a 21 percent increase from 1860 to 1958 and a 9 percent rise from 1958 to 1984. Brown and Postel (1987) note that when the amount of carbon dioxide released into the atmosphere is "above the rate at which it could be assimilated by natural systems, we have crossed one threshold" (p. 7).

The occurrence of vast fires in tropical rainforests (where the moisture level is supposed to be too high for vegetation to burn) and the rapid spread of forest damage in Central Europe suggest that we may be crossing other critical environmental thresholds. The Worldwatch report notes, for example, that in West Germany yellowing and loss of foliage represented an 8 percent loss of the nation's trees in 1982, with the percentage of tree loss moving to 34 percent in 1983 and 50 percent in 1984. While the burning of fossil fuels is believed to be behind the forest damage in Central Europe, and the crossing of acidification thresholds in lakes and soils is the cause of damage that can only be reversed over a long period of time and at great expense, other damage to the ecosystem is caused by varied cultural practices. In India, to cite an example, 380 million cattle, sheep, and goats—along with the human need for firewood—have reduced vegetation and forest cover by 16 percent over an eight-year period. The rapid destruction of tropical rainforests is yet another example of human disruption of a delicately balanced ecosystem.

THE WESTERN VIEW OF PROGRESS

The rapid growth in human population is part of the problem—the world's population has increased from 1.6 billion in 1900 to 2.5 billion in 1950 to 5.0 billion in 1986. But cultural values and ways of thinking are also a critically important factor. Although non-Western cultural practices have led to devastating disruptions of the environment—particularly in North Africa—Western cultures, particularly those perceived as the most advanced in the development of modern science and technology, are based on a root metaphor (worldview) that represents humans as not interdependent with the natural systems. Instead the environment has been viewed as a resource to be exploited and, in more progressive circles, to be "managed." At various times in modern Western history, the image of the environment has shifted from being understood in mechanistic terms, which allowed for control through technological intervention, to being understood as an economic resource with vast empty spaces into which we could dump our garbage and dangerous pollutants.

This Western mindset has another characteristic that relates to the accelerating rate of ecological damage. John Berger (1979), in his study of the difference between peasant culture and what he terms the "cultures of Progress," observes a basic difference in understanding the future and thus in assessing the meaning and purposes by which the modern Western individual determines success. The peasant, he notes, "views the future as a sequence of repeated acts of survival" (p. 204). Because they have lived economically marginal existences (due in part to the unpredictability of the natural environment), peasants developed a "conservativism not of power, but of meaning . . . preserved from lives and generations threatened by continual and inexorable change" (p. 208). The modern Western mindset, in contrast, views the future in terms of an ever-widening expansion of economic development, technological possibilities, and personal freedoms. What were at one time the luxuries of a small, exploitive social class have become, in terms of the more recently democratized culture of progress, the necessities of everyday life—even when this unlimited need for consumerism has increased the burden of work, reduced the parenting of children, and now imperils the environment with waste materials.

A problem directly related to the findings of the Worldwatch Institute is that this view of progress is being increasingly adopted throughout the world by the elite educated classes (often with degrees from Western universities), who are dedicated to the modernization of their societies. That this process of modernization is too often based on an erroneous understanding of technology and science as being culturally neutral is not the primary issue in terms of this discussion. Rather, the part of the problem we want to focus on here is the paradox whereby increases in material living standards, particularly when based on Western technologies, contribute to the deterioration of the natural systems upon which all forms of life depend. According to Brown and Postel, this paradox confronts us with the challenge of redefining how we think about progress in a manner that takes account of the quality of life that will be available for future generations:

> A sustainable future calls upon us simultaneously to arrest carbon dioxide buildup, protect the ozone layer, restore forests and soils, stop population growth, boost energy efficiency, and develop renewable energy resources. No generation has ever faced such a complex set of issues requiring immediate attention. Preceding generations have always been concerned about the future, but we are the first to be faced with decisions that will determine whether the earth our children inherit will be habitable. (1987, p. 213)

Adjusting cultural patterns around the world in order to achieve ecological balance will be an enormously difficult task, perhaps even more difficult than the politics of world peace. The uneven distribution of wealth, as well as the long tradition of treating Third World countries as suppliers of low-cost natural resources used to sustain the energy-intensive technologies and seemingly unlimited consumerism of Western societies, will cause many to view the concern about the ecological crisis as a thinly veiled attempt to deny them the opportunity to improve their living standard. As the historian Donald Worster (1985) observes: "It is ironic to find the [ecology] movement's strongest appeal among the Anglo-American middle class. This has been well noted, with not a little indignation, by the would-be middle classes of the world. Many have asked: Is the message of ecology a sermon on the virtues of poverty, to be heeded only by those who are still have-nots?" (p. 342). Can the United States, for example, which now produces 23 percent of global carbon dioxide emissions, really be expected to make the adjustments in thought processes and value orientation necessary to the development of a culture that is in ecological balance? This would constitute, as Worster notes, the overturning of the premises upon which the Industrial Revolution was based; in effect, it would represent the abandonment of the middle-class vision of unlimited economic prosperity and technological progress.

Suspicion about hidden interests is further compounded by what leading politicians in the United States view as the primary threat facing the nation. As reported in *State of the World 1987* (Brown & Wolf, 1987), "The largest international scientific collaboration in the world today is not the Global Change study, from which all nations could benefit, but the U.S. Strategic Defense Initiative or Star Wars program" (p. 199). In addition to the $9 billion already spent, another $33 billion is to be allocated to support basic research and development through 1991. For the teacher in the classroom, the contradictions and wastefulness of international politics may seem far removed from the concerns of everyday life, except as "newsbites" on nightly television. But while seemingly distant from the teacher's world, the mindset that guides the setting of national priorities will nevertheless have an impact on the resources made available to support public education. It will also influence what is perceived as the educational priorities that must be addressed in order to avoid "risk" to the nation.

Perhaps more important, at least in terms of our discussion of an ecological approach to the classroom, is the fact that the mindset that guides the nation's policy decisions in a way that is largely blind to the growing ecological crisis is also the mindset shared by teachers and writers of textbooks and software—as well as by other segments of population who have been educated in public institutions. To state the problem as it exists at the local level, where the young are going through the most vulnerable period of enculturation, the mindset that will be the basis for many people's—particularly those in teaching roles—understanding the problems of the twenty-first century is the same mindset that underlies the cultural practices that are so ecologically damaging. In effect, the major problem we face within our own culture is the double-bind whereby we cannot readily conceptualize the new patterns and practices that are ecologically sustainable because we are unconscious prisoners of the old patterns of thought. The old patterns, for most of us, are simply part of a taken-for-granted sense of reality—an aspect of "determinative memory," to recall Bateson's phrase, that causes us to think of the future in terms of assumptions and categories that were formulated in the past as a response to an even earlier problematic set of conditions.

This problem of being bound by thought patterns of the past is directly related to the constitutive role that metaphor plays in the thought process, which was the central theme of Chapter 2. The metaphorical language that characterizes the form of modern thinking that views the natural world as a resource to be managed, and material-technological progress as unlimited, has its roots in the analogic thinking of the sixteenth and seventeenth centuries. As we discussed in Chapter 4, Descartes helped establish the belief in pure thought and perception—uninfluenced by the biases of tradition, culture, and language—that is now a cornerstone of mainstream technocratic thinking. The model of thinking that has come down to us, and is ironically represented as modern, involves a reductionist way of thinking wherein the "privileged representations" can be objectively known through observation and measurement. The analogue of the individual as like an objective observer who views the world of motion and extension became encoded in the metaphorical image of the autonomously rational individual and the Cartesian belief that ideas are only as good as the data. This image of the rational process separates the "individual" not only from the influence of cultural traditions (including language) but also from nature.

Descartes not only helped lay the foundations for a new way of knowing, wherein the knower is radically separated from the known; he also contributed to the formative stage of another line of analogic thinking that connects knowledge with power over nature. His argument that knowledge of the technologies of artisans and the forces of bodies would "render ourselves the masters and processors of nature" (1637/1955, p. 119) was further strengthened by Francis Bacon's successful attempt to represent science as a means of controlling and perfecting nature for human ends. The unity of knowledge and power were to be experienced through the new form of scientific knowledge. It not only liberated the scientific and modern thinker from the earlier ethical constraints against manipulating and changing the natural environment; it also held out the promise of binding nature "to your service and [making] her your slave"—as Bacon put it (quoted in Keller, 1987, p. 242). Although the idea that nature must be subdued and dominated was later reformulated to reflect an economic concern with "efficient management," the anthropocentric view of the universe remained.

The conceptual foundations of another aspect of modern consciousness were established through the analogic thinking that viewed nature as like a machine. As discussed in Chapter 4, Kepler's statement that "my aim is to show that the celestial machine is to be likened not to a divine organism," which was the old root metaphor, "but to a clockwork" (quoted in Merchant, 1980, pp. 128–129) reflected the new metaphorical basis of thought that was to provide a way of viewing both nature and society in mechanistic terms: The human heart could thus be viewed as a "pump," the world system could be represented as a computer model that would allow predictions on "limits to growth," learning outcomes could be viewed as "products," and the brain as an "awesome computational instrument"—to cite some examples of current metaphorical thinking that are conceptually congruent with the mechanistic view of reality.

Given the last 400 years of religious, political, and cultural developments in the West, it would be incorrect to say that there is a unitary phenomenon called "modern consciousness" that is shared by everyone. There are wide variations in ways of knowing, in viewing the purpose of life, and in establishing what has authority in human experience. But it would also be incorrect to say that these multiple views of what it means to be a modern person have equal standing in the critically important political arenas of corporate boardrooms, classrooms that produce the new class of technocratic thinkers, and the legislatures that set funding priorities. There are more people visible today who view tradition (as an organic metaphor that suggests growth and renewal) as the source of the analogues that give authority to experience, who consider community to be an interdependent ecology of life forms, and who consider values to have a spiritual foundation; however, these people remain on the margins of political power. While encompassing a wide range of beliefs and lifestyles (some of which are even mildly subversive of more deeply grounded orthodoxies) the mainstream and hegemonic varieties of modern consciousness are still based on what we have loosely termed "Cartesian thinking": The individual is an autonomous being who makes intellectual and moral judgments; knowledge (the explicit and measurable variety) is the chief source of power and progress in developing technologies that will enable us to exploit nature's resources; and nature (including human beings) and society are represented in the mechanistic terms that allow for greater predictability and control.

For all the variety and what Daniel Bell (1978) terms the "syncretism" (the borrowing and mixing of cultural forms, which reflects the Cartesian view of the individual as spectator) that characterize the modern mindset, we think that the Cartesian analogues still dominate the thought process in those sectors of society that produce and legitimate the knowledge that shapes how the future is understood. The irony is that toxic and nuclear wastes (250 million tons being produced in 1985, an amount that is estimated to double in seven years), land degradation (which the United Nations Environmental Program estimates to encompass 35 percent of the earth's land surface), and the existence of more refugees from environmental breakdowns than political oppression (Schierholz, 1988) are all viewed as problems to be solved through the use of the same mindset that contributed so much to ecological imbalance. One cause of the double-bind is the failure to recognize that our thought process is in the grip of cultural patterns that were created in response to an entirely different set of social and environmental conditions.

THE BATESONIAN METAPHOR OF AN ECOLOGY

This is why the ideas of Bateson become critically important to thinking about education for the twenty-first century. The root metaphor

that he gives us is that of an "ecology"—a natural system that includes humans and other lifeforms sustained through information
and energy exchanges. Bateson's metaphor places the person and the
symbolic world of culture within a system of interdependent relations—not outside it, as is the case with the Cartesian metaphor. To
reiterate key ideas that relate directly to reconstituting our most basic
cultural beliefs: "The unit of survival is not the breeding organism, or
the family line, or the society. . . . The unit of survival is a flexible
organism-in-its-environment" (Bateson, 1972, p. 451). This commonsense notion, when compared to the cultural assumptions about
"man's" ability to develop ever more powerful technologies for the
control of nature and the creation of artificial environments as a substitute for natural systems, takes on a new and more radical dimension. We also want to reiterate two other key aspects of Bateson's
ideas: "Thus, in no system which shows mental characteristics can
any part have unilateral control over the whole. In other words, *the
mental characteristics of the system are immanent, not in some part, but in
the system as a whole*" (1972, p. 316; emphasis in original). This leads
Bateson to conclude that "*The* unit of evolutionary survival turns out
to be identical with the unit of mind" (1972, p. 483). The unit of mind
is the totality of information exchanges essential to the life processes
of the aggregate parts that make up the system—which includes humans as part of the larger biotic community.

Wendell Berry, a poet and essayist on the modern condition, is
equally critical of the Cartesian vision of unilateral control over the
environment. Responding to the ideal of the unlimited pursuit of af-
fluence, comfort, mobility, and leisure (to be gained through technological mastery), Berry writes that "this is fantastical because the basic
cause of the energy crisis is not scarcity; it is moral ignorance and
weakness of character. We don't know (as a culture) *how* to use energy
or what it is *for*" (1986, p. 13). Berry sees the problem in much the
same way as Bateson, suggesting that we have to reconstitute the conceptual and moral foundations of the dominant Cartesian culture on
the basis of a new metaphorical framework. He warns:

> A culture cannot survive long at the expense either of its agriculture or
> of its natural resources. To live at the expense of the source of life is
> obviously suicidal. Though we have no choice but to live at the expense
> of other life, it is necessary to recognize the limits and dangers involved:
> past a certain point in a unified system, "other life" is our own. (p. 47)

Instead of a thought process based on the metaphors of the machine
and the unlimited horizon of progress, Berry urges the adoption of a
different root metaphor for a sustainable form of culture:

> The definitive relationships in the universe are thus not competitive but interdependent. And from a human point of view they are analogical. We can build one system only within another. We can have agriculture only within nature, and culture only within agriculture. At certain critical points these systems have to conform with one another or destroy one another. (p. 47)

The metaphor of an "ecology" suggests not only interdependence, whereby humans and so-called more primitive forms of life are connected to the same food and information chain; it is also a basis for understanding what constitutes moral behavior. Put another way, it suggests a whole new set of moral imperatives that both clarify the limits of acceptable human behavior and creates the possibility of rediscovering a way of understanding that was integral to the lives of ancient peoples who lived in ecological balance. Evil, for example, would be reinterpreted to mean acting and thinking in a way that contributes to the deterioration of the ecosystem and thus to its life-sustaining characteristics. As any suggestion of an interconnection between moral behavior and spirituality may cause some readers to turn off from the discussion or to immediately position themselves behind the partisan canons of religious belief, it is important to see how Mary Catherine Bateson explains her father's attempt to understand the unity of an ecology as the expression of a "larger mind" that frames how we should define responsibility, love, and life itself—all essential elements of what religions have attempted to help us understand:

> Not only do we misread and mistreat meadows, oceans, and organisms of all kinds, but our mistreatments of each other are based on errors of the general order of not knowing what we are dealing with, or acting in ways that violate the communicative web.
>
> There is a bridge needed here between epistemology and ethics. In trying to understand that relationship I have always found Gregory's definition of love, offered at the Wenner-Gren Conference, especially useful, and worth repeating here:
>
> "At least a part of what we mean by the word could be covered by saying that 'I love X' could be spelled out as 'I regard myself as a system, and I accept with positive valuation the fact that I am one, preferring to be one rather than fall to pieces and die; and I regard the person whom I love as systemic; and I regard my system and his or her system as together *constituting a larger system with some degree of conformability within itself.'*"
>
> This is essentially the assertion that love is based on metaphor, a three-way metaphor that links self and other and also *self plus other*, and

uses this recognition to assert the value of the relationship as well as the value of self and other. (Bateson & Bateson, 1987, pp. 191–192)

CURRENT VIEWS ON THE PURPOSE OF EDUCATION

Given that the cumulative effect of past misuses of the environment, plus continued population growth, will likely dominate how we view the educational challenges of the twenty-first century, it is important to consider the extent to which the competing views on the purpose of public education in this country incorporate the sense of interdependency and restraint associated with being a good ecological citizen. Recent concerns about the nation's being economically and technologically at risk, as well as a host of social injustices, have resulted in public education's becoming a major focus of national debates. Neophyte teachers, as well as veterans of the classroom who have managed to keep themselves intellectually alive and sensitive to the possibilities of social reform, will be in varying degrees caught up in these debates. In some instances, teachers may attempt to adjust classroom practices in terms of the arguments that seem to have the greatest strength. We would like to identify the elements that give each of the competing arguments on the purpose of education its sense of conceptual coherence, influence what will be seen as problematic (and what will not), and establish the existential bond we know as commitment. Although the complexity of each of the identifiable arguments (which deal with aims, curriculum, and pedagogy) deserves book-length treatment, we think it is possible to identify the essential set of core assumptions and to show how they incorporate different aspects of the Cartesian way of thinking that has massively contributed to the scale of ecological damage.

Leading Arguments

Although a wide variety of views are being expressed about the problems facing education and the larger society, it seems that today three distinct arguments receive the widest media attention and exert the greatest influence on the direction of educational reform. We shall label these arguments in terms of what appears to be the distinctness of their orientation. The technocratic argument, which has its roots in the scientific management ideas of Frederick Taylor and the behaviorist theory of B. F. Skinner, characterizes the thinking that dominates the professional field of education. The academic-rationalist argument, which has an equally long history, is being currently advanced by such people as Mortimer Adler and E. D. Hirsch, Jr., who see themselves as critics of the educational establishment. The critical-pedagogy argument, heard mostly within groups advocating radical reform of society, is rooted primarily in the thinking of Paulo Freire and articulated in this country by such educational thinkers as Henry Giroux and Peter McLaren. Although each argument appears to address a different set of educational and social issues that are considered problematic, and thus each has its own set of recommendations for reforming education, we think that all three positions are based on a common set of core cultural assumptions that will further deepen rather than help resolve the ecological crisis. Before we identify the cultural assumptions that bond these positions together, we would like to identify what appears on the surface to be the distinctness of their agendas for educational and social reform.

TECHNOCRATIC ARGUMENT. The technocratic argument is exemplified in the following statement by David T. Kearns (1988), chairman and chief executive officer of the Xerox Corporation. Writing in the *Harvard Business Review* about the dangers facing businesses that must hire new workers "who can't read, write, or count," Kearns urges that "today's schools ought to look like today's smartest high-tech companies—lean, flat structures that push decision making down into the organization. Business professionals and managers are trusted with the authority to get their jobs done—and they're held accountable for performing. We have to treat teachers the same way" (p. 72). Efficiency and accountability, according to Kearns, who uses business and the liberal idea of a marketplace as the root metaphor, would require that teachers "design their own curricula, set their own specialities, and compete with other schools in a new education marketplace that would be fueled by diversity and free choice" (p. 72). This statement is important—not only because it suggests the possibility of an internal debate about the problems of basing education on the hierarchical model of early industrialism, but also because it shows how the educational priorities taken so seriously by the technicist educators have been largely set by the perceived needs of the work place.

The concern with teaching students basic skills, the emphasis on developing techniques for instruction and for managing classroom behavior, and the emphasis on basing educational reform on a scientific understanding of the classroom (i.e., collecting data) are all hallmarks of a view of education that emphasizes the importance of greater efficiency and control over educational outcomes. Ironically, this concern with the rationalization of the classroom, in order to meet the needs of the workplace and thus avoid putting the nation further "at risk," involves dealing with the student as something that is to be molded and trained through systematic reinforcement. In effect, the rationality exhibited by the experts who create the techniques and learning packages is not viewed as an attribute of students. The student's responsibility is to stay on-task and to produce the responses and behaviors that fit the teacher's prespecified educational objectives, what Hunter (1986) calls "output behavior."

ACADEMIC-RATIONALIST ARGUMENT. The academic-rationalist argument articulated by Adler and Hirsch, and increasingly supported by critics outside the educational establishment, involves an entirely different view of the individual's social responsibilities. Unlike the technicist approach, which blurs the distinction between the classroom and the workplace with its metaphorical language of process-product and management strategies, Adler and Hirsch view the primary purpose of public education as preparation for participation as an informed citizen. This involves fostering the development of personal growth, which Adler defines as "mental, moral, and spiritual" (1982, p. 16), as well as the knowledge and personal skills necessary to pursue a meaningful vocation. But the main concern is "the individual's role as an enfranchised citizen of this republic." Adler writes:

> The reason why universal suffrage in a true democracy calls for universal public schooling is that the former without the latter produces an ignorant electorate and amounts to a travesty of democratic institutions and processes. To avoid this danger, public schooling must be universal in more than its quantitative aspect. It must be universal also in its qualitative aspect. (1982, p. 17)

Thus his argument that schools should provide the same liberal arts curriculum for *all* students. The purpose of this curriculum, which is the staple of most elite private schools, is to provide essential knowledge (language, literature, history, fine arts, and so forth); intellectual skills essential for thinking, observing, and communicating; and what Adler terms the "enlarged understanding of ideas and values" (1982, p. 32) whereby students appropriate the knowledge to their own level of understanding.

Hirsch also views the development of an informed citizenry as the primary purpose of public education. As he put it, "literate culture is the most democratic culture in our land: it excludes nobody, it cuts across generations and social groups and classes; it is not usually one's first culture, but it should be everyone's second, existing as it does beyond the narrow spheres of family, neighborhood, and region" (1987, p. 21). Designating his approach to an information-based curriculum as cultural literacy, which earlier had been used to refer to the ability to decode one's own cultural patterns (Bowers, 1974), Hirsch came up with the now-famous list of factual knowledge that should form the basis of the individual's schemata of understanding. A culturally literate person, according to Hirsch, should possess a basic vocabulary of 50,000 pieces of information. By equating schema with a word or bit of factual information, Hirsch asserts that "a basic vocabulary of 50,000 schemata serves as a quickly accessible index to a much larger volume of knowledge" (p. 64) that allows the citizen to connect the events of the day to larger issues by situating them in terms of their geographical, historical, and intellectual context.

Public education, for Adler and Hirsch, must be judged in terms of passing on the accumulated knowledge that they view as essential for the reflective citizen. In giving the Anglo-Western (and masculine) view of knowledge a privileged position in the curriculum, Adler and Hirsch have come under sharp criticism—particularly from individuals and groups who are challenging this mindset as being the most enlightened and culturally advanced. We share some of the criticism directed at the Adler/Hirsch line of argument and will later identify what we regard as an even more fundamental weakness.

CRITICAL-PEDAGOGY ARGUMENT. The third perspective on the purpose of education that is likely to attract the teacher's attention is what is now being associated with the phrase *critical pedagogy*. A critical pedagogy, according to Henry Giroux and Peter McLaren, who are the most visible spokespersons of this position, exists in a tradition of emancipating thinking that includes Paulo Freire and John Dewey. As with the academic-rationalist argument of Adler and Hirsch, the advocates of a critical-pedagogy approach to public education link education to the political process. But there is a fundamental difference between the two lines of argument. Both Adler and Hirsch view the achievements of the past as the essential knowledge for individual empowerment. They also view American social, political, and economic institutions as based on essentially sound principles, arguing that they can only be made to work properly when all citizens possess a broad body of knowledge. In effect, Adler and Hirsch are articulating the traditional notion of a liberal education.

The advocates of a critical pedagogy view empowerment in very different terms.

The task of the teacher, to quote Giroux (1988), is to "make the pedagogical more political and the political more pedagogical." The teacher's proper role is that of the "transformative intellectual" who is able to recognize that "*a student's voice* is not a reflection of the world as much as it is a *constitutive force that both mediates and shapes reality within historically constituted practices and relationships of power*" (McLaren, 1989, p. 230; emphasis in original). In addition, the teacher as "transformative intellectual" must understand that "making the pedagogical more political means inserting schooling directly into the political sphere by arguing that schooling represents both a struggle to define meaning and a struggle over power relations" (Giroux, 1988, p. 127). As the unpacking of the full implications of this statement represents the core ideas of a critical pedagogy, it is important to have Giroux's full explanation:

> Within this perspective, critical reflection and action become part of a fundamental social project to help students develop a deep and abiding faith in the struggle to overcome economic, political, and social injustices, and to further humanize themselves as part of this struggle. In this case, knowledge and power are inextricably linked to the presupposition that to choose life, to recognize the necessity of improving its democratic and qualitative character for all people, is to understand the preconditions necessary to struggle for it.
>
> Making the political more pedagogical means utilizing forms of pedagogy that embody political interests that are emancipatory in nature; that is, using forms of pedagogy that treat students as critical agents; make knowledge problematic; utilize critical and affirming dialogue; and make the case for struggling for a qualitatively better world for all people. (1988, p. 127)

Rather than attempt our own summary of this position, we shall let Peter McLaren explain why a critical pedagogy is the appropriate educational response to the crises we now face: "A pedagogy of liberation has no final answers. It is always in the making. . . . It is a pedagogy which recognizes all regimes of truth to be contemporary strategies of containment. The point, Giroux reminds us, is to purge what is considered truth of its oppressive and undemocratic elements" (Giroux, Introduction, 1988, p. xx).

Critique of Common Assumptions

On the surface these three arguments on the purpose of public education in America appear to be diverse, even at fundamental odds with each other's agendas for reform. The technicist educator's concern with overcoming the student's deficit in basic skills and self-control that will further harm the nation's economic and technological capacity is, from the point of view of both the academic rationalist and the advocate of a critical pedagogy, basically wrong. But academic rationalism and critical pedagogy appear to occupy positions that are equally at odds over fundamental issues relating to the nature of emancipation, the role of public institutions, and the basic values and cultural practices that underpin everyday life. At the level of educational practice (approach to teaching and learning and to curriculum content), as well as in articulating the social purpose of public education, they indeed occupy different positions.

But at a deeper level, we want to argue that they share a core set of Cartesian/liberal assumptions and that the difference in their positions reflects the selection of certain aspects of this paradigm for amplification into a way of understanding society and the purpose of schools. In effect, the three arguments reflect three distinct ways of interpreting our present problems. That each one, while dealing with important issues and appearing to make a convincing case (depending upon which part of the Cartesian/liberal paradigm the reader takes for granted), is totally silent about the connection between cultural beliefs and practices and the ecological crisis suggests the basic limitations of the Cartesian/liberal paradigm. Its blindness to the long-term interdependence of cultural patterns and natural environment is reflected in the blind spots of the technicist, academic-rationalist, and critical-pedagogy positions. If the preliminary evidence of environmental disruption and severity of the crisis are to be taken seriously, then it would seem that all three lines of educational argument are misdirected in terms of addressing the most urgent and difficult problems we will face in the next century. When we look at the evidence and scope of accelerating environmental disruption and the breakdown in the environment's life-sustaining capacity, the most pressing educational issues cease to be the on-task rates in a well-managed classroom, the 50,000 bits of factual information that every literate American should know, or even the emancipatory possibilities of encouraging "students to develop a *pedagogical negativism*—to doubt everything. . . . (and) help students affirm their (own) judgments," to quote McLaren (1989, p. 233).

What are the bedrock assumptions that bond these seemingly conflicting positions together and lead to a common misunderstanding of what constitutes being "at risk" as a society? Although each line of argument about the social purposes of public education involves important variations in how the bedrock assumptions are to be weighted and interpreted, we think it is possible to identify three assumptions that represent a common conceptual starting point.

RELIABILITY OF THE RATIONAL PROCESS. The first assumption is that the rational process, as it is carried on in the mind of the individual, is the only reliable source of authority upon which human action should be based. This assumption, which most of us now accept as so obvious as to be little more than common sense, leads to a number of implications that separate the modern (Cartesian) person from people who are still rooted in traditional cultures. First, when this assumption becomes a basic part of one's way of thinking, the authority embedded in cultural practices, sacred texts, and bearers of the society's accumulated forms of knowledge is lessened or rejected altogether. The authority for action and belief, according to the Cartesian view of the rational process, has to be continually reestablished on the basis of the individual's rational process. For the more direct followers of Descartes, the authority of the rational process is dependent on careful observation and measurement, which yields the necessary data. The technocratic educators are representative of this more purist tradition of Cartesianism. The academic rationalists and advocates of critical pedagogy are in the more Cartesian/liberal tradition, where the emphasis is not on procedural thinking associated with developing techniques but on freeing individuals in the political sense from the authority of tradition, thus allowing them the autonomy to pursue their own self-interest (guided, it is hoped, by their own internal rational process).

In addition to overturning other cultural forms of authority, the assumption that the rational process occurs within the mind of the person has led to individuals' experiencing the world as observers—detached, reflective observers. In the area of art, this pre-Cartesian assumption has led to the cognitive style of perspectivism that puts both painter and viewer outside the painting as observers with a distinct angle of vision (Bordo, 1987). Martin Heidegger (1927/1962) refers to this observer role of the rational person as seeing the world as a picture; this stance is essential to current claims that the rational process can be objective and that we can collect objective data. Hubert Dreyfus (1981) suggests that this view of the rational person has contributed to our cultural orientation to take seriously only explicit forms of knowledge and to value ideas and techniques that are represented as context-free.

The technicist educational argument reflects a reworking of the Cartesian position whereby only those who collect the data and formulate the techniques are viewed as rational, thus their emphasis in the classroom on teaching skills to students rather than providing the knowledge that allows students to develop their own perspective (critical judgment) on the issues of the day. The academic rationalist and advocate of critical pedagogy recognize that a person is embedded in the cultural patterns and that when these patterns (of language, social interaction, beliefs) are taken for granted the individual cannot be acting in an autonomous and rationally self-directing manner—thus the need to use education to provide students with the sense of conceptual distance (viewing the world of culture as a picture) that will allow them to sort out their own preferences. In effect, their educational goal, while differing in terms of their assessment of economic and political practices, is to *achieve* as an ideal what represented Descartes' starting point: "I think, therefore I am."

Some readers may be wondering why all the fuss about an assumption that most intelligent people take for granted and that may be somewhat old-fashioned now that scientists are investigating the chemical and neurological *mechanism* of the brain. The issue of context and thought process as well as the issue of how the metaphorical nature of language encodes the mental processes of others are both central to Bateson's argument that mind (information exchanges) is immanent in the ecology of which the individual is always a part. It also relates to Bateson's point that the long-term well-being (survival) of an ecosystem is threatened when one part assumes the right to exercise unilateral control over the whole. The assumption that rationality is the possession of autonomous individuals (autonomous in the sense that they are detached observers) also carries with it the assumption that the environment is nonintelligent and thus in need of being humanized.

INDIVIDUAL AS AUTONOMOUS. The second assumption that bonds these three educational arguments together was touched on earlier in the reference to the use of education to achieve the Cartesian idea of the self-constituting individual. The radical doubt that was Descartes's starting point, where the only certainty was that thought was occurring, has led his followers (including Alder and Hirsch as well as Giroux and McLaren) to view the individual as the basic social unit. Culture, tradition, language—those nearly interchangeable metaphors for referring to a society's coding systems—are not viewed as integral to the individual's way of knowing and acting. Individual empowerment, which is almost equivalent to the older metaphor of emancipation, is to be achieved by gaining a critical understanding of the past (for Adler) and by recognizing "all regimes of truth to be contemporary strategies of containment" (to recall McLaren's words).

The Cartesian connection, which is actually more visible in the critical-pedagogy perspective than in the Adler/Hirsch positions, which still value tradition as a necessary basis of progress, is clearly evident in McLaren's recommendation that teachers should "encourage students to develop a *pedagogical negativism*—to doubt everything" (1989, p. 233).

Our concern about this view of the autonomous individual who may, in the most ideal circumstances, negotiate new meanings through dialogue with others should not be interpreted as an expression of indifference toward the failure of our social system to resolve the basic sources of inequality that physically and mentally constrain the full development of many people's lives. Rather, our chief concern here is with the reductionist view of culture that characterizes the critical-pedagogy position. Unlike Descartes, who starts with the rationalist interpretation of the metaphor "I" and thus never addresses his own cultural embeddedness, the critical pedagogues view individual's embeddedness in culture as the cause of inequality and a constraint on individuals' ability to discover their own voices. In effect, they see culture only in political terms. Giroux's summary of Freire's view of culture, which he uncritically adopts as his own position, best illustrates how a totally politicized view of culture leads to the Cartesian/liberal position wherein the emphasis is on emancipating students from their cultural embeddedness, with little attention given to the problem of relativizing meaningful and shared traditions:

> For Freire, culture is the representation of lived experiences, material artifacts, and practices forged within the unequal and dialectical relations that different groups establish in a given society at a particular historical point. Culture is a form of production whose processes are intimately connected with the structuring of different social formations, particularly those that are gender, age, racial, and class related. It is also a form of production that helps human agents, through their use of language and other material resources, to transform society. In this case, culture is closely related to the dynamics of power and produces asymmetries in the ability of individuals and groups to define and achieve their goals. Furthermore, culture is also an arena of struggle and contradiction, and there is no one culture in the homogeneous sense. On the contrary, there are dominant and subordinate cultures that express different interests and operate from different and unequal terrains of power. (1988, pp. 116–117)

The issue here is not specific injustices, such as the exploitation of the migrant farmworker or the manipulation of consciousness through the media by large corporations, but rather a total view of

culture as containing the forces of both oppression and emancipation—with each stage of emancipation being viewed as the source of
oppression to be transcended by the next generation (Freire, 1974).
This reductionist view of culture leads McLaren to state the problem
facing teachers as recognizing that

> as cultural sites, schools are contested terrains in which different values,
> conventions, and knowledges variously intersect, juxtapose, and ex-
> clude one another. Teachers and others interested in education must
> understand how the dominant culture of all levels of schooling func-
> tions to disconform and, less frequently, to legitimate or celebrate the
> cultural experiences of students who inhibit subordinate cultures. (1989,
> p. 200)

We do not disagree with the argument that culture is not monolithic and that the patterns within the dominant culture as well as
those imposed on minority social groups point to an important political dimension to culture. In fact, the earlier chapters represented an
attempt to identify hidden cultural patterns in a classroom ecology
that teachers should be aware of—patterns that range from nonverbal
communication to the conceptual-mapping characteristics of language. But we think that culture, as the lived symbolic world of individuals, is far more complex than represented by the neo-Cartesian
critical pedagogues, who view it as the existing symbolic matrix that
poses the continual challenge of emancipation through critical reflection. Persons are more deeply embedded than is recognized by the
critical pedagogues; Giroux and McLaren, for example, do not recognize the metaphorical nature of language—including how their own
metaphors of "individualism," "emancipation," "freedom," and so on
are embedded in a modernizing, Eurocentric form of consciousness.
Second, much of lived culture cannot be adequately understood
when reduced to the relativizing framework of liberal politics,
wherein the authority for belief and value becomes a matter of shifting preferences—of individuals and groups. Since most lived culture
is experienced at the taken-for-granted level, it is what gives authority
and predictability to people's experiences. In some instances, cultural
patterns will be so much a part of people's taken-for-granted experience that they will not even be aware that it is problematic—such as
the critical pedagogue's habit of arguing for the very anthropocentric
view of the universe that is partly responsible for the ecological crisis.
Third, the building of new synthesis out of conflicting cultural orientations is not as easy as the conflict model of critical pedagogy implies. Some positions, such as the traditional values of extended fam-

ilies among some culture groups, cannot be easily reconciled with the Cartesian/liberal view of the individual as a rational and thus potentially autonomous being. Transcending the old cultural patterns, by embracing the liberal view of the individual, could represent a new expression of cultural domination. The inability to resolve disagreement between the pro-choice and pro-life groups, to cite another example of how intractable some political disagreements can be, suggests that the consciousness-raising process that is to characterize the classroom may occasionally touch on bedrock beliefs that cannot be reconciled through a rational process—as the critical pedagogues appear to assume.

CHANGE AS PROGRESS. This brings us to the third shared assumption that binds together the three arguments on the purpose of education. Descartes's view of the individual as self-constituting (and thus as free of the influence of the past), as well as the procedural method of thinking that he helped to establish, contributed to the Enlightenment belief that rationally directed change puts history on a linear and progressive path. Stated more simply, nonrecognition of the multidimensionality of culture and tradition, and of how they interpenetrate individual experience, led to viewing all change as progressive. The technicist educators view each new technique, especially when grounded in supporting data, as a progressive step in educational practice. Similarly, both the academic rationalists and the advocates of a critical pedagogy view rationally empowered individuals as agents of progressive change. The idea that ancient peoples had a more complex way of understanding energy and information exchanges, and thus developed more ecologically responsive forms of culture, would simply be foreign to their view of progress as an ever-widening framework of possibility. The analogues of the past, if they have any value, are to be viewed as objects of study that will help insure that we do not repeat the mistakes of the past. The expression that people who do not know the past are likely to repeat it sums up the rationalist's view that the human drama is basically one of progressive innovation. That these groups continue to hold this view (or is it that this view continues to hold them?) in spite of mounting evidence that our innovations in technology, values, and lifestyles are contributing to global warming, ozone depletion, and acid rain (not to mention pesticide poisoning, species extinction, and the problem of disposing of toxic and solid waste) suggests the power of a culturally embedded pattern of thinking to put out of focus evidence that contradicts guiding cultural assumptions.

ECOLOGY AS AN ANALOGUE FOR EDUCATION

The ecological crisis that will increasingly occupy our attention as we move into the next century is, in large part, a crisis in cultural values and beliefs. To view the solution simply in terms of making a costly shift to more ecologically sensitive technologies may moderate the damage being done to the ecosystems, but it would be a totally inadequate response. Our profligate use of nonrenewable resources, and the concomitant creation of toxic wastes that are pumped into the atmosphere and spread across the land and water, is an outgrowth of our belief system. The most basic assumptions of the dominant culture—how we understand ourselves as individuals, the nature of the rational process, what constitutes success, the uses of technology, the value of work, the way we resolve the tension between science and moral values, and so forth—provide the conceptual and moral framework upon which materialistic and technologically driven cultural practices are based. Many of these cultural assumptions were formed at earlier stages in Western history when they seemed to be genuinely progressive steps toward the alleviation of life-shortening situations and unnecessary hardship. The ecological damage caused by earlier cultural practices seemed manageable, particularly when the discovery of the "New World" opened for exploitation vast resources of timber and other natural resources. The scale of the ecological impact was different then, and there were new territories to be colonized—thus creating a safety valve that would further strengthen the conceptual and moral foundations of what we now know as modern consciousness. As Berry (1986) points out, the European settlers could deal with their environmentally disruptive practices by simply moving on to new land and new market opportunities, thus maintaining the paradoxical myth of being free individualists who are ecologically unaccountable.

We can no longer be a transient people in search of new continents to exploit, nor can we ignore the ecological consequences of the West's cultural impact on the values, beliefs, and technological practices of a world population that is growing at exponential rates. The new frontier will not be space, as is now suggested by the special interest groups who both mystify themselves and others with the "godwords" of progress and adventure, but the reformulation of the conceptual (including Cartesian) foundations of our cultural practices. As with the awakening caused by the AIDS epidemic to the dangers of cultural attitudes that ignore the essential nature of human interdependence, we are likely to see old values and practices in a new light. This awakening to the cultural dimensions of the ecological crisis will not leave educators unaffected.

In summarizing several recent reports of the American Association for the Advancement of Science, Robert Cowen (1988) notes the unusual urgency of our situation; we cannot really wait until we have complete documentation on the extent of ecological damage before we act to mitigate the sources of the problem. The systems are too complex and dynamic, with the result that the extent of damage is continually changing; and we have only recently become aware of new dimensions of ecological disruption that need to be investigated. Waiting for conclusive evidence will simply increase the scope of the problem; as we wait for more evidence, the problematic values and beliefs will be taught to yet another generation, who will, in turn, inculcate the next generation to the materialistic expectations of being a modern individual. Nor can we wait until the political process yields a new consensus of core cultural values and beliefs. Many adults have an economic self-interest in maintaining ecologically damaging cultural beliefs; and many seem to be so deeply embedded, in terms of taken-for-granted lifestyles, that they will attempt to conserve the more nihilistic aspects of our culture. As in other forms of addiction, they will deny that the problem exists. Ironically, responding to the ecological crisis by continuing the cultural practices that contributed to it may be most visible in the knowledge-producing and -legitimating institutions, such as universities, where the Cartesian/liberal paradigm, in all its mutations, is associated with the higher values of Enlightenment thinking.

In effect, educators have a responsibility to pass on to the young a mental ecology (beliefs, values, and analogues of social practice) that will not exacerbate the crisis. But they must carry out this responsibility while possessing, like the rest of society, only a partial understanding of the path that will lead to a more ecologically responsive set of cultural patterns and practices. The problem is that of contributing to the deepest levels of cultural change when there are no agreed-upon templates. However, educators are not without analogues that can point them in the right direction. Examples exist of cultures that lived in ecological balance, including remnants of cultural groups that lived for centuries on the very land that we are destroying in mere decades with our modern practices. There are also analogues derived from shared experiences within the modern world that suggest that cooperation and an ethic of interdependence is better than an ethic of self-interest and competitive individualism. We think that Bateson's way of thinking, derived from his studies of communication in different cultural settings and animal groups, provides a more useful analogue than the ones that have dominated thinking in the West for the last four centuries: the archetypes of the machine, an anthropocentric universe, and the competitive marketplace.

The use of Bateson's ecology perspective may serve as an appropriate analogue for educators in thinking about the interconnection between culture and environment partly for reasons that relate to Wendell Berry's observations about the need for the analogues of cultural practice to be based on the same patterns that characterize the natural environment. To recall his words, "The definitive relationships in the universe are . . . not competitive but interdependent" (1986, p. 47). Understanding this interdependence, as well as finding ways to participate in the ecology as a responsible member, involves being aware of the message exchanges that are part of relationships. Since the human dimension of the ecology involves communicating largely in terms of patterns (analogues) learned from the individual's primary culture, any attempt to help students interpret more fully and intelligently the message exchanges requires that the cultural patterns be taken into account as part of the content and process of student communication. This is essentially what we have argued for as part of an ecological perspective on professional decision making in the classroom. Viewing the classroom as an ecology that is part of the larger ecology of culture and natural environment has the necessary consistency that Berry's statement calls for.

The most obvious issue, but surprisingly least recognized by the trendsetters in education, is that the conceptual basis of industrial society (and now the society of the "information age") has been based on assumptions that, if we continue to live by them, will further accelerate the rate of environmental damage. Increasing productivity to meet the expanding expectations of a consumer-oriented society translates into deforestation, further depletion of aquifers, and loss of top soil. It also adds to the toxic wastes that are reabsorbed back into the ecosystems. In effect, the evidence of environmental disruption and system breakdown is a clear message that our most basic cultural assumptions are going to have to be reexamined and, in many instances, reconstituted in ways that take into account the interdependence of culture and natural environment. For educators, transmitting the old patterns of thought (even when dressed up in progressive-sounding metaphors) would be a catastrophic mistake.

As it dawns on policy makers that the extent of environmental disruption requires more than new laws prohibiting the use of certain technologies or improper waste disposal practices, we will see increased attention being focused on the appropriateness of our cultural values and ways of thinking. This perspective will inevitably find its way to being taught in public schools and universities. New and more ecologically sensitive curricula will then be forthcoming. But while we think that increased awareness of how one aspect of the ecological crisis is encoded in the curriculum is not far off in time, we want to urge that teachers start now to reconstitute the conceptual underpinning of those aspects of the dominant culture that do not take into account the interdependence of life systems. This brings us to the encoding characteristics of language and the ways in which mental models of the past influence present thought. The assumptions that are encoded in the metaphors of "work," "individualism," "technology," "science," "progress," "modernization," "community," "data," and so forth suggest that careful attention can be given to the mental ecology of the classroom and that this process should extend from the first grade to the graduate class. The metaphors that encode the cultural schemata are present at all levels of the educational system; the level of comprehension and the context of use are what vary. The pedagogical tasks involved in asking whether the vocabulary is complex enough to convey the pattern and relationships of experience, as well as the other dimensions of primary socialization, are also part of the teacher's responsibility at all levels of the educational process—only the level of complexity will vary. Metaphors that encode the mindset of earlier people who had a mechanistic and exploitative view of the world are as problematic in the early grades as in graduate courses.

The constant awareness of the conceptual templates that students are being socialized to accept as a taken-for-granted basis of understanding needs to be supplemented by thinkers, poets, and bearers of traditions who can help recover an understanding of the analogues of how to live in sustainable and interdependent communities. E. F. Schumacher (1975), Gary Snyder (1977), Lynn Margulis (1986), William I. Thompson (1987), Wendell Berry (1986), and Carol Gilligan (1982) are just a few of the people who are helping us understand "the pattern that connects" and how these patterns of interdependence lead to a new understanding of the more ecologically problematic metaphorical frameworks. It is this orientation that we think will be forced on us by the breakdown of natural systems. The challenge will be to give up the sense of power and control that the mechanistic models of thinking appear to give educators. Ultimately, we are optimistic. We believe that they will recognize an ecological understanding of the classroom and an ecologically responsible form of culture as part of the same process and that they will help to reconstitute the cultural assumptions on which the mental ecology of the classroom is based.

References

Acheson, Keith A., and Gall, Meredith D. 1987. *Techniques in the Clinical Supervision of Teachers.* 2d ed. New York: Longman.

Adler, Mortimer J. 1982. *The Paideia Proposal: An Educational Manifesto.* New York: Macmillan.

Agar, Michael H. 1980. *The Professional Stranger.* New York: Academic Press.

Au, Kathryn Hu-Pei, and Jordon, Cathie. 1981. "Teaching Reading to Hawaiian Children: Finding a Culturally Appropriate Solution." In *Culture and the Bilingual Classroom*, edited by Henry T. Trueba, Grace Pung Guthrie, and Kathryn Hu-Pei Au. London: Newbury House.

Balzer, LeVon; Goodson, Phyllis L.; Slesnick, Irwin L.; Lauer, Lois; Collins, Ann; and Alexander, Gretchen M. 1983. *Life Science.* Glenview, IL: Scott Foresman.

Bartky, Sandra Lee. 1988. "Foucault, Femininity, and the Modernization of Patriarchal Power." In *Feminism and Foucault,* edited by Irene Diamond and Lee Quinby. Boston: Northeastern University Press.

Bateson, Gregory. 1972. *Steps to an Ecology of Mind.* New York: Ballantine.

———. 1980a. "Men Are Grass: Metaphor and the World of Mental Process." A Lindisfarne Letter published by Lindisfarne Press, West Stockbridge, MA.

———. 1980b. *Mind and Nature: A Necessary Unity.* New York: Bantam.

———, and Bateson, Mary Catherine. 1987. *Angels Fear: Towards an Ecology of the Sacred.* New York: Macmillan.

Beardsley, Monroe C. 1966. *Thinking Straight: Principles of Reasoning for Readers and Writers.* Englewood Cliffs, NJ: Prentice-Hall.

Belenky, Mary Field; Clinchy, Blythe McVicker; Goldberger, Nancy Rule; and Tarule, Jill Mattuck. 1986. *Women's Ways of Knowing: The Development of Self, Voice, and Mind.* New York: Basic.

Bell, Daniel. 1978. *The Cultural Contradictions of Capitalism.* New York: Basic.

Berger, John. 1979. *Pig Earth.* New York: Pantheon.

Berger, Peter; Berger, Brigitte; and Kellner, Hansfreid. 1974. *The Homeless Mind: Modernization and Consciousness.* New York: Vintage.

———, and Luckmann, Thomas. 1967. *The Social Construction of Reality: A Treatise in the Sociology of Knowledge.* Garden City, NY: Anchor.

Bernstein, Basil. 1971. "On the Classification and Framing of Educational

Knowledge." In *Knowledge and Control: New Directions for the Sociology of Education*, edited by Michael Young. London: Collier-Macmillan.

Berry, Wendell. 1986. *The Unsettling of America: Culture and Agriculture*. San Francisco: Sierra Club.

Birdwhistell, Ray L. 1970. *Kinesics and Context: Essays on Body Motion Communication*. Philadelphia: University of Pennsylvania Press.

Bolin, Frances S. 1987. "On Defining Supervision." *Journal of Curriculum and Supervision* 2 (Summer): 368–380.

Bordo, Susan. 1987. *The Flight to Objectivity*. Buffalo: State University of New York Press.

Bowers, C. A. 1974. *Cultural Literacy for Freedom*. Eugene, OR: Elan.

———. 1987a. *The Promise of Theory: Education and the Politics of Cultural Change*. New York: Teachers College Press.

———. 1987b. *Elements of a Post-Liberal Theory of Education*. New York: Teachers College Press.

———. 1988. *The Cultural Dimensions of Educational Computing: Understanding the Non-Neutrality of Technology*. New York: Teachers College Press.

Brophy, Jere E., and Good, Thomas L. 1986. "Teacher Behavior and Student Achievement." In *Handbook of Research on Teaching*, 3d ed., edited by Merlin C. Wittrock. New York: Macmillan.

Brown, Lester, and Postel, Sandra. 1987. "Thresholds of Change." In *State of the World 1987*, edited by Linda Starke. New York: Norton.

Brown, Lester, and Wolf, Edward C. 1987. "Charting a Sustainable Course." In *State of the World 1987*, edited by Linda Starke. New York: Norton.

Brown, Richard H. 1978. *A Poetic for Sociology*. Cambridge, England: Cambridge University Press.

Bruckerhoff, Charles. 1985. "Teachers at Work: A Case Study of Collegial Behavior in a High School." Paper presented at the annual meeting of the American Educational Research Association, Chicago, IL.

Bruner, Jerome. 1966. *Toward a Theory of Instruction*. Cambridge, MA: Harvard University Press.

———. 1985. "Narrative and Paradigmatic Modes of Thought." In *Learning and Teaching the Ways of Knowing*, edited by Elliot Eisner. Eighty-fourth Yearbook of the National Society for the Study of Education. Distributed by the University of Chicago Press.

Buber, Martin. 1965. *The Knowledge of Man*. New York: Harper & Row.

Callahan, Raymond. 1962. *Education and the Cult of Efficiency*. Chicago: University of Chicago Press.

Canter, Lee. 1979. *Assertive Discipline: A Take-Charge Approach for Today's Educators*. Los Angeles: Canter and Associates.

Carnegie Task Force on Teaching as a Profession. 1986. *A Nation Prepared: Teachers for the 21st Century*. Washington, DC: The Carnegie Forum on Education and the Economy.

Carter, Robert A., and Richards, John M. 1983. *We the People: Civics in the United States*. San Diego: Coronado.

Cazden, Courtney B. 1983. "Can Ethnographic Research Go Beyond the Status Quo?" *Anthropology and Education Quarterly* 14:33–41.

———. 1988. *Classroom Discourse: The Language of Teaching and Learning.* Portsmouth, NH: Heinemann.

Center for the Study of Instruction. 1977. *Sources of Identity: The Social Sciences, Concepts and Values.* New York: Harcourt Brace Jovanovich.

Chafe, Wallace L. 1985. "Linguistic Differences Produced by Differences Between Speaking and Writing." In *Literacy, Language, and Learning: The Nature and Consequences of Reading and Writing,* edited by David R. Olson, Nancy Torrance, and Angela Hillyard. Cambridge, England: Cambridge University Press.

Chodorow, Nancy. 1978. *The Reproduction of Mothering: Psychoanalysis and the Sociology of Gender.* Berkeley: University of California Press.

Cook-Gumperz, Jenny, ed. 1986. *The Social Construction of Literacy.* Cambridge, England: Cambridge University Press.

Cowen, Robert C. 1988. "Global Warming Requires Action Now, Study Says." *Christian Science Monitor* (December 6), 3.

Cox, M., and Lathem, E. C. 1968. *Selected Prose of Robert Frost.* New York: Collier.

Deely, John. 1982. *Introducing Semiotics: Its History and Doctrine.* Bloomington: Indiana University Press.

DeLong, Alton. 1981. "Kinesic Signals as Utterance Boundaries in Preschool Children." In *Nonverbal Communication, Interaction, and Gesture,* edited by Thomas A. Sebeok and Jean Umikes-Sebeok. The Hague: Mouton.

Descartes, René. 1955. "Discourse on Method," Part 4. In *Philosophical Works of Descartes,* edited by E. S. Haldane and G. R. T. Ross. New York: Dover. (Original work published in 1637)

Dewey, John. 1938. *Experience and Education.* New York: Collier.

Douglas, Mary. 1975. *Implicit Meaning.* London: Routledge & Kegan Paul.

———. 1978. "Do Dogs Laugh? A Cross-Cultural Approach to Body Symbolism." In *The Body Reader,* edited by Ted Polhemus. New York: Pantheon.

Doyle, Walter. 1986. "Classroom Organization and Management." In *Handbook of Research on Teaching,* 3d ed., edited by Merlin C. Wittrock. New York: Macmillan.

Dreyfus, Hubert L. 1981. "Knowledge and Human Values: A Genealogy of Nihilism." *Teachers College Record* 82 (Spring): 507–517.

Duke, Daniel. 1979. "Environmental Influences on Classroom Management." In *Classroom Management,* edited by Daniel Duke. Seventy-eighth Yearbook of the National Society for the Study of Education. Distributed by the University of Chicago Press.

———, and Meckel, Adrienne. 1980. *Managing Student Behavior Problems.* New York: Teachers College Press.

Eco, Umberto. 1979. *The Theory of Semiotics.* Bloomington: Indiana University Press.

Edwards, A. D. 1980. "Patterns of Power and Authority in Classroom Talk." In *Teacher Strategies,* edited by Peter Woods. London: Croom Helm.

Eisner, Elliot W. 1982. "An Artistic Approach to Supervision." In *Supervision of Teaching,* edited by Thomas J. Sergiovanni. Alexandria, VA: Association for Supervision and Curriculum Development.

————. 1985. *The Educational Imagination*. 2d ed. New York: Macmillan.

Ekman, P., and Friesan, W. V. 1967. "Head and Body Cues in the Judgment of Emotion: A Reformulation." *Perceptual and Motor Skills* 24: 711–724.

Emmer, Edmund T.; Evertson, Carolyn M.; Sanford, Julie P.; Clements, Barbara S.; and Worsham, Murray E. 1989. *Classroom Management for Secondary Teachers*. 2d ed. Englewood Cliffs, NJ: Prentice-Hall.

Enriquez, Evangelia, and Mirande, Alfredo. 1978. "Liberation: Chicana Style." *DeColores* 3 (Fall):3–16.

Erickson, Frederick. 1979. "Talking Down: Some Cultural Sources of Miscommunication of Interracial Interviews." In *Nonverbal Behavior: Applications and Cultural Implications*, edited by Aaron Wolfgang. New York: Academic.

————. 1982a. "Money Tree, Lasagna Bush, Salt and Pepper: Social Construction of Topical Cohesion in a Conversation Among Italian-Americans." In *Analyzing Discourse: Text and Talk*, edited by Deborah Tannen. Washington, DC: Georgetown University Press.

————. 1982b. "Taught Cognitive Learning in its Immediate Environment: A Neglected Topic in the Anthropology of Education." *Anthropology and Education Quarterly* 13: 149–180.

————. 1986. "Qualitative Methods in Research on Teaching." In *Handbook of Research on Teaching*, 3d ed., edited by Merlin C. Wittrock. New York: Macmillan.

————, and Mohatt, Gerald. 1982. "Cultural Organization of Participation Structures in Two Classrooms of Indian Students." In *Doing the Ethnography of Schooling*, edited by George Spindler. Prospect Heights, IL: Waveland.

Everhart, Robert B. 1983. *Reading, Writing, and Resistance*. Boston: Routledge & Kegan Paul.

Exline, R. V.; Gray, D.; and Schuette, D. 1965. "Visual Behavior in a Dyad as Affected by Interview Content and Sex of Respondent." In *Affect, Cognition and Personality*, edited by S. Tomkins and C. Izard. New York: Springer.

Feiman-Nemser, Sharon, and Floden, Robert E. 1986. "The Cultures of Teaching." In *Handbook of Research on Teaching*, 3d ed., edited by Merlin C. Wittrock. New York: Macmillan.

Fennell, Francis; Reys, Robert E.; Reys, Barbara J.; and Webb, Arnold W. 1988. *Mathematics Unlimited*. New York: Holt, Rinehart and Winston.

Flinders, David J. 1987. "What Teachers Learn from Teaching: Educational Criticisms of Instructional Adaptation." Unpublished doctoral diss. Stanford University.

Flood, Craig. 1988. "Stereotyping and Classroom Interactions." In *Sex Equity in Education: Reading and Strategies*, edited by Anne O'Brien Carelli. Springfield, IL: Thomas.

Foucault, Michel. 1979. *Discipline and Punish: The Birth of the Prison*. New York: Vintage.

————. 1980. *Power/Knowledge: Selected Interviews and Other Writings: 1972–1977*. Edited by Colin Gordon. New York: Pantheon.

————. 1983. "The Subject and Power." In *Michel Foucault: Beyond Structuralism and Hermeneutics*, by Hubert L. Freyfus and Paul Rabinow. Chicago: University of Chicago Press.

Freire, Paulo. 1974. *Pedagogy of the Oppressed*. New York: Seabury.

Gadamer, Hans-Georg. 1976. *Philosophical Hermeneutics*. Berkeley: University of California Press.

Geertz, Clifford. 1973. *The Interpretation of Cultures*. New York: Basic.

Gilligan, Carol. 1982. *In a Different Voice*. Cambridge, MA: Harvard University Press.

Giroux, Henry. 1988. *Teachers as Intellectuals: Toward a Critical Pedagogy of Learning*. Granby, MA: Bergin & Garvey.

Goffman, Erving. 1974. *Frame Analysis*. New York: Harper Colophon.

Good, Thomas L., and Brophy, Jere E. 1978. *Looking in Classrooms* (Second Edition). New York: Harper & Row.

Goodenough, Ward H. 1981. *Culture, Language, and Society*. Menlo Park, CA.: Benjamin/Cummings.

Goody, Jack. 1986. *The Logic of Writing and the Organization of Society*. Cambridge, England: Cambridge University Press.

Gordon, William. 1966. *The Metaphorical Way of Knowing*. Cambridge, MA: Porpoise Books.

Gouldner, Alvin W. 1979. *The Future of Intellectuals and the Rise of the New Class*. New York: Seabury.

Graff, Harvey J. 1987. *The Legacies of Literacy: Continuities and Contradictions in Western Culture and Society*. Bloomington: Indiana University Press.

Green, Judith, and Wallat, Cynthia. 1981. *Ethnography and Language in Educational Settings*. Norwood, NJ: Ablex.

Gumperz, John J. 1977. "Sociocultural Knowledge in Conversational Inference." In *Linguistics and Anthropology*, edited by Muriel Saville-Troike. Washington, DC: Georgetown University Press.

Hall, Edward T. 1959. *The Silent Language*. Greenwich, CT: Fawcett.

————. 1969. *The Hidden Dimension*. Garden City, NY: Anchor.

————. 1977. *Beyond Culture*. Garden City, NY: Anchor.

Halliday, M. A. K. 1978. *Language as Social Semiotic: The Social Interpretation of Language and Meaning*. Baltimore: University Park Press.

Harding, Sandra. 1986. *The Science Question in Feminism*. Ithaca, NY: Cornell University Press.

Havelock, Eric A. 1986. *The Muse Learns to Write: Reflections on Orality and Literacy from Antiquity to the Present*. New Haven, CT: Yale University Press.

Heath, Shirley Brice. 1982. "Questioning at Home and at School: A Comparative Study." In *Doing the Ethnography of Schooling*, edited by George Sprindler. Prospect Heights, IL: Waveland.

————. 1983. *Ways with Words: Language, Life, and Work in Communities and Classroom*. New York: Cambridge University Press.

Heidegger, Martin. 1962. *Being and Time*. New York: Harper & Row. (Original work published 1927)

Henderson, Gail. 1985. *Dimensions of Life*. Cincinnati: South-Western.

Highwater, Jamake. 1981. *The Primal Mind: Vision and Reality in Indian America.* New York: New American Library.

Hirsch, E. D., Jr. 1987. *Cultural Literacy: What Every American Needs to Know.* Boston: Houghton Mifflin.

Holmes Group. 1986. *Tomorrow's Teachers: A Report of the Holmes Group.* East Lansing, MI: Author.

Hunter, Madeline. 1986. *Mastery Teaching.* El Segundo, CA: TIP.

Hymes, Dell. 1981. "Ethnographic Monitoring." In *Culture and the Bilingual Classroom,* edited by Henry T. Trueba, Grace Pung Guthrie, and Kathryn Hu-Pei Au. London: Newbury House.

Izard, Carroll E. 1979. "Facial Expression, Emotion, and Motivation." In *Non-Verbal Behavior: Applications and Cultural Implications,* edited by Aaron Wolfgang. New York: Academic.

Johnson, Mark. 1987. *The Body in the Mind: The Bodily Basis of Meaning, Imagination, and Reason.* Chicago: University of Chicago Press.

Kearns, David T. 1988. "Help to Restructure Public Education from the Bottom Up." *Harvard Business Review* (November–December): 70–75.

Keller, Evelyn Fox. 1985. *Reflections on Gender and Science.* New Haven, CT: Yale University Press.

———. 1987. "Feminism and Science." In *Sex and Scientific Inquiry,* edited by Sandra Harding and Jean F. O'Barr. Chicago: University of Chicago Press.

Kendon, Adam. 1967. "Some Functions of Gaze-Direction in Social Interaction." *Acta Psychologica* 26: 22–63.

———. 1981. *Nonverbal Communication, Interaction, and Gesture.* The Hague: Mouton.

Lakoff, George. 1987. *Women, Fire and Dangerous Things.* Chicago: University of Chicago Press.

Leed, Eric. 1980. "'Voice' and 'Print': Master Symbols in the History of Communication." In *The Myths of Information: Technology and Post-Industrial Culture,* edited by Kathleen Woodward. Bloomington: Indiana University Press.

Lemlech, Johanna Kasin. 1984. *Curriculum and Instructional Methods for the Elementary School.* New York: Macmillan.

Lightfoot, Sara Lawrence. 1983. *The Good High School.* New York: Basic.

Longino, Helen, and Doell, Ruth. 1987. "Body, Bias, and Behavior: A Comparative Analysis of Reasoning in Two Areas of Biological Science." In *Sex and Scientific Inquiry,* edited by Sandra Harding and Jean F. O'Barr. Chicago: University of Chicago Press.

Lortie, D. C. 1975. *Schoolteacher.* Chicago: University of Chicago Press.

Lyotard, Jean-Francois. 1984. *The Postmodern Condition: A Report on Knowledge.* Minneapolis: University of Minnesota Press.

McDermott, Raymond Patrick. 1976. "Kids Make Sense: An Ethnographic Account of the Interactional Management of Success and Failure in One First-Grade Classroom." Unpublished doctoral diss., Stanford University.

McLaren, Peter. 1989. *Life in Schools: An Introduction to Critical Pedagogy in the Foundations of Education*. New York: Longman.

Mallinson, George G.; Mallinson, Jacqueline B.; Brown, Douglas G.; and Smallwood, William L. 1975. *Science: Understanding Our Environment*. Park Ridge, IL: Silver-Burdett.

Mandell, Steven L. 1983. *Computers and Data Processing Today with BASIC*. St. Paul, MN: West.

Margulis, Lynn, and Sagan, Dorion. 1986. *Microcosmos: Four Billion Years of Evolution from Our Microbial Ancestors*. New York: Summit Books.

Medley, Donald M. 1979. "The Effectiveness of Teachers." In *Research on Teaching*, edited by Penelope L. Peterson and Herbert J. Walberg. Berkeley, CA: McCutchan.

Meeks, Linda Brower, and Heit, Philip. 1982. *Health: Focus on You*. Columbus, OH: Merrill.

Mehrabian, A. 1969. "The Significance of Posture and Position in the Communication of Attitude and Status Relationship." *Psychological Bulletin* 71:359–372.

Merchant, Carolyn. 1980. *The Death of Nature: Women, Ecology and the Scientific Revolution*. New York: Harper & Row.

Michaels, Sarah, and Collins, James. 1984. "Oral Discourse Styles: Classroom Interaction and the Acquisition of Literacy." In *Coherence in Spoken and Written Discourse*, edited by Deborah Tannen. Norwood, NJ: Ablex.

Miller, Roger LeRoy, and Pulsinelli, Robert L. 1983. *Understanding Economics*. St. Paul, MN: West.

Minnesota Educational Computing Consortium. 1985. *Oregon Trail*. St. Paul, MN: Author.

Mueller, Claus. 1973. *The Politics of Communication*. Oxford, England: Oxford University Press.

Nietzsche, Friedrich. 1967. *On the Genealogy of Morals/Ecce Homo*. New York: Vintage Books. (Original work published 1888)

Noddings, Nel. 1984. *Caring; A Feminine Approach to Ethics and Moral Education*. Berkeley: University of California Press.

———. 1986. "Fidelity in Teaching, Teacher Education, and Research for Teaching," *Harvard Educational Review* 56 (November): 496–510.

Nordstrom, Carl; Friedenberg, Edgar Z.; and Gold, Hilary A. 1967. *Society's Children: A Study of Ressentiment in the Secondary School*. New York: Random House.

Ong, Walter J. 1977. *Interfaces of the Word: Studies in the Evolution of Consciousness and Culture*. Ithaca, NY: Cornell University Press.

———. 1982. *Orality and Literacy: The Technologizing of the Word*. London: Methuen.

Orr, Eleanor Wilson. 1987. *Twice as Less: Black English and the Performance of Black Students in Mathematics and Science*. New York: Norton.

Peshkin, Alan. 1988. "In Search of Subjectivity—One's Own." *Educational Researcher* 17 (October): 17–21.

Philips, Susan U. 1972. "Participant Structures and Communicative Competence: Warm Springs Children in Community and Classroom." In *Functions of Language in the Classroom*, edited by Courtney B. Cazden, Vera P. John, and Dell Hymes. New York: Teachers College Press.

———. 1983. *The Invisible Culture: Communication in Classroom and Community on the Warm Springs Indian Reservation*. New York: Longman.

Polanyi, Michael. 1964. *Personal Knowledge*. New York: Harper Torchbooks.

Reddy, Michael J. 1979. "The Conduit Metaphor—A Case of Frame Conflict in Our Language about Language." In *Metaphor and Thought*, edited by Andrew Ortony. Cambridge, England: Cambridge University Press.

Rodriquez, Richard. 1981. *Hunger of Memory*. Boston: Godine.

Rorty, Richard. 1979. *Philosophy and the Mirror of Nature*. Princeton, NJ: Princeton University Press.

Rowe, Mary Budd. 1986. "Wait Time: Slowing Down May Be a Way of Speeding Up!" *Journal of Teacher Education* 23 (January/February):43–49.

Sarason, Seymour B. 1982. *The Culture of the School and the Problem of Change*. Boston: Allyn & Bacon.

Saville-Troike, Muriel. 1978. *A Guide to Culture in the Classroom*. Rosslyn, VA: National Clearinghouse for Bilingual Education.

Schierholz, Tom. 1988. "Study Brings the 'Greenhouse Effect' Home." *The Christian Science Monitor* (November 20): 3.

Schön, Donald A. 1979. "Generative Metaphor: A Perspective on Problem-Setting in Social Policy." In *Metaphor and Thought*, edited by Andrew Ortony. Cambridge, England: Cambridge University Press.

———. 1983. *The Reflective Practitioner*. New York: Basic.

Schumacher, E. F. 1975. *Small Is Beautiful: Economics As If People Mattered*. New York: Harper & Row.

Schwab, Joseph J. 1969. "The Practical: A Language for Curriculum." *School Review* 77 (November): 1–23.

Scollon, Ron. 1982. "The Rhymic Integration of Ordinary Talk." In *Analyzing Discourse: Text and Talk*, edited by Deborah Tannen. Washington, DC: Georgetown University Press.

———. 1985. "The Machine Stops: Silence in the Metaphor of Malfunction." In *Perspectives on Silence*, edited by Deborah Tannen and Muriel Saville-Troike. Norwood, NJ: Ablex.

Scollon, Ron, and Scollon, Suzanne B. K. 1981. *Narrative, Literacy and Face in Interethnic Communication*. Norwood: NJ: Ablex.

———. 1984. "Cooking It Up and Boiling It Down: Abstracts in Athabaskan Children's Story Retelling." In *Coherence in Spoken and Written Discourse*, edited by Deborah Tannen. Norwood, NJ: Ablex.

———. 1985. "The Problem of Power" (monograph). Haines, AK: The Gutenberg Dump.

———. 1986. *Responsive Communication: Patterns for Making Sense*. Haines, AK: Black Current.

Scribner, Sylvia, and Cole, Michael. 1981. *The Psychology of Literacy*. Cambridge, MA: Harvard University Press.

Sergiovanni, Thomas J. 1987. "The Metaphorical Use of Theories and Models in Supervision: Building a Science." *Journal of Curriculum and Supervision* 2 (Spring): 221–232.

Siegman, Aron W. 1979. "The Voice of Attraction: Vocal Coordinates of Interpersonal Attraction in the Interview." In *Of Speech and Time*, edited by Aron W. Siegman and Stanley Feldstein. Hillsdale, NJ: Erlbaum.

Simons, Herbert D., and Murphy, Sandra. 1986. "Spoken Language Strategies and Reading Acquisition." In *The Social Construction of Literacy*, edited by Jenny Cook-Gumperz. Cambridge, England: Cambridge University Press.

Sinclair, J., and Coulthard, M. 1975. *Towards an Analysis of Discourse: English of Teachers and Pupils*. Oxford, England: Oxford University Press.

Smith, Howard A. 1984. "State of the Art of Nonverbal Behavior in Teaching." In *Nonverbal Behavior: Perspectives, Applications, Intercultural Insights*, edited by Aaron Wolfgang. New York: Hogrefe.

Smyth, W. John. 1986. *Learning about Teaching through Clinical Supervision*. London: Croom Helm.

Snyder, Gary. 1977. *The Old Ways: Six Essays*. San Francisco: City Lights.

Sommer, Robert. 1969. *Personal Space: The Behavioral Basis of Design*. Englewood Cliffs, NJ: Prentice-Hall.

Sprick, Randy. 1986. *Discipline in the Secondary Classroom*. West Nyack, NY: Center for Applied Research in Education.

Taba, Hilda. 1962. *Curriculum Development: Theory and Practice*. New York: Harcourt Brace Jovanovich.

Tannen, Deborah. 1986a. "Relative Focus on Involvement in Oral and Written Discourse." In *Literacy, Language, and Learning: The Nature and Consequences of Reading and Writing*, edited by David R. Olson, Nancy Torrance, and Angela Hildyard. Cambridge, England: Cambridge University Press.

———. 1986b. *That's Not What I Meant!* New York: Morrow.

Thompson, William I., ed. 1987. *Gaia, A Way of Knowing: Political Implications of the New Biology*. Great Barrington, MA: Lindisfarne Press.

Tyler, Ralph W. 1949. *Basic Principles of Curriculum and Instruction*. Chicago: University of Chicago Press.

Vannatta, Glen D., and Stoeckinger, John. 1980. *Mathematics: Essentials and Applications*. Columbus, OH: Merrill.

Vogt, Lynn A.; Jordon, Cathie; and Tharp, Roland G. 1987. "Explaining School Failure, Producing School Success: Two Cases." *Anthropology and Education Quarterly* 18 (December): 276–286.

Vygotsky, Lev Semenovich. 1962. *Thought and Language*. Cambridge: MIT Press.

Warren, Richard L. 1982. Schooling, Biculturalism, and Ethnic Identity: A Case Study. In *Doing the Ethnography of Schooling*, edited by George Spindler. Prospects Heights, IL: Waveland.

Wax, Murray; Wax, Rosalie; and Dumont, Robert, Jr. 1964. "Formal Education in an American Indian Community." Supplement to *Social Problems* 11 (Spring): 54–55.

Wolcott, Harry. In press. "On Seeking—and Rejecting—Validity in Qualitative Research." In *Quantitative Inquiry in Education: The Continuing Debate*, edited by Elliot W. Eisner and Alan Peshkin. New York: Teachers College Press.

Wolfgang, Aaron. 1979. "The Teacher and Nonverbal Behavior in the Multicultural Classroom." In *Nonverbal Behavior: Applications and Cultural Implications*, edited by Aaron Wolfgang. New York: Academic.

Worster, Donald. 1985. *Nature's Economy: A History of Ecological Ideas*. Cambridge, England: Cambridge University Press.

Index

About the Authors

C. A. BOWERS teaches education and social thought in the College of Education at the University of Oregon. His previous publications include *The Progressive Educator and the Depression: The Radical Years* (1969), *Cultural Literacy for Freedom* (1974), *The Promise of Theory: Education and the Politics of Cultural Change* (1984), *Elements of a Post-Liberal Theory of Education* (1987), and *The Cultural Dimensions of Educational Computing: Understanding the Non-Neutrality of Technology* (1988). His current interests concern the interconnections among education, belief systems, and the ecological crisis. He received his Ph.D. from the University of California, Berkeley.

DAVID J. FLINDERS is Assistant Professor of Education in the Department of Curriculum and Instruction at the University of Oregon. He has published articles in *Curriculum Inquiry, The Journal of Curriculum and Supervision,* and *Educational Leadership,* and his dissertation won a national award from the Association for Supervision and Curriculum Development. His interests concern curriculum foundations and qualitative classroom research. He received his doctoral degree from Stanford University in 1987.